F. W. Garforth is a Senior Lecturer in the Department of Educational Studies at the University of Hull.

He is the author of *Education and Social Purpose* (Oldbourne, 1962) and *The Scope of Philosophy* (Longman, 1971). He is editor of *Locke's Thoughts Concerning Education* (Heinemann, 1964), *John Locke's Of the Conduct of the Understanding* (Teachers College Press, New York, 1966), *John Dewey: Selected Educational Writings* (Heinemann, 1966), *Bede's Historia Ecclesiastica* (Bell, 1967), *Education for the Seventies* (University of Hull Institute of Education, 1969), and *John Stuart Mill on Education* (Teachers College Press, New York, 1971).

John Stuart Mill's
Theory of Education

John Stuart Mill's Theory of Education

F. W. GARFORTH

Department of Educational Studies
University of Hull

BOOKS
10 East 53d St., New York 10022
(a division of Harper & Row Publishers, Inc.)

First published in 1979 by Martin Robertson & Company Ltd.
108 Cowley Road, Oxford OX4 1JF.
Published in the U.S.A. 1979 by
Harper & Row Publishers, Inc. Barnes & Noble Import Division

Library of Congress Cataloging in Publication Data

Garforth, Francis William.
John Stuart Mill's theory of education.
Bibliography: p.
1.   Mill, John Stuart, 1806-1873.   2.   Education-Philosophy.
3.   Utilitarianism.   I.   Title.
LB675.M5172G37   1979   370.1   78-31807
ISBN 0 06 492332 0

Typeset by Pioneer Associates, East Sussex.
Printed and bound by Richard Clay Ltd.,
at The Chaucer Press, Bungay, Suffolk.

for
Francesca

Contents

Acknowledgements   ix

Preface   xi

PART I: PERSONAL AND HISTORICAL   1

PART II: SCIENTIFIC FOUNDATIONS   27

      1   Experientialism   29

      2   Science and Human Nature   36

      3   Association Psychology   46

      4   Ethology   59

      5   The Practical Arts   67
          Philosophical Issues

PART III: THE EDUCATIVE PROCESS   83

      1   Introductory   85
          Philosophical Issues

      2   Environmentalism   107
          Philosophical Issues

      3   Method   142
          Philosophical Issues

4   Content   183
Philosophical Issues

5   Liberal Education   203
Philosophical Issues

Notes   231

Bibliography   251

Index   263

Acknowledgements

I am greatly indebted for guidance, correction and encouragement to my colleague John Lawson, who read the manuscript at an early stage in its composition and since then has patiently answered my many questions on historical details. My thanks are also due to the staff of the Brynmor Jones Library of the University of Hull for their help in procuring for me copies of some of Mill's less accessible writings; to the staff of the Institute of Education Library of Hull University for assistance in various ways; and to the University of Toronto Press and its editors, whose volumes of Mill's Collected Works have considerably eased my labours and whose *Mill News Letter* is an invaluable source of information on all aspects of Mill studies. I wish, too, to express gratitude to my publishers, and in particular to Mr Edward Elgar for his advice during my preparation of the final version of the manuscript.

As on previous occasions my wife has made life easier for me by sharing the burden of proof correcting and indexing.

Preface

This book has two principal purposes. One, obviously enough, is to introduce the reader to the educational thought of a great man who is best known for his work in other fields — political economy, logic and the theory of science — and known to most only for his books *On Liberty* and *Utilitarianism*. Mill has not hitherto been regarded as an educational thinker or as having made any useful contribution to educational theory. However, it is clear from his writings that education was never far from his mind; for Mill's central motivating purpose throughout his life was, in his own words, 'the improvement of mankind', and he saw education as an essential instrument to this end. This belief in the potency of education he accepted initially from his father, James Mill, who, together with Bentham and other utilitarians, attributed to education almost unlimited power to modify and improve human behaviour; Helvetius' dictum, 'L'éducation peut *tout*', they accepted as part of their utilitarian doctrine. But for John Stuart the belief was more than a credal article passively accepted from his elders; it became for him an autonomous commitment, the positive affirmation of his own thought and experience. It is true that, with the exception of the *Inaugural Address* (whose dominant theme is liberal studies at university), he has left no extended writing on education; but comment on it recurs throughout his works, both in his major books, *A System of Logic* and *Principles of Political Economy,* and in his many lesser books, essays and articles. There is enough of it, certainly, to permit the deduction of a coherent theory of education and its processes; and to present this theory io what the present book aims to do.

There is a second purpose, however, which is not so obvious. Some twenty-five years ago the now familiar 'revolution in philosophy' began to penetrate educational studies. Educational philosophy was transformed from an examination of the theories and doctrines of the 'great educators' into a critical analysis of the language and concepts of education, of its methods, of its aims and their justification. Clarification of ideas and the neutral display of logical relationships took the place of prescription and exhortation. At the forefront of the revolutionary movement in education were, in Britain, Professors Peters, Hirst, Dearden and O'Connor. Peters's *Ethics and Education,* Hirst and Peters's *The Logic of Education,* Dearden's *The Philosophy of Primary Education* and O'Connor's *An Introduction to Educational Philosophy* are now established texts in educational philosophy, familiar to all students of this area of educational studies. In the United States Professor Israel Scheffler has performed a similar role; his *Conditions of Knowledge* and *The Language of Education* are no less familiar.

It is my belief that the impetus of this movement has faded and that a fresh approach to problems in educational philosophy is needed. I am not suggesting that the critical study of language and concepts is no longer necessary, nor that educational thinking has been clarified so definitively that we can dispense with the services of Professor Peters and his associates; and nothing I say here should be understood as in any way disparaging the enormous value of the work and writings of these philosophers. There will always be a need, not least in education, for clarification and resolute testing by logical criteria; this has always been, and will remain, a central function of philosophy in any area of its application. However, I am far from sure that the best entry into philosophical problems, whether generally or in education, is by subjecting them to aseptic logical scrutiny in isolation from their human context. At some point such scrutiny is essential, but not perhaps initially or for all students.

For human beings are contextual; so too are their problems, philosophical and otherwise. Problems of justice, freedom, knowledge, obligation, personal identity and, in education, of authority, equality, autonomy, creativity, curriculum, morality — all these arise initially, become problematic, in actual situations, in the context of which they derive both their meaning and the motivation for their solutions. What I am implying is that the problems of educational philosophy, for many if not most students, are best approached (that is, with insight and understanding) through a study which involves them with actual persons speaking from their personal and historical context. For a few the logical may be the correct initial approach; for most the contextual approach would seem more appropriate; for all the discipline of rigorous logical analysis is essential to any claim to be engaged in educational *philosophy*.

What I am suggesting, then, is not that we should return to the 'great educator' studies of a generation ago; rather that philosophical issues in education should be seen first in a personal and historical context — that is, in actual educational writers — and only then abstracted, generalised and subjected (with, I believe, far greater understanding and sense of practical relevance) to critical scrutiny. In this way it should be possible to secure the best of both worlds — the pre- and the post-revolutionary — in educational philosophy.

J. S. Mill seems particularly suited to such an approach. He was a great man in his own right, offering us that vision of greatness which he himself thought (though the words are not his but A. N. Whitehead's) an essential part of any education worth the name. He was among the most influential thinkers of his time, widely known and widely respected for his personal integrity and the sincerity of his ideals. Further, as I have already noted, because he saw education as an indispensable means to his goal of human improvement, he was deeply, continually and critically concerned with problems of educational purpose and process. Indeed, most of the problems which feature in current texts and journals of educational philosophy can be found in one guise or another in his writings.

I offer this book, then, both as a study of Mill's educational thought and as a contextual approach to philosophical issues in education. It can be used for the first alone or for the first leading to the second. To assist this latter purpose I have appended to Part II and to each chapter of Part III a brief statement of issues which arise in the preceding pages and which seem appropriate for further study as problems in educational philosophy. I have also added suggestions for reading relevant to these problems — a far from complete list but sufficient to enable the student, with or without tutorial guidance, to pursue them further.

Loch Cluanie, July 1978

PART I
Personal and Historical

John Stuart Mill was born in 1806. His father, James, was a Scotsman who, after studying for the ministry at the University of Edinburgh, failed to find a parish and decided to seek his fortune in London as a writer and journalist. Within a few years he was earning enough to marry and start a family; John was the first of nine children. His mother receives no mention in the final published form of John's *Autobiography*; a derogatory reference to her in an earlier version was expunged. Lacking academic training, overshadowed by her husband's brilliance and preoccupied with the care of a large family, she could contribute little to John's intellectual needs; it was his father who dominated his upbringing. Details of John's life can be found in Packe's biography and, more recently, in Robson's *The Improvement of Mankind* and Mazlish's *James and John Stuart Mill*; brief surveys are readily available in books on various aspects of his work. There is, of course, his own posthumously published *Autobiography*, and we now have Stillinger's edition of the early draft which includes the comments on his mother. Of particular interest is the critical account written by his younger contemporary, Alexander Bain. All these books are listed in the bibliography. In the paragraphs that follow no more is intended than to survey some of the more significant events and circumstances of his life and education.

James Mill established a reputation for himself by writing a history of British India. Published in 1817, the book was an immediate success; it was also instrumental in securing for him a post in the India Office (then under the East India Company), where he rose ultimately to a position of the highest responsibility. At the age of seventeen John was able to follow him into the same office and the same career — a career which, by good fortune, left him ample leisure for his voluminous writings of later years. By this time James had become a convinced utilitarian and a close friend of Jeremy Bentham, the foremost utilitarian theorist of the time; he had also adopted the principles of association psychology (see below, pp.46-57), which he saw as a principal means, through education, of attaining the goal of human happiness. These two creeds, utilitarianism and associationism, he strove to impart to John, who did indeed remain committed to them, though not without modification, throughout his life.

John's own education was extraordinary, if not unique. He went neither to school nor to university; until the age of fourteen he was educated almost entirely at home, either by or under the supervision of his father. At the age of three (so we are told in the *Autobiography*) he was set to learning Greek; at eight he embarked on Latin; by fourteen, when his formal education ended, he had read more of the classics than the modern university student at the end of his undergraduate course. Arithmetic, algebra and geometry were also part of his curriculum, followed by as much of the higher mathematics as his father could teach him. Apart from formal lessons he read widely, especially in history but also in science and English literature. He was particularly encouraged to read 'books which exhibited men of energy and resource in unusual circumstances, struggling against difficulties and overcoming them';[1] this left him with a permanent admiration for human greatness in any area of achievement and a respect for the heroic as an essential stimulus to progress. 'Of children's books,' he tells us, 'any more than of playthings, I had scarcely any'; but his father borrowed for him, among others, *The Arabian Nights, Don Quixote* and *Robinson Crusoe*, the last of which delighted him throughout boyhood.[2]

However, books were not the only medium of his education in these early years. He accompanied his father in daily walks through the country lanes round London, repeating to him the lessons he had learnt the day before and stories from the books he was reading for himself. Thus, Greek and arithmetic and English history were mingled in his early memories with 'green fields and wild flowers'[3] — a delightful and enviable recollection. Moreover, what he learnt from his father he was required to impart to his younger brothers and sisters; although he disliked the task, looking back on it he recognised its value in giving him a clearer grasp and a more thorough retention of what he himself had learnt.

From about the age of twelve he entered upon a more advanced course of instruction. This began with a thorough grounding in the traditional logic of Aristotle and the scholastic logicians, whose value as a training in disciplined reasoning James Mill regarded highly. Though not convinced at the time, John later appreciated this early drilling in logic as one of the most important parts of his education, than which 'nothing in modern education tends so much, when properly used, to form exact thinkers, who attach a precise meaning to words and propositions'.[4] His classical studies continued, but in greater depth and detail; much of his time was given to careful reading and analysis of the Athenian orator Demosthenes and of the major dialogues of Plato; both of these authors, he explains, he could now read 'with perfect ease'.[5] To Plato he owed a lifelong debt; no writer, he asserts, contributed more to his 'mental culture'[6] — not through his philosophical theories (which he rejected) but through the Socratic method of discussion and argument (see below, pp.175-177,) At the age of thirteen he was taken through a complete course of political economy. Since there was no introductory textbook, his father taught him by means of lectures delivered during their country walks; each day's lecture he was made to write and rewrite in his own words until it was clear and precise. (Later James Mill used these notes of John's as the basis for his *Elements of Political Economy.*) A further task imposed on him was to help his father correct the proofs of his massive *History of British India* — an implausible task, surely, for a boy of twelve, but one which, he says, 'contributed largely to my education in the best sense of the term'.[7]

At the age of fourteen his formal education ended. He spent the next year in France and when he returned, although his studies continued under his father's general direction, 'he was no longer my schoolmaster'.[8] His year in France was important in two ways. He was the guest of Sir Samuel Bentham, Jeremy Bentham's brother; for the summer of 1820 Sir Samuel rented a chateau in the south within reach of the Pyrenees, to which they made one prolonged excursion. This first introduction to mountain scenery made a deep impression on John and coloured his tastes throughout his life (as can be seen, for instance, in the letters he wrote to his wife during his travels in Greece in 1855). He was also introduced to French life and culture which, even at that age, he found in pleasant contrast to what he knew of English society. He retained a lifelong love of France and the French people. He learnt to speak and write the language fluently, and ultimately he bought a house at Avignon which he used for holidays and finally for his retirement.

After his return from France he embarked on what might be

regarded as a programme of university studies and activities, without actually going to university. He read deeply in law and psychology and worked his way through the writings of Jeremy Bentham; as a result of this last he not only became a doubly convinced utilitarian but found that now at last he had a gospel to preach — the principle of utility: the greatest happiness of the greatest number — something to which he could devote the entire purpose of his life and thereby effect enormous advances in human well-being. Through his father's influence and that of his friends John was able to associate with numerous men of learning and distinction; he formed a small debating group which he called the 'Utilitarian Society', began writing letters and articles for various journals, allied himself with a political group known as the Philosophical Radicals, was arrested for distributing birth-control leaflets in the streets of London,[9] and altogether threw himself with all the fanaticism of youth into proclaiming the ideals to which he felt committed.

But there was a cloud on the horizon. He could sense in himself that all this enthusiastic zeal for human improvement had only an intellectual basis; it had no root, he tells us, 'in genuine benevolence or sympathy with mankind'.[10] The fact is — and it was at last dawning on him — that his upbringing and education had been deficient on the emotional side. His relationship with his mother was unsatisfactory; his father's nature — on the surface at least — was coldly intellectual, distrustful of emotion and of any passionate expression of feeling. Intellectually John was as able as his father, but at heart he was something of a romantic and a mystic, and his education omitted (though he did not realise it at the time) certain elements of imagination and emotion for which his nature craved. It cost him a nervous breakdown at the age of twenty. Mill himself calls this 'a crisis in my mental history'[11] — and indeed it was, a turning point in his development, an assertion of his own personality against his father's. To us, looking at it objectively, it is a fascinating and instructive event in his personal growth; to him it was a period of depression from which he eventually emerged with a new sensitivity to spiritual and aesthetic values and a new interpretation of the gospel of utilitarianism. He was greatly helped in his recovery by reading, for the first time, the poetry of Wordsworth, which seems exactly to have suited his mental condition.

There is much in John's education that we can rightly condemn (though we should bear in mind that psychology and pedagogy have made great advances in the intervening years and that by the standards of his time James Mill might well be regarded as progressive). Indeed, one might doubt whether, after such an upbringing, he could have anything of value to say on education; this book will, the writer hopes, prove such doubt unfounded.

Certainly he was emotionally deprived, lacking both a father's tenderness and the mutuality of mother-child affection. Companionship too was wanting, except within his own family and until, at fourteen, he was released from his father's immediate supervision. His education was over-academic; it forced upon him a level of learning beyond a child's understanding and a load of learning which no child should be expected to support. It gave no place to practical skills — it was 'more fitted for training me to *know* than to *do*.[12] Yet whatever its faults, it had positive merits which John readily acknowledged: his year's residence in France, the discipline of deductive logic, the vision of greatness in the classical and historical writers. Above all it gave him two things of enormous worth: first, through the sheer quantity of knowledge he acquired it gave him 'an advantage of a quarter of a century over my contemporaries';[13] second, it forced upon him, by his father's deliberate intent, the habit of finding out for himself and the need to develop the skills for so doing.

Another crisis in Mill's life, though not immediately recognised as such, occurred when, at a dinner party in the summer of 1830, he met the wife of John Taylor, a prosperous City merchant. Harriet Taylor, already the mother of two children, was an attractive, vivacious and intelligent woman; for Mill, who had little experience of women outside his own family, she seemed to fill a deep emotional emptiness in his own life and also to be a paragon of all the virtues that he imagined a woman could possess. In the *Autobiography* he describes her in terms of exaggerated adulation and in his letters to her he assumes a tone of almost pathetic subservience. They soon became close friends, intimate friends; they fell in love. For nineteen years this relationship continued, during which time Harriet never lost her respect for her husband or abandoned her obligations to him and to her children. John Taylor resigned himself to the situation, and Harriet and Mill spent much of their time together both in London and elsewhere. Surprisingly (by present standards) they never slept together during these years; we have only their own testimony for this, but Mill was certainly a man of conspicuous honesty, even to his own detriment, and there is no reason to believe otherwise. John Taylor died in 1849; the two were married in 1851, and Harriet died seven years later at Avignon while they were travelling to the Mediterranean. After her death Mill found comfort in his stepdaughter Helen, who became virtually his secretary and housekeeper until Mill himself died in 1873.

Precisely what was the nature of their intellectual relationship and what the extent of Mill's indebtedness to Harriet is still a matter of speculation; it is discussed in the biographical works already mentioned and in the books by Hayek, Himmelfarb (*On Liberty and Liberalism*), Kamm and Pappé which are listed in the bibliography. During the years of their friendship and subsequent marriage they considered together every topic that interested them — poetry, sex, marriage, the status of women, poverty, economics, freedom and many others. To her can probably be attributed Mill's increasing emphasis on individuality, expressed most notably in *On Liberty* which, he insists, was a 'joint production', drafted, written and revised in close collaboration.[14] Most of his books owe something to her, one notable exception being his *A System of Logic*. Together they planned an ambitious schedule of writing which included, in addition to *On Liberty*, most of his later writings, the publication of which she did not live to see — *Utilitarianism, Considerations on Representative Government, The Subjection of Women, Auguste Comte and Positivism, Three Essays on Religion,* the *Autobiography* and the section of *An Examination of Sir William Hamilton's Philosophy* in which Mill discusses causation and the will. In 1858, the year of her death, the Government took over the India Office and Mill resigned his post; this left him with the leisure to write the projected books, a task which occupied him for much of the following ten years.

It also left him free to engage in direct political activity; thus, when the bulk of his writing was finished, he was persuaded to stand as an independent Liberal candidate for Westminster in the General Election of 1865. Characteristically he refused to canvass, to contribute to election expenses or to commit himself to the policies of any political party. However, he agreed to make two speeches during his 'campaign', one to the electors, the other to the voteless working people who, he insisted, had as much right as the rest to hear his views. At the latter meeting he was faced with a placard which quoted him as referring to the working classes as 'habitual liars';

asked if he had written this, he answered immediately, 'I did', and was greeted, after a moment's silence, with tumultuous applause.[15] Mill was a conscientious and, where he felt deeply, outspoken Member of Parliament. Among his contributions to debate two are especially noteworthy: in a long and eloquent speech during the passage of the 1867 Representation of the People Bill he defended his proposal to extend the franchise to women; and in a debate on capital punishment he spoke for its retention for 'atrocious cases',[16] strictly on the humanitarian grounds that it was kinder to the criminal than lifelong incarceration. On education he had little to say, his contribution being confined mainly to brief comments during the committee stage of the Public Schools Bill (p.20 below) and a plea for the better education of girls in his speech on female suffrage (p.21 below). At the General Election of 1868 he was not re-elected.

During these later years of his life Mill was able greatly to extend his public activities. To causes he believed in he gave generously of his time; among these were the Association for Land Tenure Reform, the Women's Suffrage Society (of which Helen Taylor, his step-daughter, was a founder member) and the National Education League. The University of St Andrews elected him its Rector for 1866 (without his prior consent) and in the following year he made there, in his inaugural address, his most extensive pronouncement on education. He was no less energetic in opposing what he saw as wrong; thus he sided with the North in the American Civil War against the 'aggressive enterprises of the slave-owners', condemned the treatment of negroes in Jamaica (many years earlier he had bitterly attacked his former friend, Thomas Carlyle, for his attitude to 'niggers'), and joined with others in prosecuting its Governor, Edward John Eyre, for alleged brutality.[17] In giving evidence to a Royal Commission on venereal disease he caused consternation by condemning as the guilty parties not the prostitutes who offered their services but the men who sought them.[18] Throughout this time he maintained an increasingly exacting correspondence (as the published volumes of his letters testify), giving always a clear, considered reply to any serious request or inquiry. Yet he found time also for travel and for his lifelong botanical interests; wherever he went he collected and pressed flowers, of which he had amassed several large volumes by the end of his life. Much of his time in these last years he spent at Avignon, writing, revising his books and enjoying a leisurely and detached retirement. It was here that he died on 7 May 1873.

Mill's lifetime coincided almost exactly with the establishment of a national system of elementary education in England and Wales. In 1806 the state had no part and no interest in education; by 1873 there had been created a foundation on which to build the complex structure of state schools that exists today. Schools there were, of course, at the beginning of the century, widely diverse in kind and efficiency. There were charity schools, founded by philanthropic enterprise for the instruction of the poor in religion, morals and the elements of literacy. Sunday schools performed a similar function, though their emphasis was primarily religious and moral; promoted by Robert Raikes and other evangelicals in the 1780s, they became widely established throughout England and Wales by the end of that century. For the middle classes there were the endowed grammar schools. Some of these, if their master was able and dedicated, provided a sound basic education for university or the professions, but many had stagnated into incompetence; their curriculum was dominated by the classical languages, whose drudgery Locke had complained against in his *Thoughts concerning Education* (1693), to be echoed in Mill's *Inaugural Address* two centuries later (p.190 below). There were also numerous private schools and academies which, by providing a wider, more practical and vocationally orientated curriculum, appealed especially to the growing commercial and industrial element among the middle classes. For the rich and the aristocracy there were the famous schools, Eton, Harrow, Westminster, Winchester and a few others — the 'public schools' as they came to be known; here too, as in the grammar schools,classics dominated the curriculum and was assumed to provide an education suitable for the sons of gentlemen. Apart from the charity schools, the Sunday schools and similar institutions for the instruction of the poor, most of these schools, and all of the famous few, provided only for boys; private schools for girls existed from the 1790s, but the institutional education, as we now understand it, of girls of the middle and upper classes was still in the future.

The only universities in England and Wales at the beginning of the nineteenth century were Oxford and Cambridge; these were not then, as they are now, centres of excellence in academic and professional learning. Students and tutors were generally required to be members (the latter ordained and celibate members) of the Anglican Church; and since both came predominantly from the aristocratic and wealthy classes, the universities were a preserve of ecclesiastical and social privilege, conservative and resistant to change. Their statutes were out of date, their curricula narrow (and, as in the schools, mainly classical), their examinations often trivial; in their complacent seclusion they made no response to the pressing social and industrial needs of the time. Mill was scathing in his criticism of them (he attended neither himself): Oxford, he wrote in the *Monthly Repository* of 1834, 'is as effete as the Pope'; the two universities were 'among the last places where any person wishing for education, and knowing what it is, would go to find it'.[19] It is not surprising, he writes elsewhere, that England has lost the intellectual distinction she once had.[20]

During the latter part of the eighteenth century it had become increasingly apparent that such educational facilities as existed were inadequate for the needs of a profoundly changing society. Britain was in the throes of becoming an industrial nation; rapid growth of population, together with its increasing concentration in urban centres, where there was neither cultural tradition nor social structure, gave rise to grave problems of housing, health, poverty, morality and crime; in this unprecedented situation children were among the worst sufferers. There was change even in the countryside; bigger farms, the enclosure of common land and new methods of agriculture were destroying established patterns of life and creating a class of displaced and disaffected rural poor. Adding their weight to these social pressures were new ideas and new movements which gave further impetus to a demand for education. Echoes of the French Revolution reverberated in Britain long after its worst excesses, haunting the upper classes with fears of rebellion and inciting the more intelligent among the mass of the population to fight for political democracy and improved conditions of life. Social stability, it was realised, implied indoctrination with traditional values; the extension of political rights required a literate and informed population. Rousseau and Helvetius, the former with his gospel of 'Follow nature', the latter with his 'L'éducation peut *tout*', had stimulated fresh thinking about education, its power, its purposes and its methods. The latter appealed especially to the utilitarians, led by Jeremy Bentham and James Mill, who saw in education an instrument essential to the pursuit of their goal of human happiness through social reform: '. . . all the difference which exists, or can ever be made to exist, between one *class* of men and another is wholly owing to education'.[21] Another powerful influence was the evangelical movement; originating with the Wesleys and their circle of preachers, it had spread to the established Church and become there an attempt to revitalise its Christianity and at the same time protect society against the dangers of moral corruption and revolution. Response to this recognised need and concomitant demand for more and improved education had taken many forms. New charity schools were founded, while those already in existence acquired a new significance; Sunday schools, as mentioned above, were founded in large numbers nationwide in the last two decades of the eighteenth century; new private schools and academies provided for the aspirations of the middle classes. In addition to formal schooling there were other important sources of educational influence and provision. Corresponding societies, mainly of working-class membership, were established in London (1792), the Midlands and the North to facilitate the exchange of information and ideas. Literary and philosophical societies (philosophical in the sense of scientific) were founded in Manchester (1781), Newcastle (1793) and other large towns; as well as organising lectures and meetings, they built up libraries (the Newcastle Society had over 9,000 books) which were especially important in making more widely accessible the new political, social and educational thinking. Books and pamphlets, now more cheaply produced, were another significant educational influence — and deliberately so used, as, for instance, by the evangelicals, whose tracts and pamphlets, aimed at inculcating basic Christian beliefs and virtues, were sold in vast numbers.

But all this was not enough. For the time being the middle and upper classes could safely be left to provide for their own children. They had the money and the schools; they supported established values and the *status quo* and consequently were no danger to social stability. The lot of the poor, however, especially in the major industrial areas, was desperate; if ever they were to become efficient workers and, eventually, participant citizens, they must be given at least the elements of literacy and numeracy and imbued with basic moral habits of hard work, honesty, obedience and respect for the law. Such was the thinking of those who cared — infused in many, undoubtedly, with a genuine humanitarian regard for children and concern for human improvement.

It should not be assumed that the current of opinion was unreservedly in favour of improved educational provision for the poor. There were many who resisted it: some argued that educating the masses would encourage insubordination and disrupt the existing social hierarchy; others feared the political consequences of universal literacy — an informed populace would demand the franchise and a voice in government; others again insisted that the nation's children were an indispensable source of cheap labour for Britain's growing industries. The tide, however, was turning against them; moreover, an instrument was at hand which seemed ideal for distributing the elements of education efficiently and at minimum cost. This was the monitorial system. Its essence was simple enough: a schoolmaster, trained in the operation of the system, was put in charge of a number of monitors or assistants (who might be no more than eleven years old), each of whom had charge of a group of ten or a dozen younger children. The master drilled the monitors in the various items of instruction, and the monitors in their turn drilled the groups. It was mechanical, almost mindless, in its operation, but it was hailed with enthusiasm for its 'beautiful and efficient simplicity'[22] — and also, of course, for its cheapness — and welcomed, among others, by the utilitarians (but not by J.S.Mill, for whose views, see below, P.160). It was introduced into schools by Joseph Lancaster, a Quaker, and Andrew Bell, an Anglican clergyman, each of whom was claimed by his supporters as its inventor. In 1808 the non-denominational Royal Lancasterian Society (later the British and Foreign School Society) was founded and in 1811 the Church of England's National Society, each of them dedicated to the instruction of the poor by the monitorial system. Before the mid-century the system had been overtaken by more enlightened methods of teaching (though still crude by today's child-centred criteria); but the two Societies, assisted from 1833 by state grants, remained the main providers of mass education until the 1870s. By that time there had been established a structural basis on which the state, when it finally assumed responsibility for elementary education, was able to build an extended and improved system of schooling.

Among the critics of monitorial methods was Robert Owen, whose schools, established at New Lanark in the early 1800s for the younger children of his cotton workers, were a major influence in nineteenth-century education. While accepting that the monitorial schools were useful in increasing the extent of educational provision, he claimed that his own schools were superior: instead of regimented instruction backed by a code of rewards and punishments, there were kindness and understanding, freedom for children to find their own activities or work together in groups; the curriculum included stories, games, singing and dancing, nature study and various practical pursuits; methods of teaching were adapted to the children's age and interests; there was emphasis on the spirit of the school community — sympathy, co-operation and service to others. Owen's experiments in infant education led to a nationwide infant school movement and the founding of a number of societies to promote these new ideas and establish schools based on them.[23] In all this there is clear evidence of the influence of Rousseau, Helvetius and Pestalozzi, whose writings on education and pedagogy were widely read in Britain in the early decades of the century. Especially important was Pestalozzi's insistence, in his many books and manuals, on sensory and practical experience as the basis of learning. The work of Owen and the many others who contributed to the infant school movement not only added to the momentum of the demand for more and better education; it also had the result of giving to infant education an enlightened technique and attitude to children which distinguished it from, and eventually percolated into, the more formal, authoritarian regime of the elementary schools.

Meanwhile it was becoming obvious that the government could not isolate itself indefinitely from responsibility for the nation's education. The voluntary societies, however well-meaning, lacked the resources to match the immensity of the problem; they could not compel attendance at school, nor could they prevent the exploitation of child labour (and consequent illiteracy) in factories and work-houses. Thus, as the century progressed, the government's involvement grew from tentative and reluctant beginnings to a firm commitment, in the 1870 and subsequent Acts, to a national, compulsory and publicly financed system of elementary education. That it took so long was due, in addition to the sources of opposition mentioned above, to dissension about the control and financing of schools and to sectarian rivalry between the religious denominations. The Church of England resented the state's intrusion into what it regarded as its own exclusive guardianship of children's spiritual and educational welfare; the nonconformists were jealous of the Anglicans; many rate- and taxpayers resisted state subsidies for schools.

It is impossible in this brief historical introduction to do more than merely sketch the progress of state intervention in education and indicate some of its principal landmarks. The first instance of such intervention was the Health and Morals of Apprentices Act in 1802, which sought to control the working hours and conditions of child workers and to ensure that they received a minimum of instruction in the three Rs; it was followed by a similar Act in 1819. However, their educational provisions could not be enforced and were ineffective. A more positive step was taken in 1816, when Henry (later Lord) Brougham secured the appointment of a select committee 'to inquire into the education of the lower orders of the Metropolis' — later extended into a wider survey of popular education throughout the country. Its report, some two years later, was valuable in pointing to the many existing deficiencies and abuses in educational provision and in its recommendations for remedying them. Nevertheless, a Bill which Brougham introduced in 1820 'for better providing the means of Education for his Majesty's subjects' in England and Wales failed because of nonconformist opposition. It included provision for rate-assisted parochial schools, but virtually gave control of them to the Church of England.

Utilitarians played a major part in the promotion of education at this time. In Parliament it was mainly the work of two men, J. A. Roebuck and Joseph Hume, both of whom were Members for most of the years between 1830 and 1850; they were supported by George Grote during the few years of his Parliamentary career. In 1833 Roebuck moved a resolution requesting

> That this House, deeply impressed with the necessity of providing for a due education of the people at large; and believing, that to this end the aid and care of the State are absolutely needed, will, early during the next Session of Parliament, proceed to devise a means for the universal and national education of the whole people.[24]

This, the first attempt to secure legislation for a national system of education, was argued in a speech remarkable for its clarity, earnestness of purpose and educational wisdom. But it was not accepted. He succeeded, however, to the extent of persuading Parliament to make its first grant to education — a sum of £20,000 to be distributed through the National and British Societies. Henceforth grants were made annually.

Further select committees reported during the 1830s and proved beyond doubt that educational provision for the poorer classes was seriously deficient in both quantity and quality. In 1837 Brougham, now in the Lords, made another attempt to introduce legislation aimed at further developing a national education; this too was unsuccessful. There was now much unease, not only about the state of education but also about the use and misuse of the annual Parliamentary grants. Consequently in 1839 there was appointed (in the face of strong opposition) a Committee of the Privy Council responsible for supervising the distribution and use of the grants, which were now made conditional on inspection. At first the Committee, through its inspectors, was concerned primarily with general oversight of the need for and provision of schools and with the suitability of school buildings — site, teaching rooms, heating, playing space, etc. Gradually its work was extended to include matters of curriculum and pedagogy; grants were made available for furniture and apparatus. It also gave attention to staffing and the improvement of professional standards; grants were made to augment teachers' salaries and to provide a pension scheme; the Societies were assisted in building their denominational training colleges; and — a vital move — in 1846 a pupil-teacher scheme was established which replaced monitors with apprentices and helped to ensure an adequate supply of teachers.

The appointment of this Committee proved to be a watershed in the development of education in England and Wales. Henceforth the state was inextricably involved in education; it could not now withdraw from its responsibilities. In the Committee and its inspectorate there existed the germ of what was later the Board of Education, then the Ministry of Education and finally the Department of Education and Science. It could only be a matter of time before this initially tentative supervisory role became a full-blooded assumption of government responsibility for the nation's education. Especially significant was the Committee's intervention to promote teacher-training facilities. These had existed earlier for the training of monitors, but they were inadequate and there was no means of inspection to ensure their quality. The truth was now dawning that an efficient national system of education requires as an integral and indispensable element in its structure a supply of trained teachers.

Another significant step towards a literate and informed populace was the Public Libraries Act of 1850, which permitted a ½d. rate to subsidise the provision of libraries. The need for ready access to books, not least for those who could not afford to buy them, had long been felt. It had been partially met by the circulating libraries, private subscription libraries and those established by the Literary and Philosophical Societies, Mechanics' Institutes and other organisations (many of them specifically for working-class readers). Even schools were beginning to acquire them, and the Committee's first instructions to its inspectors in 1840 required them to report on this. The Act of 1850 merely enabled; it did not compel. Resistance to it was keen, and twenty years later only some forty towns had opened public libraries. Nevertheless, it was an important move, which Mill must have welcomed; for he always insisted that education is not confined to schools and institutions, and in 1845, writing in the *Edinburgh Review,* he hailed 'the cheap libraries, which are supplying even the poorest with matter more or less instructive and, what is of equal importance, calculated to interest their minds'.[25]

The inability of voluntary effort to satisfy the nation's educational needs was now apparent — except to the voluntaryists themselves, who were opposed in principle to government intervention and resisted, often with fanatical zeal and remarkable lack of concern for the children who were the victims of the system, any attempt to enlarge the area of state intervention. A Bill of 1843, aimed at improving the lot of factory and pauper children, failed because of nonconformist opposition. Some voluntaryists demanded the total withdrawal of government grants and regulations. Freedom was at stake, they claimed; and in the words of one of them, it was indeed possible for 'voluntary Christian zeal to provide the means of education and religious instruction'.[26] In the end they were proved wrong, but not before they had delayed for more than a generation the creation of a national system of education.

Meanwhile there was growing dissatisfaction with the condition of elementary education. The existing system of grants for voluntary provision was now firmly established; year by year increasing sums of money were spent on it. Yet its effectiveness was seriously in doubt, and over all hung the unresolved controversy of state provision versus voluntaryism and the ability of the latter to meet the demand. In 1858 a Royal Commission was appointed 'to inquire into the present state of popular education in England, and to consider and report what measures, if any, are required for the extension of sound and cheap elementary instruction to all classes of the people'. Its Report, published in 1861, recognised the value of what the religious denominations had achieved but was critical of the standards of instruction, of the level of attendance and of the early age of leaving (comparatively few stayed beyond eleven years); further, the existing organisation under the Committee of Council was too complex, it did not reach the areas most in need and its results were incommensurate with the cost. The Commission recommended retaining voluntary provision but with increased grants paid partly from taxation and partly from local rates; the level of local grants was to depend on the results of examinations conducted by the inspectors in reading, writing and arithmetic. This latter measure introduced the notorious principle of 'payment by results', roundly condemned by many leading educationists of the time, including Matthew Arnold and T. H. Huxley — but not by J. S. Mill, who, writing on the abuses of endowments, described it as a 'real principle of efficiency' and claimed that a teacher's pay should bear some relation to the number and proficiency of his pupils (see below, p.22). The Revised Code of 1862, introduced by Robert Lowe, Vice-President of the Committee of Council, retained the voluntary system, rejected rate-aided grants, but accepted payment by results. The educational effects of the last were profound and damaging: it encouraged rote learning, testing and concentration on examination requirements to the detriment of an extended, educationally appropriate curriculum; and it established an impoverished notion of elementary education which took generations to eradicate.[27]

The Revised Code could be no more than a delaying action; not only was it unsatisfactory in itself, but its operation showed conclusively that a grant-supported voluntary system could not supply the education the country needed. Moreover, public opinion was shifting away from voluntaryism towards acceptance of state intervention. Many local societies were formed to promote a national, compulsory system of education; their activities were co-ordinated in the National Education League, founded in October 1869. The culmination of this veering of opinion and the efforts accompanying it was the Education Act of 1870, introduced into Parliament as a Bill by W. E. Forster. The aim of the Act was to provide schooling 'for all the children resident in [any] district for whose elementary education efficient and suitable provision is not otherwise made'. It retained the voluntary schools but provided for the appointment of School Boards, locally elected and supported from local rates, to supplement, where necessary, deficiencies in voluntary provision. The Act did not make elementary education either compulsory or free; compulsion (from five to thirteen years) was left to the decision of the Boards (in regard only to their own schools); they were also given power to decide the payment required of parents (a maximum of 9d a week),and to waive it altogether for the very poor. A conscience clause, introduced into the Bill by W.F.Cowper-Temple (and retained almost in its original wording to the present day), prohibited denominational teaching of any kind in rate-aided schools.

Thus was the foundation laid for a universal, and eventually both compulsory and free, education for the nation's children. It should be noted, however, first that it was elementary, second that it was intended for the poor. The need for the state to concern itself with secondary education (not simply as a chronological stage, but as a higher level of education) was apparent before the 1870 Act. The Taunton Commission, reporting in 1868 on endowed schools, had recommended a national system of secondary schools, graded according to the age of the children attending; it also recognised that 'real ability [should] find its proper opening',[28] thus suggesting the notion of a 'ladder' enabling the more able children to proceed from elementary to secondary schooling. Between 1870 and the end of the century the need for such a 'ladder' — both as logically implied by the elementary schools and as a matter of educational justice — became irresistible; elementary schools began to extend their studies to higher levels and ages; scholarships facilitated the entry of their pupils to grammar schools. Eventually the state's responsibility for secondary education was acknowledged in the Education Act of 1902, which gave to counties and county boroughs the power to provide 'education other than elementary and to promote the general co-ordination of all forms of education'. That the 1870 Act legislated for the poor confirmed and prolonged what has been referred to as a 'two-nation' organisation of education — elementary for the lower classes, secondary for the middle and upper. This, despite the existence of 'ladders', scholarships and other means of enabling 'poor' and 'working-class' children to enjoy the benefits of secondary and higher education, has been a major criticism of English education in the century since.

The state of the existing secondary schools (endowed, grammar, proprietary, private and 'public') was a cause of concern during the first half of the nineteenth century and after. Endowments were misused, standards lax, schools ill-organised and inefficient. Curricula were narrow and overloaded with Latin and Greek, while science and mathematics were neglected. This was not true of all the schools; enlightened heads like Thomas Arnold at Rugby and Edward

Thring at Uppingham anticipated the need for reform and made for themselves and their schools a well-deserved reputation; and they were not alone. However, there was sufficient disquiet to lead to the appointment of two Commissions, the Clarendon in 1861 and the Taunton (officially the Schools Inquiry Commission) in 1864, to investigate, respectively, the nine major public schools and the endowed schools. The Report of the Clarendon Commission, published in 1864, was followed by the Public Schools Act of 1868; the Taunton Commission's Report led to the Endowed Schools Act of 1869. Both Acts sought to remedy existing abuses and deficiencies; the latter in particular aimed at reforming the charities on which the endowed schools were founded, and among its recommendations was the extension of charities to include the education of girls.

Universities were not neglected during this period. Mention has already been made of the state of Oxford and Cambridge, the only universities in England and Wales at the beginning of the century. A Royal Commission was appointed to investigate them in 1850. It reported in 1852, and the ensuing Acts (1854 for Oxford, 1856 for Cambridge) introduced important reforms, including competition for fellowships and scholarships and the admission of nonconformists to the B.A. (not to the M.A., however, which meant in effect that university government was still Anglican-dominated and dissenters could still be barred from fellowships). Changes in the administration of the universities opened the way for further reform of courses and examinations. By 1859 Mill himself, who had so vehemently censured them earlier, was able to admit that what he had written of them had 'in a great measure ceased to be true'.[29] It was not until 1871 that religious tests were finally abolished, with the one exception of degrees in divinity.

The failure of Oxford and Cambridge to reform themselves led to a move to establish a university in London; the result was University College, which received its first students in 1828. The initiative came from Thomas Campbell, the poet, who was supported by Liberals, nonconformists, secularists, utilitarians and others; they objected to the social and religious exclusiveness of Oxbridge and wanted a university which had no religious tests and gave due place to science and technology. James Mill, after some initial hesitation, became one of the most active of them; he was elected to the first council of the College in 1825. This 'Godless institution in Gower Street' (as Thomas Arnold dubbed it) was strongly opposed by Anglicans, who accordingly established King's College (opened in 1831) as an institution committed to the doctrines of the Church of England. The two were brought together by royal charter in 1836 within a University of London, which had the power to grant degrees (denied previously to the separate colleges).

Reaction against the 'Godless' London College contributed also to the creation of the University of Durham, which was established by Act of Parliament in 1832, initially as an ecclesiastical foundation endowed from the revenues of the see. In 1851 came Owens College, Manchester, which received its charter as a university in 1880; a College of Physical Science was established in Newcastle in 1871. Meanwhile the University of London was expanding rapidly, affiliating to itself colleges of various kinds throughout Britain and the Empire. A development of great importance was its power to grant external degrees, at first through the affiliated colleges, but from 1858 to individual students. In Wales, St David's College, Lampeter, founded in 1827 for the education of Anglican ordinands, received a charter to grant at first (1852) the B.D., later (1865) the B.A. Colleges were established at Aberystwyth in 1872, Cardiff in 1883 and Bangor in 1884, and the three were brought together as a federated University of Wales in 1893. By the end of the century university colleges had been founded in nine of the major cities in England, all of them sooner or later to become universities in their own right.

An obvious question concerns the part Mill played in this parallel process of reform and development leading towards a universal, state-supported system of education. Directly, not a great deal, if participation is assumed to involve political action and formal proposals for legislation; from this he was debarred until his retirement from the India Office in 1858. Even during his years in Parliament he was preoccupied with other matters, notably a just and representative franchise which seemed to him of prior importance to, and an essential foundation for, universal education. In the debates on the Representation of the People Bill he pleaded for working-class representation on the grounds that this would accelerate the provision of popular education — in a very few years 'there would be in every parish a school rate, and the school doors freely open to all the world'.[30] During the committee stage, in a long speech supporting female suffrage, he complained of the lack of educational opportunity for girls, and this despite the lip-service paid to the importance of mothers as educators of future men.[31] In a debate on the Civil Estimates in 1867 he emphasised the need for technical education and commended the practice in other countries of offering it as 'a reward for the good use of the advantages of elementary education'.[32] As a Member of Parliament he was most directly involved in education during the committee stage of the Public Schools Bill; however, his contributions were brief, the most important being concerned with the abuse of endowments and their appropriation for the education of a privileged minority.[33]

Mill's reputation and his known interest in education led to many requests, both private and official, for his advice and opinion. He was asked to contribute a paper to an official report on examinations for the Civil Service; this he did, recommending examinations as a stimulus to merit and 'mental cultivation' and a protection against partiality.[34] Another official request came from the Schools Inquiry Commission seeking his views on certain matters concerning endowments. Among his recommendations were payment by results, regular inspection, a thorough training to improve the quality of teachers, and their certification by universities or other approved institutions (interestingly, he insists that training be closely linked with schools 'where the art of teaching may be practically acquired'). He adds a further recommendation that promotion should depend on proved competence tested by results, arguing that the best guarantee of efficiency is 'the assured prospect of removal'![35] During the nationwide controversy which accompanied the passage of the 1870 Education Bill he was invited to address a meeting of the National Education League on a motion deploring the proposal that School Boards should be able to establish denominational schools at public expense. In his speech he expressed the hope that denominational schools would not remain 'as a permanent institution', but as long as they existed, then 'those who make use of religious teaching [must] pay for it themselves instead of taxing others to do it'.[36] Finally, it should be borne in mind that for many years his work in the India Office included drafting letters of advice and policy concerning education in the Native States. In this way he was directly involved with practical issues, albeit in another country and at a great distance, and had some personal responsibility for shaping educational development.[37]

Indirectly Mill's contribution to education in Britain was lifelong and cumulative, adding impetus through half a century to the powerful current of thought (not confined to utilitarians) which was fed by social and economic pressures as well as by moral and intellectual ideals. The fundamental importance of education was an essential item of utilitarian belief: James Mill was committed to it; John too accepted it as integral to his own thinking. This can be seen, for instance, in his early articles, 'On Genius' and 'Civilisation', and in his 'Notes on the Newspapers' contributed to the *Monthly Repository* in 1834. It appears in his letters throughout his life: 'Nous travaillons toujours', he writes in one of them, 'à la cause de l'éducation'.[38] It is reaffirmed in his major works, *A System of Logic* and *Principles of Political Economy*, in lesser writings, such as *Representative Government* and *The Subjection of Women*, and in a large number of essays, articles and reviews. He saw education (rightly conceived, of course) as a creative force, an essential means to truth, to intellectual rigour, to strength of character, to the release of individual potential. He saw it too as indispensable to his ideal of an informed, responsible and fully enfranchised democracy.

Inevitably he was committed to universal education, both as an individual right and as a social and political necessity, and to some form of national system. As for state intervention, this too he came eventually to accept. At the time of the first grant for education in 1833 he had thought that, with this assistance, voluntary effort could provide at least a sufficient quantity of schooling. As the years passed and the problems grew, it became apparent to him, as to others, that even this was beyond the capacity of voluntary provision, that the state must play a greater part, even to the extent of compulsion. He was well aware of the dangers — indoctrination, bureaucracy, the loss of freedom, the stifling of variety, experiment and individual initiative. Carried too far, state intervention, he believed, becomes a potent instrument for moulding citizens into servile conformity and consequent mediocrity: 'A government which can mould the opinions and sentiments of the people from their youth upwards can do with them whatever it pleases'.[39]

Nevertheless, he was persuaded that the dangers were outweighed by the need. Already in the 1840s, when he was writing *Principles of Political Economy*, he was convinced of the economic need for popular education to improve the quality of labour and increase the potential of industrial skills. He saw it too as vital to the goal of universal suffrage: power in the hands of the uneducated was a source of danger — 'no lover of improvement can desire that the *predominant* power should be turned over to persons in the mental and moral condition of the English working classes'.[40] He believed, further, that state intervention was necessary to assist research and scholarship, much of which was beyond the means of private resources. He suggests too a role for government in compensating the inequities which handicap the race of life: 'In racing for a prize the stimulus to exertion on the part of the competitors is only at its highest when all start fair'.[41] If the state does nothing to help the weaker, the handicap becomes a dispiriting burden. It was perhaps the qualitative deficiency of the voluntary provision that most troubled him: instruction alone was not enough — even if it was good instruction, which often it was not; education is not merely for life but 'that we may live well', and for this the positive intervention of government was essential.[42]

In reviewing the arguments for and against, Mill makes a valuable distinction between 'authoritative' and 'non-authoritative' intervention. The former limits and controls the free agency of individuals by precise regulation, centrally imposed and administered; the latter relies on advice and persuasion and provides a standard and an example by exhibiting them in its own institutions. He draws another important distinction between the right to direct and the right to enforce education. That he allowed the latter he makes clear in *Principles of Political Economy* and *On Liberty*: if parents will not accept responsibility for educating their children, the state must impose it. Direction, however, is another matter: though the state may require education, it must not prescribe how or from whom it shall be obtained; if voluntary provision fails, then the state must, 'as the less of two great evils', provide schools and colleges, but 'it must neither compel nor bribe any person to come to them'.[43] Nor should it have a monopoly of education: state education should be one among many competing experiments; by providing an example and a stimulus it should help the rest to achieve 'a certain standard of excellence'.[44]

Although it would be difficult to pin-point detailed illustration, there can be little doubt that Mill's views, expressed with persistence and often with vehemence, contributed significantly to the mounting pressure for educational reform and a national system of schooling. Mill himself was respected even by his opponents for his intellectual power, his personal integrity, his commitment to truth and his devotion to the cause of human improvement; his utterances could not be lightly disregarded. His books and articles were widely read; his *System of Logic* and *Principles of Political Economy* (of which eight and seven editions respectively were published during his lifetime) were, within their fields, perhaps the most influential books of the century, and both contain important comment on education. *On Liberty*, with its vital third chapter, 'Of individuality, as one of the elements of well-being', and its guarded but conclusive acceptance of government intervention in education, was read, according to one nineteenth-century estimate, by 'hundreds of thousands' and 'produced a profound impression on contemporary thought'[45] (though it had a hostile reception from many critics).

If asked to single out the most valuable and also the most characteristic elements in Mill's influence, the present writer would point, first, to his insistence on the importance of individuality and of education as the means of liberating it. This is the message of chapter iii of *On Liberty*: 'Human nature is not a machine to be built after a model. . ., but a tree, which requires to grow and develop itself on all sides, according to the tendency of the inward forces which make it a living thing'.[46] Without this release of human potential in all its variety and inventiveness there can be no social progress: 'The initiation of all wise or noble things comes and must come from individuals'.[47] Second, there is his emphasis on quality. It is this emphasis that distinguished his own utilitarianism from that of James Mill and Bentham — the *quality* of happiness, not simply its quantitative assessment — and it extends, as has already been noted, to his concept of education. Buildings, books and equipment are, of course, indispensable, but in the final count what matters is the quality of educational experience — 'mind must be taught by mind'; and from this follows the obvious need for teachers of the highest competence and character and (as will be apparent later) for an environment which supports their efforts.

PART II
Scientific Foundations

CHAPTER 1

Experientialism

There are two major traditions within European philosophy, the rational and the empirical, representing distinct and incompatible views of the origin and nature of knowledge. The rationalist philosopher maintains that there are certain truths and principles which human reason can discover for itself, unaided by sense experience; such truths, whether regarded as self-evident or as apprehended by some special faculty of intuition, are *a priori*, independent of and prior to experience. The empiricist, by contrast, rejects this epistemological self-sufficiency of reason: knowledge is *a posteriori*, derived ultimately from the data of sensory experience; reason can select, arrange and interpret these data, but it cannot from its own resources create or initiate knowledge. From the fourth century BC to the Renaissance the rationalist tradition was dominant; the empirical, after flourishing briefly among the scientists of Alexandria and other cities of the Greco-Roman world, was eclipsed by its rival and reappeared only fitfully until the twelfth and thirteenth centuries. From that time on, however, it was increasingly recognised that knowledge, certainly of the external world, is not attained by imposing on that world the preconceptions of human reason but by observation and experiment, by recording and generalising from data supplied by sense perception and by the various instruments which extend its range.

Among the leaders in this revival of empiricism were two thirteenth-century Englishmen, Roger Bacon and William of Ockham; another, some three centuries later, was Francis Bacon, who sought to elaborate an effective method for science based on observation, experiment and inductive generalisation. He was followed by John Locke, who is commonly regarded as the founder of modern empirical philosophy and to whose *Essay concerning Human Understanding*

Mill himself attributes 'a revolution in the philosophy of the human intellect'.[1] Locke asked the fundamental epistemological question: whence come the materials of knowledge? His answer was clear and emphatic: 'from EXPERIENCE ; in that all our knowledge is founded and from that it ultimately derives itself'.[2] It is an answer, however, which raises further baffling problems, and in the attempts of George Berkeley, David Hume and others to solve them a strong British empirical tradition was established which has persisted with little intermission to the present time. It is to this tradition that the Mills and their fellow utilitarians belong.

John Mill states his own position unequivocally. In a letter to a friend, written when he was nearing completion of his *Logic*, he excuses himself from the task of deducing some all-embracing explanatory cosmic system from the known laws of phenomena: 'Mine professes to be a logic of *experience* only, and to throw no further light upon the existence of truths not experimental than is thrown by showing to what extent reasoning from experience will carry us'.[3] In the *Autobiography* he says of the same book that it presents a doctrine which 'derives all knowledge from experience'; he continues: 'The notion that truths external to the mind may be known by intuition or consciousness independently of observation and experience is, I am persuaded, in these times the great intellectual support of false doctrines and bad institutions'.[4] He writes elsewhere that 'the one really grave charge' that can be made against mathematics is that 'it leads men to place their ideal of science in deriving all knowledge from a small number of axiomatic premises, accepted as self-evident, and taken for immediate intuitions of reason'.[5] Finally, in the essay on Coleridge he contrasts the rationalist and empiricist epistemologies and concludes thus:

> As to the fundamental difference of opinion respecting the sources of our knowledge . . . the truth on this much-debated question lies with the school of Locke and Bentham. The nature and laws of things in themselves or of the hidden causes of the phenomena which are the objects of experience appear to us radically inaccessible to the human faculties. We see no ground for believing that anything can be the object of our knowledge except our experience and what can be inferred from our experience by the analogies of experience itself; nor that there is any idea, feeling or power in the human mind which, in order to account for it, requires that its origin should be referred to any other source.[6]

It should be noted, however, that Mill did not himself use 'empirical' or 'empiricism' to describe his position; for him these words carried a pejorative sense, indicating a limited and ineffective method of scientific investigation greatly inferior to his own as set out in the *Logic*. Science, he believed, must not only observe and record, it must also discover the underlying regularities of cause and effect which enable us to explain and predict. 'Empiricism' is a mere enumeration of facts which neither explains nor accounts for them; thus he writes of 'empiricism and unscientific surmise', of 'bad generalisation *a posteriori* or empiricism properly so called'; and in a footnote in *Sir William Hamilton's Philosophy* he defends Francis Bacon against 'a slovenly misconception' which attenuates his teaching to a mere empiricism — rather, he was a 'philosopher who laboured to construct a canon of scientific induction by which the observations of mankind, instead of remaining empirical, might be so combined and marshalled as to be made the foundation of safe general theories'.[7] Since, therefore, adhering firmly to the Lockean tradition, he believed the sole source of knowledge to be experience, his epistemology is most appropriately described as *experiential* (a word he does not himself use of it). Whereas empiricism, for him, was a mere piecemeal sorting out of data, lacking coherence and logical demonstration, experientialism would suggest a correct scientific method leading to valid conclusions bound together in a system of general 'laws'.

In the passages quoted above, where Mill declares his experientialism, he is evidently at the same time disclaiming the contrary, rationalist, view which holds that some knowledge at least is accessible to intuition independently of sense experience. There was, in fact, a strong contemporary current of intuitionist philosophy, and he waged a constant war against its exponents. Chief of these was Dr William Whewell, Professor of Moral Philosophy at Cambridge from 1838 to 1855, whose powerful influence made him a prime target of Mill's attack; a less extreme adversary was Sir William Hamilton, whom he nevertheless describes as 'the great fortress of the intuitional philosophy in this country'[8] and against whom he directed the artillery of a massive 600-page volume of refutation. In contrast Mill clung resolutely to the primacy of sense experience, rejecting rationalist claims for intuitive knowledge of, for instance, the relation of cause and effect, personal identity and mathematical, moral and theological propositions.

Yet some critics have argued that Mill's commitment to experientialism was not as wholehearted as is generally assumed; one of them, R. P. Anschutz, asserts categorically that 'in the last resort he must be regarded as primarily a rationalist.'[9] Undoubtedly one can find in Mill's writings passages which suggest a leaning towards the rationalist/intuitionist viewpoint — for instance, the desire for certainty (which is characteristic of the rationalist tradition) and a cognate desire for a coherent system of interrelated laws to explain the phenomenal world. Nor is this surprising, for Mill had been steeped in Plato, the arch-rationalist, from his earliest years, and (like Plato) he was himself fundamentally a mystic (as Laski acknowledges in his introduction to the *Autobiography*)[10] and therefore prone to probe beneath the surface of phenomena. However, that he desired and consistently strove towards an experientialist epistemology is obvious enough; other writings apart, the whole effort of his *Logic* was directed to this end; what is perhaps questionable is the extent of his success.

A System of Logic Ratiocinative and Inductive (to give it its full title) was his attempt to construct a logic and a scientific method consistent with his assertion of experientialism. Now Mill was far more than a philosopher and epistemologist. At heart he was a reformer, and it was his earnest and lifelong desire to improve human society, both in its material conditions and in its cultural quality. Thus, the conception of science which emerges from the *Logic* and his other writings is both theoretical and practical: science aims at the discovery of truth, but it is also an essential instrument of social advance. It is 'the first principle of all intelligent action,' he writes in the essay 'Nature', 'to know and take heed of the properties of the things we have to deal with, so far as these properties are capable of forwarding or obstructing any given purpose.'[11] Only by the scientific study of nature can we learn whether and by what means our purposes can be achieved; to choose these purposes, however, is not the task of science. There is a distinction, as Mill rightly emphasises, between facts and values, and a corresponding distinction between statements and imperatives: 'Propositions of science assert a matter of fact: an existence, a co-existence, a succession, a resemblance. . . A proposition of which the predicate is expressed by the words *ought* or *should be* is generically different from one which is expressed by *is* or *will be*.'[12] Matters of fact he assigns to science, matters of value to what he calls 'art' and ultimately to a supreme 'art' or body of doctrine which he names alternatively 'the Art of Life', 'the Doctrine of Ends' and 'Teleology' (see below, pp.69-71). He makes the same distinction in the essay 'Of the Definition of Political Economy': science differs from art

> as the understanding differs from the will, or as the indicative mood in grammar differs from the imperative. The one deals in facts, the other in precepts. Science is a collection of *truths*; art, a body of *rules*, or directions for conduct. The language of science is, This is, or, This is not; This does, or does not, happen. The language of art is, Do this; Avoid that. Science takes cognizance of a *phenomenon*, and endeavours to discover its *law*; art proposes to itself an *end*, and looks out for *means* to effect it.[13]

The practical function of science, then, is to promote the attainment of human purposes by providing relevant factual information. Its theoretical function is also indicated in these quotations: to examine phenomena, to discover the uniformities or 'laws' underlying them, to make factual pronouncements, to establish truth. 'Propositions of science,' Mill has told us, 'assert matters of fact' and 'any facts are fitted, in themselves, to be a subject of science'.[14] Science does more than this, however; it seeks also to *relate* facts, building them into a system of causal laws which can both explain and predict. In *Sir William Hamilton's Philosophy* he writes of science as 'a system of truths flowing out of, and confirming and corroborating, one another; in which one truth sums up a multitude of others and explains them, special truths being merely general ones modified by specialities of circumstance.'[15] A similar view is implied in his analysis of 'nature', where he describes it as 'a collective name for all facts, actual and possible' and continues:

> The word suggests, not so much the multitudinous detail of the phenomena, as the conception which might be formed of their manner of existence as a mental whole, by a mind possessing a complete knowledge of them; to which conception it is the aim of science to raise itself by successive steps of generalisation from experience.[16]

The nearest approach to this ideal is found in what he regarded as exact sciences such as astronomy and Newtonian mechanics, where the phenomena 'have been brought under laws comprehending the whole of the causes by which the phenomena are influenced . . . and assigning to each of those causes the share of effect which really belongs to it';[17] it then becomes possible to predict future phenomena with precision and certainty. Other sciences, such as meteorology, fall short of this perfection, and even more so 'the science of human nature', that is, of man and man in society. Ideally, then, science, whether as a whole or in its separate branches, is experience unified into a coherent body of knowledge in which particular facts can be explained by reference to 'laws' of increasing generality; these 'laws' are themselves systematically interrelated, and from them particular facts can be deduced and therefore predicted.

It would be outside our present purpose to expound in any detail the procedures by which Mill hoped to construct from the experiential data of sensory perception the explanatory and predictive systems of the separate sciences and of scientific knowledge as a whole. For this the reader should turn to the books recommended[18] (and, of course, to the *Logic* itself). Suffice it to say here that his principal means to this goal was a refined and strengthened process of induction relying on the uniformity of nature as its 'ultimate major premise'.[19] The traditional deductive syllogistic logic, though able to demonstrate the implications and the consistency or otherwise of its premises, could not establish the truth of the premises themselves; these it must accept as given. Above all, it could not provide the factual generalisations which are the foundation of scientific laws and central to Mill's conception of science. His aim, therefore, was to displace from its hitherto dominant position that 'smaller logic which only concerns itself with the conditions of consistency' and to substitute the 'larger [i.e. inductive] logic which embraces all the general conditions of the ascertainment of truth'[20] — not, be it noted, to dismiss the former entirely, for the logic of consistency has an indispensable part to play, as Mill clearly recognised, in the search for truth. Induction could, he believed, provide proof as cogent as that of the syllogism: 'Induction is proof. . . The business of inductive logic is to provide rules and models. . . to which if inductive arguments conform, those arguments are conclusive. . . .'[21]

This claim for certainty is indeed a crucial weakness in his inductive theory. It rests on his assumption of the uniformity of nature: 'the proposition that the course of nature is uniform is the fundamental principle. . . of induction. . . the ultimate major premise in all cases of induction'.[22] Now the uniformity of nature can mean two different things: either that regularities observed in past experience reflect a metaphysical order of reality 'behind' phenomena and in some way productive of them; or that such regularities can reasonably (but not *certainly*) be expected to recur in the future. The first of these is incompatible with experientialism, since what is 'behind' or 'beyond' phenomena is inaccessible to sensory experience; the second lacks the logical cogency which Mill requires in his 'ultimate major premise'. In fact it is now commonly accepted that inductive conclusions, indispensable though they are to the advancement of scientific knowledge, are incapable of the proof that Mill was seeking; for it is always logically possible that conclusions derived from experiential evidence may be refuted by further experience; hence it is the inconclusive ground of non-refutation, not proof in any final demonstrative sense, that gives induction such validity as it has. He does, however, as must any thoroughgoing experientialist, confess to the ultimate inability of experience to explain experience (for instance, 'that final inexplicability' of self-consciousness); and he would surely have agreed with his eminent predecessors Locke and Hume that 'as to a perfect *science* of natural bodies. . . we are. . . so far from being capable of any such thing, that I conclude it lost labour to seek after it', and 'no philosopher who is rational and modest has ever pretended to assign the ultimate cause of any natural operation'.[23]

Here we must leave Mill's attempt to construct an experientialist theory of science and scientific method and turn to further difficult problems which arose in the application of his conclusions to the nature and activities of human beings.

CHAPTER 2

Science and
Human Nature

It has already been emphasised that Mill was at heart a reformer; the underlying motive of his activities, theoretical and practical alike, was 'the improvement of man'.[1] This is obvious from even a cursory reading of his *Autobiography*, and it is underlined again and again throughout his writings. His adolescent ambition, sharpened by his reading of Bentham and his association with the *Westminster Review*, was 'to be a reformer of the world'.[2] His mental crisis of 1826 and subsequent experience enlarged and deepened this ideal from a somewhat ethereal, intellectualised notion into a profound commitment of heart as well as mind. It became, as J. M. Robson says,[3] the unifying element in his thought, and though not equally conspicuous in all his written works, it is the essential clue to a comprehensive understanding of them. The *Logic* itself was by no means a pure intellectual exercise in the pursuit of truth; of Mill's passionate devotion to truth there can be no doubt, but always he looked beyond to its essential role in elevating human experience. He was also intensely interested in logic and in devising a correct methodology for science, but it was to be a science with practical potential for the betterment of humanity, a science whose purposes would be subordinate to the supreme 'Art of Life'.[4] Moreover, although the application of science to society comes last in the *Logic*, it is clear from the *Autobiography* that this was no afterthought but a stimulus, almost from the start, to thinking out an acceptable theory of scientific investigation.[5]

Now the improvement of society requires a knowledge of causal laws not only in the natural sciences but also in society itself and in man — especially in man, for Mill believed that social phenomena are ultimately dependent on the causal laws of individual psychology. Therefore, having devised, as he confidently thought, a satisfactory logical theory and methodology for the natural sciences, he had now to consider whether these were equally applicable to the study of society and the human mind; in his own words, 'whether moral sciences exist or can exist; to what degree of perfection they are susceptible of being carried; and by what selection or adaptation of the methods brought to view in the previous part of this work that degree of perfection is attainable'.[6] Other sciences are now firmly established; they have assembled, each in its own sphere, a body of knowledge which commands considerable (and some, like astronomy and the physical sciences, almost universal) consensus. Even in physiology, despite much remaining uncertainty and controversy, there is a large area of accepted fact; but 'the laws of mind and in even a greater degree those of society'[7] are so far from such consensus that it is disputed even whether they are capable of scientific study. Quite apart from considerations of human improvement, it is intolerable that 'matters so much the most important with which human intellect can occupy itself' should 'remain the only subject which philosophy cannot succeed in rescuing from empiricism' (Mill's meaning of the last word, of course).[8]

An essential prerequisite to any improvement in society, so Mill believed, is improvement in the quality of the individuals who compose it; for him this was an article of faith as well as of scientific method.[9] Individual improvement depends on numerous factors, some of them environmental (for instance, economic and educational opportunity), some of them personal (such as motivation and intelligence); but a fundamental need is to understand the laws of mind and behaviour, to provide a systematic and scientifically validated psychology, since without this it is impossible to promote individual development in the directions desired. One must know both what human nature is and is capable of and by what means it can be guided to the goals chosen for it (or, to put it another way, social improvement depends in part on human educability, and this, once it has been shown to exist, depends in turn on accurate knowledge of the psychological means by which it can be actualised in educative processes). Mill had no doubt of the importance of psychology: 'a true psychology', he writes in *Sir William Hamilton's Philosophy*, 'is the indispensable scientific basis of morals, of politics, of the science and art of education'; and in his *Inaugural Address* of 1867 he recommends its study to the students of St Andrews University.[10] But how scientific *can* it be? Are the methods which he had elaborated for the natural sciences applicable to the human mind? 'Any facts,' he insists, 'are fitted in themselves to be a subject of science' — provided they are obedient to constant causal laws; but human nature presents peculiar difficulties. For one, it is 'the most complex and most difficult subject of study on which the human mind can be engaged';[11] for another, it cannot be fully investigated by experimental methods — and even if it could, would not yield the same accuracy of result as the natural sciences. But there is a more fundamental problem than this, which must be resolved before any attempt can be made at constructing a scientific psychology.

The problem has two aspects, one philosophical, the other scientific. The first is the question of whether individuality and freedom are possible in a world of causally ordered events; the second is whether a scientific method which relies on causal uniformity is applicable to entities assumedly characterised (and Mill does assume this) by individuality, freedom and choice. Negatively, as it were, Mill must rebut the view that causation is incompatible with human freedom and dignity; positively he must show that the facts of human nature are like all other facts in being susceptible of scientific enquiry and of generalisation into ultimate causal laws. He examines the problem in chapters ii and iii of *Logic* VI and also, in a different context of controversy, in *Sir William Hamilton's Philosophy* (6th edition, chapter xxvi). In an earlier Book of the *Logic* he declared his commitment to causal uniformity with a rigour which smacks of determinism: 'The whole of the present facts are the infallible result of all past facts, and more immediately of all the facts which existed at the moment previous. . . If the whole prior state of the entire universe could again recur, it would again be followed by the present state.'[12] He now reaffirms his belief in 'that constancy of causation, which is the foundation of every scientific theory of successive phenomena' and asserts its inclusion of human activities 'like all other natural events': 'The law of causality applies in the same strict sense to human actions as to other phenomena. . . No one who believed that he knew thoroughly the circumstances of any case, and the characters of the different persons concerned, would hesitate to foretell how all of them would act.'[13]

However, this belief is misleadingly referred to as 'the doctrine of philosophical necessity', a nomenclature which 'provides one of the most signal instances in philosophy of the abuse of terms'. 'Necessity' here is no more than a metaphor, but it is misinterpreted as a compelling force 'too powerful to be counteracted at all', whereas all it means is 'uniformity of order' and 'capability of being predicted'. Thus, 'when we say that all human actions take place of necessity, we only mean that they will certainly happen if nothing prevents'.[14] There is no compulsion in any normal sense, but rather a uniform sequence, so that if a friend who knows us well knows all our circumstances too, he will confidently predict how we will act. 'Any *must*,' Mill writes in *Hamilton's Philosophy*, 'any necessity other than the unconditional universality of the fact, we know nothing of.'[15] Thus interpreted, philosophical necessity does not 'conflict in the smallest degree with what is called our feeling of freedom' (any more than does the theological doctrine of divine foreknowledge);[16] nor does it detract from human dignity. Only when it is interpreted in a stronger, *compulsive* sense — when the inference is that what *does* happen *could not have happened otherwise*, as if there were 'some peculiar tie or mysterious restraint exercised by the antecedent over the consequent' — only thus interpreted is 'necessity' degrading and contrary to our consciousness of freedom. In fact,

> we know that we are not compelled, as by a magical spell, to obey any particular motive. We feel that if we wished to prove that we have the power of resisting the motive, we could do so, (that wish being, it needs scarcely to be observed, a *new antecedent*); and it would be humiliating to our pride and (what is of more importance) paralysing to our desire of excellence, if we thought otherwise.[17]

Such an interpretation is also, Mill maintains, wholly unwarranted by his own account of causal uniformity; rather, it is akin to oriental fatalism, which not only accepts whatever happens as inevitable but abandons all effort to resist or change it.

There is a modified form of fatalism, however, which is more plausible and therefore more insidious. This is the doctrine of the Owenites, followers of the social and educational reformer, Robert Owen: our actions are the inevitable result of our characters, and since our characters are formed for us by environment and circumstances, what we do is determined by forces outside our control. Even if we *will* a change in our circumstances that might modify our character for the better, the act of will is itself the product of character and circumstances and therefore non-voluntary.

Mill's answer to the Owenites contains the crux of his argument against the incompatibility of causal uniformity with human freedom and thus against objections to the scientific study of human nature.[18] It is true that 'our actions follow from our characters, and that our characters follow from our organisation, our education and our circumstances', but it does not follow that our actions are the *inevitable* consequences: 'The causes . . . on which action depends are never uncontrollable; and any given effect is only necessary provided that the causes tending to produce it are not controlled.' Moreover, although a man's character is 'in the ultimate resort' formed for him by circumstances, he still has a part to play 'as one of the intermediate agents': 'His character is formed by his circumstances . . . but his own desire to mould it in a particular way is one of those circumstances, and by no means one of the least influential.' Thus, we do have the power to intervene, to inject into circumstances new factors which will modify our characters and so change the direction of will and desire. Mental illness apart, it is never the case that human actions 'are ruled by any one motive with such absolute sway that there is no room for the influence of any other'; if parents and educators can form character by manipulating the circumstances which shape it, we also can do it for ourselves by the same means, provided we so desire; and Mill is certain that we *can* so desire, so long as we are not paralysed into inertia by believing it to be impossible: 'we are exactly as capable of making our own character, *if we will,* as others are of making it for us.' And even though our *willingness* depends in part on circumstances (upbringing, education, accident), we still have the feeling 'of our being able to modify our own character, *if we wish*'; this is 'the feeling of moral freedom which we are conscious of', the fulfilment of which requires mastery over habit and temptation and the achievement of 'confirmed virtue'.

This leads Mill to a different line of argument (already hinted at in the quotation above — 'we know that we are not compelled. . . .'), that the feeling of being able to modify our characters is central to what we call 'moral freedom'.

> A person feels morally free who feels that his habits or his temptations are not his masters, but he theirs; who even in yielding to them knows that he could resist; that were he desirous of altogether throwing them off, there would not be required for that purpose a stronger desire than he knows himself to be capable of feeling.[19]

Without this feeling of moral freedom and the conviction that it is not mere illusion, morality would become a charade, the acting out of imperatives which we cannot claim to be our own. Yet this consciousness of moral freedom does not nullify the reality of psychological or behavioural causation. 'A volition,' Mill writes in *Sir William Hamilton's Philosophy* (here using 'moral', as often, in the sense of 'psychological'), 'is a moral effect, which follows the corresponding moral causes as certainly and invariably as physical effects follow their physical causes. Whether it *must* do so, I acknowledge myself to be entirely ignorant. . . All I know is that it always *does*.'[20]

To sum up: Mill argues, first, that causal uniformity is not the same as necessity interpreted in a rigid determinist or fatalist sense; second — and this is the central point — that it is always open to human volition, yet without exemption from causal uniformity, to intervene in the sequence of cause and effect, to introduce 'a new antecedent', in order to modify the course of events; and third, as a supporting argument to the latter, that the possibility of such intervention is essential to a genuine morality. These arguments are far from convincing. Though he rightly denies that causal uniformity implies any mysterious constraining force of inevitability, he comes close to such a view himself in his insistence on the universality of the fact of causation (the 'always *does*' of the above passage). More crucially, however, he does not explain how the will *can* intervene to divert the causal sequence nor how it *does*. Volition, Mill insists, is as much a part of causal sequence as any other event; true, it can redirect the course of causal sequence, but this redirection is itself part of a causal sequence. There seems here to be not only a conjunction of incompatibles, but also an unexplained mechanism of change. How is the train of events diverted from one line to another? How are the points changed (to continue the metaphor), and who or what operates the switch? It would seem that volition needs temporarily to be released from causation in order to initiate a new sequence — to jump, as it were, from one line to another; but this would imply exemption from causal sequence and would be inconsistent with Mill's emphatic commitment to causality and the uniformity of nature. One is left with the uneasy feeling that human volition has been given a special dispensation of exemption from, or intervention in, the laws of cause and effect ('his own desire to mould it in a particular way'); that to include human volition along with

ˌpurely material factors among the 'circumstances' which form
character is a convenient ambiguity which by-passes the fact that
will and desire also have their place in the cause/effect process. On
the other hand, if the will is wholly and inescapably subject to
causality, it is difficult to avoid the Owenite conclusion that our
characters are made *for* us and not, as Mill must insist in order to
defend his ideal of human educability and human improvement, *by*
us.

Mill's stand on causal uniformity is further prejudiced by his
conception of the social role of the gifted individual. He was impressed
from his early childhood by what he read of great men and great
exploits; this was part of the attraction for him of ancient Greece and
Rome, of Plutarch's *Lives* and of the voyages of discovery. Later this
romantic attachment of childhood developed into a considered view
of the essential contribution of the great man or woman to human
progress. Thus, in *Representative Government* he insists that
originality and invention are essential to progress, and that it is a
first claim on any government to stimulate the qualities that promote
them — energy, courage, imagination and the rest.[21] The same
message is central to *On Liberty*, where he states his faith in the
manifold wealth of human genius and its powers of origination; and
it appears also in the *Logic* (VI, xi, 3), where he suggests that 'the
volitions of exceptional persons . . . may be indispensable links in the
chain of causation.'[22]

It is difficult to see any way out of the impasse. Mill's position as
social reformer and logician of science requires that human behaviour
be causally explicable and causally predictable; but his concept of
individuality demands freedom — freedom for choice, for initiative,
for spontaneity of growth. One possible escape he suggests himself,
namely, a regress of causes 'into the region of the unknowable'[23] —
which amounts to an admission that there is a limit to explanation.
Another is implicit in his very assertion of behavioural predictability:
if all the facts (of character and circumstances) were known, then
human action 'might be unerringly inferred'; but Mill is saved from
the consequences of this by the impossibility of ever knowing *all* the
relevant facts or even which *are* relevant; predictability — and
determinism with it — is therefore in principle incapable of proof. It
is easy to accuse Mill of conceptual jugglery, of a convenient ambiguity
of statement or even (as has his biographer, Michael Packe) of
bending logic — nor is he entirely guiltless; but two things can be

said in mitigation. First, the problem of reconciling free will with causal uniformity is still debated and still unsolved; second, he is surely right in pointing to morality as the key area in which the problem is most acute and a solution both most urgently needed and most likely to be found.[24]

Assuming, then, that human behaviour is not exempt from scientific investigation, Mill turns to practical issues of method. He begins with a distinction between exact and inexact sciences. In the former general laws are thoroughly established and systematised, and the phenomena they encompass, together with all apparent irregularities, can be fully explained and accurately predicted; astronomy is an eminent example. The latter, whether through the inaccessibility or complexity of the data or the difficulty of relating them, have not yet reached this degree of perfection; among these are meteorology and the science of human nature. Of the last he writes:

> The phenomena with which this science is conversant being the thoughts, feelings and actions of human beings, it would have attained the ideal perfection of a science if it enabled us to foretell how an individual would think, feel, or act throughout life, with the same certainty with which astronomy enables us to predict the places and the occultations of the heavenly bodies. It needs scarcely be stated that nothing approaching to this can be done.[25]

There are two principal reasons: first, it is impossible to discover all the facts relevant to prediction; second, action is the joint product of circumstances (the facts of the situation) and character, and character is itself the product of a vast diversity of factors whose aggregate influence is 'never in any two cases exactly similar'; once again, therefore, prediction is blunted. A third reason, which he mentions in chapter v of *Logic* VI, is the difficulty of exposing human beings to experiment (more acutely felt in Mill's time than ours!). Progress is possible, however, towards the ideal: some general laws of human nature can certainly be established; so too can narrower generalisations and uniformities derived directly from observation ('empirical laws'). Combining these we can make generalised assertions which are 'true in the main' and provide a basis for predictions 'which will *almost* always be verified'. Moreover, in dealing with large numbers of persons it becomes possible to establish statistical generalisations which, though only probable 'when asserted of individual human beings indiscriminately selected', become 'certain when affirmed of the character and collective conduct of masses'. Finally, every effort must be made to form deductive links between such general laws as are known and the lesser generalisations, so that these latter 'can be exhibited as corollaries from the universal laws of human nature on which they rest'. Thus, within the limits he states and by adapting procedure to the peculiar difficulties of its subject matter, Mill is confident that human nature is an appropriate subject for science.

It is not part of his purpose, Mill makes clear, to speculate about 'the mind's own nature'; psychological enquiry is not concerned with such questions as 'what the Mind is' and how it differs from 'Matter', but with mental phenomena, 'the various feelings or states of consciousness of sentient beings', including 'thoughts, emotions, volitions and sensations, the last being as truly states of mind as the three former'.[26] 'It remains incontestable,' he writes, 'that there exist uniformities of succession among states of mind, and that these can be ascertained by observation and experiment'; the province of psychology is to investigate them, to establish 'the laws, whether ultimate or derivative, according to which one mental state succeeds another — is caused by, or at least is caused to follow, another'.[27] He does not underestimate the difficulties of the enterprise. Experiment is limited by considerations of humanity as well as by the intractability of subject matter — indeed, he doubts even if it is possible. Observation, too, has its problems: Locke was right to insist that 'the origin of our ideas' is the crux of psychological inquiry and the theory of mind; but their origin in the infant mind is inaccessible to the external observer at the actual time of its occurrence, and in the adult it is so overlaid by and absorbed into subsequent experience that introspection cannot isolate it. These original mental contents can therefore only be inferred as residual elements in the phenomena of mature consciousness. (Mill underestimates the possibilities of both experiment and observation; the former is clearly not inconsistent with human freedom and dignity, and much valuable information has, in fact, come from controlled observation of even the youngest babies; but it would be unreasonable to censure him for this).

He will not allow psychology to be subsumed under physiology: it may well be — indeed, it is 'extremely probable' — that every 'mental state' has a 'nervous state for its immediate antecedent and proximate cause',[28] but there is no proof of this; the existing state of ignorance about the nervous system precludes the possibility of deducing mental laws from physiological; at least for the time being, therefore, mental phenomena must be studied as such in a distinct science of mind. Nor is psychology to be confused with logic: the latter is 'the theory of the ascertainment of objective truth'; there is a natural link between the two in 'the theory of the particular mental operations whereby truth is ascertained or authenticated', namely, conception, judgement and reasoning, but they remain separate disciplines.[29] Finally, Mill displays his usual epistemological caution in avoiding extravagant claims for psychology; here, as in other fields of inquiry, he recognises limits, certainly in the present state of knowledge, to human questioning. Thus, there are two ultimates in analysing the complexity of mental phenomena: one is 'the difference between a fact and the thought of that fact' — a difference which is polarised chronologically in memory and anticipation; the other, closely linked, is self-consciousness, the awareness that the succession of mental states in memory up to the present moment of consciousness belongs uniquely to a self who is *myself* (see p.56).[30] As is noted elsewhere, Mill was not insensitive to the 'narrow region of our experience' and the consequent mystery which thwarts intellectual penetration.[31]

CHAPTER 3

Association Psychology

It was part of the aim of the *Logic* to place 'metaphysical and moral science on a basis of analysed experience, in opposition to the theory of innate principles'.[1] The reference in the latter part of the quotation is to the intuitionist philosophy, which manifested itself in psychology no less than in other fields of knowledge and to which Mill was uncompromisingly hostile (p. 31 above). Applied to psychology, intuitionism held that mental phenomena are not wholly explicable in terms of simple sense data, as Locke, Hume and their empiricist successors maintained; rather, there are certain fundamental elements in mental experience which are directly or intuitively present to the mind. Mill describes it as an *a priori* psychology and contrasts it with his own *a posteriori* experientialist psychology:

> The *a priori* thinkers hold that in every act of thought, down to the most elementary, there is an ingredient which is not given *to* the mind, but contributed *by* the mind in virtue of its inherent powers. The simplest phenomenon of all, an external sensation, requires according to them a mental element to become a perception and be thus converted from a passive and merely fugitive state of our own being into the recognition of a durable object external to the mind. . . Experience, instead of being the source and prototype of our ideas, is itself a product of the mind's own forces working on the impressions we receive from without and has always a mental as well as an external element. Experience is only rendered possible by those mental laws which it is vainly invoked to explain and account for.[2]

(The Kantian influence in this is obvious, and German thinkers had been powerful contributors to the *a priori* psychology; at the time of the review Mill claims that 'the sceptre of Psychology has decidedly returned to this island', where both kinds were now flourishing).[3]

46

A crucial point of difference between the two psychological schools was the origin of the awareness of self in contradistinction to a world external to it; here, as Mill clearly recognised, the characteristic differences between the opposing psychologies are most forcibly illustrated, and he devotes about a fifth of *Sir William Hamilton's Philosophy* to attacking the intuitionist position and elucidating his own (it is, incidentally, one of the more interesting areas of what is, for the modern reader, a somewhat arid volume of controversy). Partly, of course, this is a philosophical problem, but the means by which this duality of consciousness is produced in the mind is a psychological question, and Mill's exposition of it will be considered below. Though central, it is not the only problem, however, for the intuitionists claimed that all the basic constituents of consciousness contained a mental contribution; for instance, the so-called primary qualities of matter — solidity, extension and shape — the notion of distance and likewise more sophisticated concepts such as infinity in space and time. All these 'ideas' (in Locke's terminology) or ingredients of consciousness they held to be in some way and to some extent given *a priori* and not wholly acquired from experience. Mill was saved the trouble of working out his own alternative to intuitionism, for he found it ready-made in the well established association psychology in which he had been thoroughly instructed by his father and which he was able to accept with little modification as his own.

The fundamental tenet of association psychology is that mental content is built up from elementary ingredients contributed by sensory experience, which are linked together according to ascertainable 'laws'. This theory was far from new in Mill's time — indeed, it had a venerable history which can be traced back to certain hints in Plato (who used the acknowledged fact of mental association to argue his own intuitionist Theory of Forms); this is hardly surprising, since it is a matter of common experience, regularly utilised as a mnemonic device, that ideas *are* associated in or by the mind — that, for instance, recollection of a particular event or person recalls with it numerous related items such as the state of the weather or the colour of a dress. It was Aristotle who first attempted a systematic study of association and tried to formulate the principles which govern it. His account of it develops from an explanation of the act of recollection in the *de Memoria*:[4] mental processes he asserts, always take the form of a series or train; their association in this series may be either *necessary* (e.g. in logic or mathematics, where *a* entails *b*; and perhaps in biology, where one stage of growth necessarily precedes another) or *habitual*. Association by habit can be powerful but is not inevitable — individuals differ in this respect. It occurs when objects or events experienced are similar, contrasted or contiguous in space or time; in such instances the recollection of one tends to recall others associated with it in any of these ways, and the more frequently they are experienced together, the stronger becomes the mind's tendency to associate them. Little was added to this initial analysis until the seventeenth century, when Thomas Hobbes embarked on a fresh investigation of mental states and their relationships, eschewing the traditional intuitionism and founding his inquiry on a firm experientialist basis in sensory experience. He paved the way for others, first of whom was John Locke, the inventor of the phrase 'association of ideas'. Locke makes a distinction similar to Aristotle's between necessary and habitual association:

> Some of our ideas have a natural correspondence and connexion one with another. . . Besides this, there is another connexion of ideas wholly owing to chance or custom: ideas that in themselves are not at all of kin come to be so united in some men's minds that it is very hard to separate them; they always keep in company, and the one no sooner at any time comes into the understanding, but its associate appears with it; and if they are more than two which are thus united, the whole gang, always inseparable, show themselves together.[5]

About the means of association (similarity, etc.) he has little to say, though he does explore 'simultaneous association', the fusing of several associated simple ideas into a single, complex, unitary conception. After him came Berkeley, who added causality to the three modes of association named by Aristotle, and Hume, who likewise included causality and who used association as the principal instrument of his sceptical enquiry into the concept of cause. 'Were ideas entirely loose and unconnected,' Hume writes,

> chance alone would join them; and 'tis impossible the same simple ideas should fall regularly into complex ones (as they commonly do) without some bond of union among them, some associating quality by which one idea naturally introduces another. This uniting principle among ideas is not to be considered as an inseparable connexion; . . . we are only to regard it as a gentle force which commonly prevails. . . .[6]

Although association psychology was not confined to Britain, it was here principally that it was developed from the experientialist foundations laid by Locke and Hume; and it was by British thinkers that it was elaborated into a systematic psychology which aimed to account for the full range of mental processes. The first of these was David Hartley, a contemporary of Hume's; after him came numerous others, of whom the most notable were Thomas Brown, James Mill, Alexander Bain (all Scots) and Herbert Spencer. There is no need to follow its progress at the hands of these exponents, but a summary of its doctrines as they were in the early part of the nineteenth century is essential to an understanding of John Mill's psychological assumptions.

Association psychology is essentially an experientialist or (in the modern sense) empiricist account of mental phenomena. The primary data of experience are sensations registered upon the nervous system and these give rise (deliberately a vague expression — see on) to 'ideas' or mental occurrences which are the ideational, as distinct from the sensational, aspect of consciousness. The fundamental principle of associationism is the tendency of these latter to link with one another to form either trains (or series) of mental items or unitary complexes wherein the items are bound into a simultaneous whole. By some exponents association was regarded as a 'force' which encouraged or impelled the linkage of mental items; others denied the existence of any linkage or union between the items, asserting that they remained contiguous (though still separate) in the mind simply because of the prior repeated concurrence of the initial sensations; others again held a position between these two, accepting a union of some kind but rejecting any impelling 'force'. A further distinction can be made between a 'mechanical' and a 'chemical' account of association, particularly in regard to the unitary complexes; the former held these to be a combination of separate elements temporarily held together but resolvable into their original particularity; the latter regarded the combination as in some way transforming and transcending the particularity of the separate items, just as a chemical compound like water is qualitatively distinct from its component elements.

All associationists agreed that mental processes had a physiological basis in the nervous system, but they had no clear view as to the nature of this basis or the relation between sensations (events in the nervous system) and 'ideas' (events in the mind); indeed, this remained a standing problem for which they devised no satisfactory solution. J. S. Mill himself leaves it an open question; he admits, as has been noted (p.44), the probability that every mental state has a nervous state for its immediate antecedent, but knowledge of these nervous states is too scant to allow any inference to be drawn from them of the mental states 'of which they are supposed to be the generators or causes';[7] hence his conclusion in favour of a distinct 'science of mind'. However, there was considerable agreement about the factors which promote association: similarity (one experience tends to recall another which resembles it) and contiguity (a sensation or idea tends to recall others which formerly occurred in close proximity to it in space or time). Contrast, which Aristotle and others included, was rejected by J. S. Mill as superfluous, on the grounds that it was implied by similarity; causality found few adherents after Berkeley. In addition, the strength of association could be influenced by the intensity, duration and recency of the original experience, by the frequency of its repetition, by the pain or pleasure accompanying it and by factors of heredity and life experience in the individual person.

The fundamentals of association psychology were well established by the end of the eighteenth century; they were also widely known beyond the immediate circle of its exponents, and their influence was apparent in other areas of thought than psychology, for instance in ethics and jurisprudence. A new analysis of mental phenomena was needed now, which not only assumed the basic principles of association psychology, but developed them in detailed exposition of specific topics. James Mill was among the leaders in this new phase, and his *Analysis of the Phenomena of the Human Mind*, published in 1829, became the classic of nineteenth-century associationism, as Hartley's *Observations on Man* (1749) had been of the eighteenth. James Mill's interest was not merely theoretical; like his son, he was an ardent reformer and saw association psychology as an essential instrument for his purposes. The rival psychology of intuitionism, holding as it did that certain elements of mental experience are contributed *a priori* from the innate constitution of the mind, leaned inevitably towards a conservative view of human nature as resistant to change. At worst it could become a bastion of self-interested opposition to reform, a plea for indolence, an apology for the *status quo*; as J. S. Mill writes in his *Autobiography*, 'there never was such an instrument devised for consecrating all deep-seated prejudices', and he saw it as 'one of the chief hindrances to the rational treatment of great social questions and one of the greatest stumbling-blocks to human improvement'.[8] Associationism, on the other hand, implied a view of human nature as essentially malleable, educable; if mental experience, if outlook, attitude and character, are built from ingredients associatively linked, then by changing the environment and consequently the sensory experience which contribute the ingredients, the pattern of character can be shaped initially, and possibly even re-shaped, towards improvement. As part of his education, therefore, into the role of social reformer John Mill was set to read Hartley's *Observations* and other associationist writings, and between 1822 and 1829 he read, part by part as it was written, the manuscript of his father's *Analysis*. Many years later he wrote in *Sir William Hamilton's Philosophy* that 'hardly anything universal can be affirmed in psychology except the laws of association.'[9]

His adherence to associationism was not uncritical, however; nor did he accept without reserve the conclusions expressed in the *Analysis*. He nowhere presents a full and systematic account of his own version, regarding this as unnecessary in view of the work done by his father and others; but its principal features can be sketched out from a reading of *Logic* VI, parts of *Sir William Hamilton's Philosophy* and the notes which he wrote for the 1869 edition of the *Analysis*; there is also a useful summary in his review article, 'Bain's Psychology'. All that concerns us here is its outline and main emphases. Among the fundamental psychological laws (possibly *the* fundamental laws, though he does not say so) are the following:

> Whenever any state of consciousness has once been excited in us, no matter by what cause, an inferior degree of the same state of consciousness, a state of consciousness resembling the former but inferior in intensity, is capable of being reproduced in us without the presence of any such cause as excited it at first.
>
> These ideas or secondary mental states are excited by our impressions [i.e. sensations], or by other ideas, according to certain laws which are called Laws of Association.[10]

That is, mental constituents can be recalled to, or can recur in, consciousness without a repetition of the sensory experiences which initially caused them; and these constituents tend to link up in associated trains. Of the 'laws of association' similarity and contiguity are basic; their effect is increased by the intensity and/or frequency of the original experience, so much so that the resulting association may become virtually inseparable. Absolute indissolubility he rejects — not only would it be contrary to normal experience, but it would also amount to the unacceptable admission that character can be damaged beyond hope of reformation. That associated ideas can be virtually inseparable was important as part of his attack on intuitionism; for this *apparent* inseparability deludes us into believing that they are *actually* and *existentially* inseparable and are apprehended as such by an intuitive act of perception.

To the commonly agreed laws Mill added a supporting 'law of obliviscence': ideas which remain for long periods unrecalled and unattended to may disappear from consciousness, thus causing gaps in a series of recollected ideas; in this way he could explain not only lapses of memory but also the ability to leap from one idea to another (as we often do) without passing through a long chain of intermediate ideas. His associationism also included four emphases which are both interesting in themselves and psychologically important.

First, in explaining the nature of complex clusters of associated ideas he stresses what he calls 'mental chemistry'. Two associationist views of such complexes are possible: one is 'physical' or 'mechanical' — each idea retains its separate identity but is linked or bonded with the others into a coherent whole; the other is that they are fused, by a process similar to a chemical reaction, into a new entity which transcends its particular components and can be said 'to *result from*, or *be generated by*, the simple ideas, not to *consist* of them'.[11] Though Mill is unwilling to apply this chemical analogy to all mental experience — the mind's 'abstruser conceptions, its sentiments, emotions and volitions'[12] — it clearly offers a more satisfactory account of some mental processes than the mechanical model and is more in keeping with his own views on individuality and genius.

Second, he recognises the importance of attention, and in explaining its relation to volition he strengthens associationist theory of conative phenomena. In a protracted note to chapter xxv of the *Analysis* (II, pp. 372ff.) he complains of the inadequacy of his father's account of attention and attempts to show how the accepted laws of association can explain voluntary and effortful attention (where an object is not in itself sufficiently attractive to hold it spontaneously) and the fatigue which results from prolonged voluntary attention.

Third, in an even longer note (twenty-one pages!) to volume I, chapter xi he corrects and improves on his father's analysis of belief. It is not, as James Mill thought, simply a case of inseparability of ideas resulting from habitual association; belief involves (or *should* involve) an appeal to evidence, to reason; moreover, it incorporates an element of volition which makes it more than a mere linkage of two ideas however supposedly inseparable: 'We believe a thing when we are ready to act on the faith of it; to face the practical consequences of taking it for granted; . . . the association which leads to action must be, in some respect or other, different from that which stops at thought.'[13] He concludes, therefore, that there is an 'ultimate and primordial' distinction between imagining and believing, between holding a thought or a flow of thoughts in consciousness and believing it to be true to fact, a 'reality of nature'.[14] In this distinction we reach 'the central point of our intellectual nature, presupposed and built upon in every attempt we make to explain the more recondite phenomena of our mental being'.[15]

Finally, in a section of *Logic* VI which strikes a remarkably modern note, Mill shows his awareness of individual differences and considers the reasons for them: 'The commonest observation shows that different minds are susceptible in very different degrees to the action of the same psychological causes.' These differences are not 'ultimate facts, incapable of being either explained or altered'; on the contrary,

> It is certain that, in human beings at least, differences in education and in outward circumstances are capable of affording an adequate explanation of by far the greatest portion of character, and that the remainder may be in great part accounted for by physical differences in the sensations produced in different individuals by the same external or internal cause[16]

— a conclusion necessary to Mill's faith in human educability by the manipulation of environment. He adds as an afterthought that certain mental facts do not fit readily into these possible explanations, notably the instincts; but this does not prevent him from affirming optimistically that instincts 'may be modified to any extent or entirely conquered in human beings, and to no inconsiderable extent even in some of the domesticated animals, by other mental influences and by education'.[17]

The deficiencies of associationism as a total psychology are obvious enough and some of them will be noted below. Meanwhile it may be helpful to offer an illustration of Mill's use of it as an explanatory theory in what he regarded as a crucial problem for both psychology and philosophy. It is the former aspect which concerns us here; reference to the latter can be found on p. 79 below. In chapter x of *Sir William Hamilton's Philosophy* Mill attacks the intuitionist view that the distinction of ego and non-ego is known immediately in the very act of perception. He quotes him thus:

> We are immediately conscious in perception of an ego and a non-ego, known together, and known in contrast to each other. This is the fact of the Duality of Consciousness. It is clear and manifest. When I concentrate my attention in the simplest act of perception, I return from my observation with the most irresistible conviction of two facts, or rather two branches of the same fact: that I am, and that something different from me exists. In this act I am conscious of myself as the perceiving subject, and of an external reality as the object perceived; and I am conscious of both existences in the same indivisible moment of intuition. . . We may, therefore, lay it down as an undisputed truth that consciousness gives, as an ultimate fact, a primitive quality: a knowledge of the ego in relation and contrast to the non-ego; and a knowledge of the non-ego in relation and contrast to the ego. The ego and non-ego are thus given in an original synthesis, as conjoined in the unity of knowledge, and in an original antithesis, as opposed in the contrariety of existence.[18]

Mill's task is to show that consciousness of self and others is equally, and more convincingly, explicable by association psychology. He makes two initial postulates which, he claims, 'are proved by experience': one is that 'the human mind is capable of expectation . . . that after having had actual sensations we are capable of forming the conception of possible sensations';[19] the other is the basic laws of association — similarity, contiguity and inseparable association suggesting an existential union of ideas. What is meant, he now asks, by belief in an external world?

> We mean that there is concerned in our perceptions something which exists when we are not thinking of it; which existed before we had ever thought of it, and would exist if we were annihilated; and further, that there exist things which we never saw, touched or otherwise perceived, and things which never have been perceived by man.[20]

How does the belief arise? At any one time we are conscious of only a small number of present sensations; but we are aware, as a result of past experience and memory, of a vast number of *possible* sensations which we might have if we could place ourselves in the appropriate circumstances. These possible sensations are not isolated but are grouped (by normal association) into an enormous variety of complexes which themselves tend to form associative links with one another; there is thus built up in consciousness a continually extending substratum of *possible* sensations which underlies the sensations *actually* present in consciousness. These possibilities of sensation are not linked haphazardly but follow causal sequences which impose on the possible sensations in their various groupings a constancy of order and relation. In this way there is built up the conception of an ordered world of permanent possibilities of sensation, whose initial origin in sensory experience is forgotten and which is 'independent of our will, our presence, and everything which belongs to us'.[21] Moreover, 'we find other people grounding their expectations and conduct upon the same permanent possibilities on which we ground ours'; they do not experience the same actual sensations, but they have the same *possibilities* of sensation. 'The world of possible sensations succeeding one another according to laws is as much in other beings as it is in me; it has therefore an existence outside me; it is an external world'; and these groups of possibilities, he adds, are 'the fundamental reality in nature'.

Now present sensations, however vividly experienced, are fleeting and impermanent:

> Thus our actual sensations and the permanent possibilities of sensation stand out in obtrusive contrast to one another; and when the idea of cause has been acquired and extended by generalisation from the parts of our experience to its aggregate whole, nothing can be more natural than that the permanent possibilities should be classed by us as existences generically distinct from our sensations, but of which our sensations are the effect.[22]

Hence comes the contrast between ego and non-ego. However, this does not explain the conception of a *permanent* self underlying immediate consciousness and including it. By similar arguments, therefore, Mill goes on to show that just as the actual world can be explained as a permanent possibility of sensation, so too 'the belief I entertain that my mind exists when it is not feeling, nor thinking, nor conscious of its own existence resolves itself into the belief of a permanent possibility of these states.'[23] There remains a problem which Mill does not overlook: not only are we conscious of present and possible sensations, we are also conscious of *ourselves as the subject of them*; mind or consciousness is not simply a series of feelings but a series of feelings which is conscious of itself as being one. This presents him with a paradox which he cannot solve, 'a final inexplicability' which must be accepted as an 'ultimate fact'.[24] However, he has, so he believes, proved his point that the contrast in consciousness of ego and non-ego can be explained perfectly well by the laws of association without recourse to intuition.

To anyone looking back at it from a century or more later association psychology presents an oddly amateurish appearance, one of naivety almost, a relic from a period of unsophisticated innocence. It had no experimental foundation; it lacked the support of controlled and carefully documented observation; and despite Mill's disdainful contrast of Sir William Hamilton's 'introspective in contradistinction to the psychological method' and his claim that in associationism alone could be found 'the true conditions of psychological investigation', in fact the associationists themselves relied for the evidence of their conclusions principally on what would now be called introspection.[25] This has a place in certain kinds of psychological inquiry, but is far too limited and unreliable to be acceptable as a major instrument of research — and in any case, as Mill recognised (p.44 above), it can tell us little about the minds of children. Clearly it is no substitute for the quantitative experimental and observational techniques of the present time (which is not to deny a limit even to *their* penetration of the human mind). This is not the only weakness of association psychology; another is its failure to subject to critical analysis such concepts as 'mind', 'mental state', 'consciousness', 'idea', 'expectation' and many others which are essential to its theoretical structure. Yet another is its over-reliance on physical or mechanical models for interpreting mental phenomena — as if the mind were a kind of Newtonian universe of interacting forces or, more simply, a bag of marbles ('ideas') dispensed from experience and three-dimensionally patterned by some mysterious process of inter-attraction. (In time, it is true, this model was modified, not only by the 'chemical' account of complex ideas (p. 52 above) but also, and much more profoundly, by dynamic, evolutionary models suggested by Darwin and other biologists; this is apparent in the later writings of Alexander Bain, also Mill's biographer, and Herbert Spencer). A further weakness, derived in part from this mechanical model, was its inadequate account of volition: association suggests a passivity rather than an activity of mental processes, and it is difficult to see how, from the combining of mental items (even in 'chemical' compounds) there can come a spontaneous, self-assertive force which wills and chooses. Mill was aware of the problem and discusses it in his review of Bain's two volumes of psychology; the substitution of organic, evolutionary models was a step towards a more convincing explanation of the conative aspect of mind.[26] Again, it was clear to the associationists that their work was hampered by inadequate knowledge of the nervous system (p.49 above),and that there was little hope of unravelling the relation between mental and sensory experience without further very considerable advance in this area; on the other hand, it was to their credit that they recognised and insisted on the existence of such a relation — however ethereal in some of its flights, mind had firm roots in physiological soil.

A point of particular interest in Mill's account of associationism is its suggestion of the need for a theory of the un- or subconscious as an explanatory hypothesis; again and again he seems poised on the brink of a Freudian leap into a new concept of mind, only to withdraw as the vision fails him. For instance, in chapter xv of *Sir William Hamilton's Philosophy* he examines the professor's view that there are unconscious states of mind, 'latent mental modifications', which nevertheless influence our conscious thoughts and actions; 'the sphere of our conscious modification,' he quotes from him, 'is only a small circle in the centre of a far wider sphere of action and passion of which we are only conscious through its effects.'[27] In countering this view Mill virtually accepts it, for he uses language which implies just such an unconscious sphere of mental processes — 'capability' of recall, 'powers and susceptibilities of which we are not conscious', 'the unconscious result of association'. In the end he is forced to agree with Sir William to the extent of admitting 'his unconscious mental modifications in the only shape in which I can attach any very distinct meaning to them, namely unconscious modifications of the nerves'.[28] Similar assumptions are implied in Mill's own account of mind which he proposes in an earlier chapter as superior to that of the intuitionists: 'The belief I entertain that my mind exists when it is not feeling, nor thinking, nor conscious of its own existence, resolves itself into the belief of a permanent possibility of these states.'[29] But what *is* this 'permanent possibility' if not a kind of unconscious mental substratum whose underlying permanence contrasts with, and also feeds and sustains, the flow of consciousness? Whatever its weaknesses as now apparent, Mill believed that association psychology supplied the correct interpretation of mental phenomena and was therefore the only acceptable basis for a scientific theory of character formation and of practical education. His account of this theory is the next subject for consideration.

CHAPTER 4

Ethology

To his own satisfaction at least Mill believed he had now formulated a theory of science and of scientific method which could provide genuine knowledge not only of the physical world but also of the far greater complexity of human nature; he further believed that a systematic science of mind, both explanatory and predictive, already existed in association psychology, to whose basic principles he firmly adhered. However, because his interest was not merely theoretical or academic, he could not stop here. To understand human beings was not enough; he wanted also to change them for the better and by thus improving individuals to effect the improvement of society: 'the worth of a state . . . is the worth of the individuals composing it.'[1] Now human beings are contextual; they live in a mesh of circumstances which are different for each of them and whose interplay with factors of heredity and upbringing produces the enormous observable variety of character and behaviour. Causality is operative here, of course, as everywhere else, and ultimately, Mill believed, behaviour depends on the fundamental causal laws of psychology; but so extreme is the complexity of that interplay of influences in each individual's situation that these basic psychological laws are of little immediate help in explaining and predicting his behaviour:

> Suppose that all which passes in the mind of man is determined by a few simple laws: still, if those laws be such that there is not one of the facts surrounding a human being, or of the events which happen to him, that does not influence in some mode or degree his subsequent mental history, and if the circumstances of different human beings are extremely different, it will be no wonder if very few propositions can be made respecting the details of their conduct or feelings which will be true of all mankind.[2]

59

Certainly, Mill is saying, there are primary psychological laws which are the ultimate determinants of behaviour; but it is impossible *in vacuo* and out of context to know how these will affect the details of individual behaviour. All men are subject to the laws of association, but the behavioural impact of those laws in any individual flows from the conjunction with the situational factors pertaining to that individual; or in modern terms, all men have instinctive tendencies to fear, aggression, self-preservation and sex, but how these tendencies express themselves depends on a variety of social, cultural and personal factors.

It might be suggested, as a logical consequence of Mill's position, that every individual's situation is unique and that it is impossible, therefore, to generalise at all from basic psychological laws and situational factors to particular items or even types of behaviour. He does not accept this, however:

> Human beings do not all feel and act alike in the same circum-stances; but it is possible to determine what makes one person in a given position feel or act in one way, another in another; how any given mode of feeling and conduct compatible with the general laws (physical and mental) of human nature has been or may be formed. In other words, mankind have not one universal character, but there exist universal laws of the formation of character.[3]

By 'universal laws' Mill does not here mean the basic laws of association (or any other conceivable) psychology, but general laws of behaviour which are always (or at least usually) true of a given combination of the basic psychological laws with a particular pattern of circumstances (including character). Thus, if a is a psychological law, x a pattern of circumstances and y a form of behaviour, one might generalise that $a + x = y$, and this equation would constitute a universal law of the formation of character. It is on the basis of such laws, Mill continues, 'that every rational attempt to construct the science of human nature in the concrete and for practical purposes must proceed'.[4]

Evidently, then, there is need of a subsidiary science whose orientation would be practical rather than theoretical and whose task would be to discover and systematise these laws of the formation of character; they could then be implemented in controlling and modifying behaviour in order to produce a desired kind or quality of character. Such a science Mill outlines in chapter v of *Logic* VI; the name he gives to it is 'ethology' (from the Greek ἦθος ,'custom', 'character'), and it was his intention, once the *Logic* was finished, to elaborate this outline in his next book. 'With parental fondness,' writes Alexander Bain, 'he cherished this subject for a considerable time, regarding it as the foundation and cornerstone of sociology. . . A few months later he wrote: "I do not know when I shall be ripe for beginning 'Ethology'. The scheme has not assumed any definite shape with me yet." ' In fact it came to nothing, and he was soon deeply involved in writing his *Principles of Political Economy*. Bain comments: 'I do not believe there was anything to be got in the direction that he was looking'[5] — and Mill himself may well have come to the same conclusion. In *Logic* VI, however, he has no doubt of the possibility of 'a science of ethology founded on the laws of psychology . . . though little has yet been done, and that little not at all systematically, towards forming it'.[6] Although it scarcely yet exists, the time is ripe for its creation; there is already available a mass of empirical data, and the causal laws of mind, the major premises of ethology, are now firmly established; admittedly, there are areas of uncertainty in 'the natural differences of individual minds' and their relation to peculiarities of environmental circumstance, but these can be discounted in a broad survey (such as was intended) of 'mankind in the average or *en masse*'. He concludes, therefore, that

> most competent judges will agree that the general laws of the different constituent elements of human nature are even now sufficiently understood to render it possible for a competent thinker to deduce from those laws, with a considerable approach to certainty, the particular type of character which would be formed in mankind generally by any assumed set of circumstances.

How far Mill was justified in this optimistic assessment is a question which will be considered later.

As to the purpose of ethology, he makes it plain that what he intends is not a descriptive science merely but one which can be made instrumental to prescribed goals:

> The subject to be studied is the origin and sources of all those qualities in human beings which are interesting to us, either as facts to be produced, to be avoided, or merely to be understood; and the object is to determine from the general laws of mind, combined with the general position of our species in the universe, what actual or possible combinations of circumstances are capable of promoting or of preventing the production of those qualities.[7]

Ethology must be harnessed to the production of effects 'which it is desirable to produce or to prevent', to values and purposes beyond itself; when fully developed and when thus value-orientated, it constitutes 'the foundation of the corresponding art', which is education, and practical education will then consist in transforming the principles of ethology into 'a parallel system of precepts' and the adaptation of these to the peculiarities of individual circumstances.[8] Education, 'in the widest sense of the term', refers to 'the formation of national or collective character as well as individual';[9] ethology is thus linked to purposes of potentially enormous extent, which may include the shaping of a whole nation or culture to conform with chosen patterns of value. But what values, and chosen by whom? These are crucial questions which Mill does not attempt to answer here, though answers can be found elsewhere in his writings, for instance in *Utilitarianism, On Liberty* and *Representative Government*. They will be considered briefly below; for the moment it is sufficient to note his insistence on ethology's need for prescriptive direction.

We have yet to consider Mill's account of the methods appropriate to ethological science and of its status in relation to the fundamental science of psychology. In his account of science, it will be remembered, Mill distinguishes between causal laws, which are primary and fundamental and to which all natural phenomena are ultimately causally related, and empirical laws, which are local or limited generalisations from experience. In chapter v of *Logic* VI he refers to these latter as 'truths of common experience', 'familiar maxims', 'the common wisdom of common life'. Though they hold true within the limits of observation and offer valuable practical guidance, their truth is not absolute but dependent on primary causal laws; only in so far as their logical dependence on these latter can be established are they acceptable as scientifically valid and predictively reliable:

> The empirical law derives whatever truth it has from the causal laws of which it is a consequence. If we know those laws, we know what are the limits to the derivative law; while if we have not yet accounted for the empirical law — if it rests only on observation — there is no safety in applying it far beyond the limits of time, place and circumstance in which the observations were made.[10]

What is the position, then, of Mill's 'laws of the formation of character'? It is clear that these are not ultimate causal laws, but it is not so clear that they are to be regarded as empirical laws. In fact,

Mill seems to be placing them somewhere in between: at one point he describes ethology as 'the exact science of human nature' and justifies this by adding that 'its truths are not, like the empirical laws which depend on them, approximate generalisations, but real laws'; a little later he describes the principles of ethology as 'middle principles', like Bacon's *axiomata media*, to be distinguished 'on the one hand from the empirical laws resulting from simple observation, and on the other from the highest generalisations'.[11] To the present writer Mill's account of them seems neither wholly clear nor consistent; no doubt it would have been otherwise had he developed this preliminary sketch into his proposed book on ethology.

In other respects, however, his intention is unambiguous. Like the laws which it formulates, ethology is a derivative science; whereas psychology is the science of the primary laws of mind, which it establishes by induction from experimental and observational data, ethology is 'altogether deductive', deriving its laws from previously established psychological laws; it is 'the ulterior science which determines the kind of character produced in conformity to those general laws by any set of circumstances, physical or moral'[12] (for the meaning of 'moral', see p.37 note 6). Mill proceeds to show that this cannot be otherwise. There are only two ways, he asserts (in v, 3) of establishing laws of nature — by experiment (including observation) and by deduction from more general laws. For ethology experiment, in the restricted modern sense, has only a limited efficacy: it is impossible to impose on human beings the rigid controls required by scientific accuracy and equally impossible to record the infinite number and variety of relevant data. Observation suffers from similar disabilities: however meticulous the investigation, the very complexity of human character and circumstance ensures the existence of unknown residual factors, ignorance of which may vitiate the whole inquiry. In any case, neither experimental nor observational conclusions can be more than empirical laws, lacking scientific status until logically linked with primary causal laws. However, although precise scientific conclusions are beyond the reach of ethology, a knowledge of 'tendencies', of statistical conclusions derived from the study of mankind *en masse*, are certainly within its compass; for practical purposes of influencing behaviour these may well be sufficient; at least they offer material for further theoretical inquiry. Ethology can be scientifically justified, therefore, only as a *deductive* discipline; as such it has a twofold task, or two methods of procedure: first, it must derive whatever conclusions are practicable from the experimental and observational study of human nature and seek to establish appropriate logical connections between these and known primary laws; second, it must study these primary laws, argue from them to the likely results of their operation in given circumstances and then compare these hypothetical conclusions with 'the recognised results of common experience'[13] (and presumably of observation and experiment too). Working thus from two directions, it will be possible, so Mill believes, to establish a system of ethological laws logically deducible from psychological laws and verifiable by experiential evidence. Such verification, it should be noted, is integral to Mill's concept of deduction as a means of establishing ethological laws or any similar deductive system; it is an essential safeguard against logically invalid or facile hypothesising.

How far is his conception of an ethological science acceptable? In answering this it is necessary to distinguish between ethology as such (whatever name one chooses to give it) and the particular form and methodology which Mill ascribed to it. He was right in seeking a science, or a branch of a science, whose task would be to examine human behaviour in its actual setting of circumstance and social relationships, to interpret it in the light of known psychological laws (or others conjecturally suggested) and to formulate a system of subsidiary laws and principles which could be used for explanation and prediction. Something akin to this would seem to be the province of social psychology and applied psychology as we know them. However, in his assessment of what such a science could achieve in relation to contemporary knowledge of psychological laws and the factual data then available he was excessively optimistic. Even today, with a vast accumulation of psychological and environmental data at our disposal, it would be foolhardy to claim 'a considerable approach to certainty' for conclusions about the impact on character and behaviour, even 'in mankind generally', of 'any assumed set of circumstances'.[14] The continuing controversy about the influence of the mass media, of pornography and of punishment is sufficient warning of this. True, he amply acknowledged the complexity of the data, both human and environmental, which ethology would need to examine; and in the practical application of ethological laws he grants that a knowledge of *tendencies* alone may be possible and may well be sufficient. Nevertheless, he seems to have underestimated seriously the degree of unpredictability which besets all human calculations, even with the aid of the most refined techniques of computerised extrapolation (as, for instance, in present forecasts of population growth). The influence on character of environment and circumstance is not simply a pressure exerted from without on a pliable material; it is a *mutual* influence, an *inter*relationship, as Mill was at pains to emphasise in his defence of free will (pp.39-40). Moreover, environment is not material only but *personal*; it consists very largely — and very importantly — of other people and *their* characters, a fact which complicates still further the task of unravelling the baffling intricacy of interacting influences and thus of arriving at reliable generalisations and predictions about human behaviour. Perhaps it was Mill's increasing realisation of this that led him to despair, as Bain says, of making any headway with ethology and to turn instead to political economy.

It seems, too, that Mill was misled by his uncritical acceptance of a model of the human mind shaped after physical, mechanical and chemical analogies. The blame for this is not entirely his; it stems in part from the association psychology (p.56 above) which he accepted as the only possible alternative to intuitionism; where he can be faulted, perhaps, is in his failure to undertake, or even to see the need for, a thorough analysis of the concept of mind by which to test the adequacy of the model he was using. However it may be, the result was an oversimplified version of mental operations and modifications; the mind becomes, as a nineteenth-century critic put it, a kind of 'primitive psychoplasma', alike in all men (except, as Mill grants, for certain 'natural differences' which he does not specify) and manipulable in response to carefully calculated external pressures.[15] 'He was all his life,' wrote Alexander Bain,

> possessed of the idea that differences of character, individual and national, were due to accidents and circumstances that might possibly be, in part, controlled; on this doctrine rested his chief hope in the future. He would not allow that human beings at birth are so very different as they afterwards turn out.[16]

Such a view ignores, or minimises, the mind's spontaneity in initiating new lines of thought and behaviour, not in passive obedience to external stimuli, but dynamically from its own imaginative resources; and it is a view which is difficult to reconcile with Mill's insistence on individuality and the cultural importance of genius. Partly for the same reason, partly because of his conception of science and scientific law, Mill overemphasised the deductive status of ethology, its dependence for logical justification on primary causal laws. True, he insisted on empirical verification of ethological laws as an essential part of their validation, and on the necessity for accepting tendencies rather than proven certainties in generalising or predicting about human nature. One must accept, too, that he was right in pointing to the fundamental role of primary psychological laws in social as well as more restrictedly individual situations; but his ideal of a neat system of deductively derived and empirically verified behavioural laws was certainly unrealisable in his own time, and may well be at any time. However, these criticisms should not be allowed to obscure the many points of value in Mill's account of ethology; the very concept of such a science, anticipating modern social psychology; his insistence on the complexity of the data and the vast number of variables; his acceptance of tendencies as practically viable substitutes for an unattainable certainty of prediction; his acknowledgement of the problems facing the experimental investigator; his recognition of the non-normative character of science and the dependence of ethology, therefore, for its practical application on an art of education embodying prescribed values and purposes. This last, 'the imperative mood . . . characteristic of art',[17] is the next topic to be considered.

CHAPTER 5

The Practical Arts

Ethology, though practically orientated, is still basically a theoretical account of laws and tendencies; its province is the indicative mood of factual statement (which may, of course, include hypothesis); strictly, it is not its task to implement its own theoretical findings nor to state the ends to which they should be directed. Practical implementation is the work of the corresponding art,[1] namely education, which uses ethological laws as means to achieving clearly defined purposes. These purposes, though formulated within education as a practical art, are judged and controlled by criteria supplied, as will be seen, by an overriding teleology or theory of values. The characteristic mood of art, Mill declares, is the imperative; it is this which distinguishes it from the indicative mood of descriptive science: 'whatever speaks in rules or precepts, not in assertions respecting matters of fact, is art'; and he has written earlier of practical education as the transformation of ethological principles into 'a parallel system of precepts'.[2] Once again, Mill has not made himself entirely clear; precept in education can be of a limited technical kind, empirically based and aimed primarily at efficient performance — for instance, pedagogical precepts as to the correct use of voice, questioning and visual aids; the term can also refer to wider moral and social purposes to which the pedagogical precepts are subordinate as means. Both of these categories are imperatives; both are essential to education; but it is the latter which govern the whole process and give it a dominant value orientation, and it is these principally that he has in mind. Although Mill points to the art of education as the practical counterpart of the science of ethology, he never undertook a detailed exposition of their relationship or a systematic account of education as the practical implementation of ethological principles. The general contours of the latter, had he ever accomplished it, can be inferred from the references to education which abound in his writings and will become apparent in Part III below. He does, however, in the final chapter of *Logic* VI, outline in general terms, first, the relation between science and the practical arts and, second, the sources of the value criteria which give direction to the latter; what he writes there is both interesting in itself and important for the light it throws on his conception of education.

His first step is to make the distinction, already noted, between the 'moods' of science and the practical arts — the former indicative, the latter imperative: 'Propositions of science assert a matter of fact, an existence, a co-existence, a succession or a resemblance'; propositions of art (in the sense to which Mill confines it for his present purpose) 'enjoin or recommend that something should be' — they are a class by themselves, generically different from the propositions of science.[3] This is a correct and important distinction; it is an aspect of the 'is/ought' controversy familiar to students of twentieth-century philosophy. It should not, however, be taken as an exhaustive description of either side; science as a human activity contextually situated in time and place is no more value-free than the practical arts are restricted, at least in their content, to propositions in the imperative mood. The relation between them Mill describes as follows:

> The art proposes to itself an end to be attained, defines the end, and hands it over to the science. The science receives it, considers it as a phenomenon or effect to be studied, and having investigated its causes and conditions, sends it back to art with a theorem of the combination of circumstances by which it could be produced. Art then examines these combinations of circumstances, and according as any of them are or are not in human power, pronounces the end attainable or not. The only one of the premises, therefore, which art supplies is the original major premise, which asserts that the attainment of the given end is desirable. Science then lends to art the proposition (obtained by a series of inductions or of deductions) that the performance of certain actions will attain the end.[4]

Thus art concludes that certain activities are not only desirable but also practicable; it then converts the 'theorem' of science into practical rules or precepts aimed at successful performance of the activities in question. However, Mill admits that perfection is unattainable in the formulation both of the scientific 'theorem' and consequently of the practical rules, which 'a wise practitioner' will therefore regard as provisional; and he castigates those who posit 'large and sweeping practical maxims', argue from them to particular applications and thus pride themselves on being 'logical and consistent'.[5] Not only is it necessary to refer constantly to the science or sciences which supply the guiding theorems; there is also a need to examine the results of practical activity, since 'success itself may conflict with some other end which may possibly chance to be more desirable'.[6]

Mill summarises his argument so far in a paragraph which merits quotation in full:

> The grounds, then, of every rule of art are to be found in the theorems of science. An art, or a body of art, consists of the rules, together with as much of the speculative propositions as comprises the justification of those rules. The complete art of any matter includes a selection of such a portion from the science as is necessary to show on what conditions the effects which the art aims at producing depend. And art in general consists of the truths of science arranged in the most convenient order for practice, instead of the order which is the most convenient for thought. Science groups and arranges its truths so as to enable us to take in at one view as much as possible of the general order of the universe. Art, though it must assume the same general laws, follows them only into such of their detailed consequences as have led to the formation of rules of conduct, and brings together from parts of the field of science most remote from one another the truths relating to the production of the different and heterogeneous conditions necessary to each effect which the exigencies of practical life require to be produced.[7]

A particular art, then, be it education or any other, relies on science for three things: to provide a theoretical justification of the practicability of its chosen purposes; to offer a body of theoretical knowledge as a necessary means to achieving these purposes; and to suggest, in general terms only, how this knowledge might best be utilised. At this point art takes over, considers the recommendations of science in relation to particular circumstances and the resources available and decides whether or not its goals are attainable; if they are, it adapts and arranges whatever areas of scientific knowledge are appropriate to the requirements of practice. (Mill suggests, but does not develop the point, that an intermediate set of scientific principles may be needed to bridge the gap between 'the higher generalities of science'[8] and the particular requirements of art.)

Although the scientist is indispensable in linking the ends chosen by art to the means of attaining them, the choice of ends is outside his competence; science is non-normative: 'Whether the ends themselves are such as ought to be pursued, and if so, in what cases and to how great length, it is no part of his business as a cultivator of science to decide, and science alone will never qualify him for the decision.' 'The definition of the end itself,' Mill asserts, 'belongs exclusively to art and forms its peculiar province.' Every art has 'one first principle or general major premise' which states the goal proper to that art — health for medicine, buildings for the builder, beautiful or imposing buildings for the architect (Mill's examples). It is not simply that the doctor *approves* of health or the builder of his house; emotional incentives are insufficient justification for the doctor or builder himself, let alone for anyone else. Approbation must be justified, and for this are needed 'general premises determining what are the proper objects of approbation and what the proper order of precedence among those objects'. Thus Mill is led naturally and inevitably to the idea of a supreme art ('unfortunately still to be created'), an 'Art of Life in its three departments, Morality, Prudence or Policy, and Aesthetics; the Right, the Expedient, and the Beautiful or Noble in human conduct and works'.[9] The name he gives to it is 'Teleology, or the Doctrine of Ends' (Greek τέλος). The ends of the separate arts (health, etc.) are seldom in dispute; but when there is a question of precedence or supremacy among them, teleology must be called to give judgement:

> There is, then, a *philosophia prima* peculiar to art, as there is one which belongs to science. There are not only first principles of knowledge, but first principles of conduct. There must be some standard by which to determine the goodness or badness, absolute and comparative, of ends or objects of desire. And whatever that standard is, there can be but one.[10]

The startling problems of ethical philosophy raised by this declaration are outside the scope of the present discussion; but assuming that there *must* be such a standard and only *one*, there can be no doubt what Mill will conclude this to be: 'the promotion of happiness is the ultimate principle of teleology.' He is careful to add, however, that happiness need not be the immediate goal of every specific action; pain or unhappiness must sometimes be chosen as conducive to greater ultimate happiness, whether for the individual or for mankind. Here again he merits quotation at length for the nobility of the ideal he cherishes and his resolute rejection of a utilitarianism which falls short of it:

The cultivation of an ideal nobleness of will and conduct should be to individual human beings an end to which the specific pursuit either of their own happiness or of that of others (except so far as included in that idea) should, in any case of conflict, give way. But I hold that the very question, what constitutes this elevation of character, is itself to be decided by a reference to happiness as the standard. The character itself should be, to the individual, a paramount end, simply because the existence of this ideal nobleness of character, or of a near approach to it, in any abundance would go further than all things else towards making human life happy, both in the comparatively humble sense of pleasure and freedom from pain, and in the higher meaning of rendering life, not what it now is almost universally, puerile and insignificant, but such as human beings with highly developed faculties can care to have.[11]

In chapter xii of *Logic* VI there is no specific mention of education and the reader must infer for himself how Mill might have interpreted for that particular practical art the general principles he here enunciates. For instance, it is interesting to speculate what 'general major premise', what single supreme objective he would consider distinctive of education as health is of medicine. There is no obvious or easy answer; indeed, there may be no answer at all, for different cultures, and the same culture at different times, have proposed such varied goals for their educational endeavours as military efficiency, intellectual achievement, 'the good life', conformity to tradition and personal development. In view of what he writes elsewhere. Mill would perhaps have chosen 'individuality' (see below. pp.88-9). but an individuality obedient to the criterion of that 'ideal nobleness' which he upholds in the penultimate paragraph of the *Logic*. One may question, too, whether a *philosophia prima,* a teleology of values and purpose, is either possible or desirable in a democratic society of the kind Mill envisaged, and *a fortiori* in the plural society of today; and whether it is consistent with Mill's own dialectical conception of the pursuit of truth (pp.175-7 below) and with the freedom for dissent which he defends so passionately in *On Liberty*. It conjures up the somewhat distasteful picture of a praesidium of philosopher-kings miraculously in agreement and dispensing value judgements to the denizens of a Platonic cave. Perhaps this is unfair, but certainly there is more than a hint of Plato here (as there is also of Aristotle, not only in the title *philosophia prima*, but also in the idea of a specific goal for every art). Mill, it must be remembered, was steeped in Plato during childhood, and the experience gave him a vision of the Good accessible only to the most resolute endeavour and comprising intellectual, moral and aesthetic truth; the vision never wholly faded, and traces of it can be found in many aspects of his thought. Fortunately, philosophers rarely agree; this and the realities of life outside totalitarian societies make it unlikely that his ideal of an authoritative teleology will ever be realised.

Where Mill is entirely right, however, is in pointing to the need for firm value direction, and this not only from within education as a practical art but from outside it too — for if his conception of a *philosophia prima* is unacceptable (whether in the guise of metaphysics, religion or political ideology), some degree of control by social or cultural values is essential in any national system of education. For a principal function of a nation's schools is to promote social cohesion by initiating children into accepted values. Whether happiness should be included in these values, either as one among others or the one supreme, is arguable; Mill had no option but to posit the latter, not only as a convinced utilitarian but also as a pupil and admirer of Plato, whose aim in the *Republic* was 'so far as possible the happiness of the whole community' and who, it should be added, was profoundly conscious of the role of values in promoting social unity.[12]

Mill is right, too, in insisting on the non-normative character of science in relation to practical art. Science is not in itself value-free (a point already noted), for it incorporates at least the ideal of objective truth; but it has no right, logical, moral or any other, to determine the purposes for which that truth should be used by such arts as politics, medicine and education; in relation to these the function of science is instrumental. Now, as Mill very wisely says, 'in purely physical science there is not much temptation to assume this ulterior office' of recommending practical goals, 'but those who treat of human nature and society invariably claim it; they always undertake to say, not merely what is, but what ought to be.'[13] Perhaps not *invariably*, but the temptation noticeably exists in the tendency of educational psychologists and sociologists to exceed their legitimate factual bounds and assume the role of teleological mentors. As individuals, of course, they have as much right to do so as any other citizen — indeed, an *obligation* to do so, not only because of their superior knowledge, but also because the dialectic of value debate is essential to cultural improvement; they do not, however, have this right as scientists committed to the discovery and accurate presentation of fact.

Finally, Mill anticipates present-day educational philosophy in pointing to the danger of sloganised principles which decay into thoughtless catchwords of unanalysed practice. His examples are taken from French politics, but his warning is equally applicable to English education, whose history is bedevilled by such slogans, from Juvenal's *mens sana in corpore sano*, beloved of earlier generations of educators, to the 'child-centredness' of contemporary educational jargon. Initially liberalising in suggesting fresh purposes, approaches and attitudes to children, they are transformed by thoughtless repetition into sterile and restrictive clichés. To maintain their invigorating power they must constantly be subjected to analysis, to rational justification and to amendment, as Mill suggests, by reference to 'the principles of the speculative science'.[14]

For Mill, a complete system of science must include not only the individual human being but society too; therefore, before moving on in Part II to the practical details of his educational thought, some mention must be made of his attempt to extend the range of science to include what he chose to call (adopting 'a convenient barbarism'[15] coined by Comte) by the name of 'sociology'. Here again his concern was not simply for truth, important though this was, but also to establish a reliable means to human betterment, which would be subordinate, like ethology and its associated arts, to the ultimate imperatives of a Doctrine of Ends.

Individual character is a product of circumstances; but these, as he was at pains to emphasise, are subject to (and include) human volition; they can be controlled and shaped to serve deliberate purposes. To be utilised thus, however, they must be understood — *scientifically* understood, in terms of explanatory and predictive laws. Circumstances include the whole context of human existence, physical, organic and socio-cultural; the first two of these had long been subjected to scientific study, and in certain areas — Mill mentions mechanics and astronomy — had been structured into coherent causal systems. Although every part of this context has its influence on character, by far the most powerful formative impact comes from the last; it is by understanding and controlling this especially, therefore, that humanity will be improved. Always, however, the study of social phenomena must be in conjunction with acknowledgement of the known psychological laws of individual human nature; for the process of betterment is reciprocal, social change improving man, and man, thus improved, contributing to further social advance. Moreover, it was these same psychological laws (as we shall see in a moment) that Mill believed to be the primary causal determinants of social phenomena.

He was well aware that the difficulties involved in creating a social science were enormous. Its complexity would be far greater even than that of the psychology and ethology of individuals, for 'a nation . . . exposes a larger surface to the operation of agents, psychological and physical, than any single individual'; the causal factors are proportionately more numerous, even to the extent of defying 'our limited powers of calculation'.[16] There were further problems in assembling reliable data, in the resistance of these data to quantitative expression, in the virtual impossibility of controlled experiment; and underlying all was the problem of free will, perplexing here no less than in psychological science. However, he insists that social phenomena, like all other phenomena, are governed by causal laws and therefore admit of scientific investigation and the possibility, in principle at least, of scientific proof; sociology *can*, therefore, achieve the status of a science. It is unnecessary for our present purpose to expound in any detail Mill's attempt to justify this conclusion and to devise a methodology for social science; suffice it to note the following.

First, he was convinced that the primary causal laws of social phenomena are the same as those of individual human nature but operating, of course, in a far wider and more intricate setting:

> All phenomena of society are phenomena of human nature generated by the action of outward circumstances upon masses of human beings. . . Men . . . in a state of society are still men. . . Human beings in society have no properties but those which are derived from, and may be resolved into, the laws of the nature of individual man.[17]

(It is arguable that Mill is mistaken here, that human beings *en masse* are not the same, psychologically speaking, as human beings in their individuality; it is also arguable that men and women never shed their sociality, never *are* individuals, and that the distinction Mill makes is therefore false. These are questions which cannot, unfortunately, be pursued here.) Second, he believed sociology to be ideally a deductive science, inferring from the primary psychological laws to the intermediate laws which result from their operation in

society, and further inferring from these to more limited generalisations of the commonsense or practical kind ('empirical laws' — p.62
above) and from these finally to particular effects in particular
circumstances. This, the ideal, Mill calls 'the Physical or Concrete
Deductive Method'.[18] Third, any such inference must be submitted
to empirical verification, and this in two possible ways: either by
checking the conclusions of deduction against the evidence of
experiment and observation, or by provisionally establishing conclusions from empirical evidence and then linking them inferentially
with the primary causal laws; either way the logical coherence is
complete and the conditions of a genuine science fulfilled. The latter
process may in certain situations of extreme complexity be the only
one possible, and Mill in fact regards it as a method in its own right,
naming it 'the Inverse Deductive or Historical Method'.[19]

Two further points are worthy of note. Mill agrees with (and
commends) Comte in his assertion of the role of the intellect in social
progress: 'The state of the speculative faculties, the character of the
propositions assented to by the intellect, essentially determines the
moral and political state of the community.'[20] Though not among the
more powerful of human propensities, and hardly a dominant motive
save in a few exceptional individuals, the pursuit of truth is
nevertheless, he declares, the main determinant of social progress.
Next, he emphasises repeatedly the significance of outstanding
individuals in initiating social and cultural advance. He develops this
idea in chapter xi of *Logic* VI, in a passage remarkable for its insight
and cultural sensitivity — and remarkable, too, for its contrast with,
even contradiction of, the strict logical and causal coherence which
he requires for sociology as a science: even the most rigorous of
universal laws, he here insists, can be converted by human will 'into
instruments of its designs, and the extent to which it does so makes
the chief difference between savages and the most highly civilised
people'.[21]

Book VI of the *Logic*, with its proposals for a psychology and a
sociology both linked to deliberate goals and finding practical
expression in education and other forms of environmental control,
can be seen as a remarkable attempt to apply behavioural and social
engineering (to use modern terms) to the quest for human improvement:

We may hereafter succeed not only in looking far forward into the
future history of the human race, but in determining what artificial

means may be used, and to what extent, to accelerate the natural progress in so far as it is beneficial, to compensate for whatever may be its inherent inconveniences or disadvantages, and to guard against the dangers or accidents to which our species is exposed from the necessary incidents of its progression.[22]

Embryonic though it is, and despite its weaknesses and dangers, there is in Mill's conception a certain grandeur which commands respect. Much of it he owes to his father, to Bentham and to Comte (whose *Système de Politique Positive* he later severely censured); much too, no doubt, to Plato, whom, as we have noted above, he could read 'with perfect ease'[23] at the age of fourteen and whose ideal of an ordered society founded on rational investigation of man, society and the universe and on commitment to the highest values can hardly have failed to impress him. One can see here too an anticipation of the behavioural shaping by psychological reinforcement which is familiar now in the works of B. F. Skinner, its best-known contemporary exponent — though Skinner's reduction of love and altruism to 'the smooth flow of positive reinforcement', as R. S. Peters has described it in reviewing *Beyond Freedom and Dignity*,[24] is but a vapid substitute for the richness of Mill's ideal.

Immense and tantalising questions are suggested by the notion of a scientific behavioural and social technology as adumbrated in *Logic* VI. How far, if at all, can human nature be re-shaped? Are we not limited, in fact, merely to changing the expression, the outward manifestation, of what is basically the same in all of us? And is it possible to do even this much without exercising an authority which amounts to tyranny, a denial of that freedom and dignity which, *pace* Skinner, are still for most of us essential to meaningful existence? To what goals shall we harness our ethology, our social technology? Who shall choose them for us and how ensure that the choice is wise? If happiness is the goal, what does it consist in? And have we — whether a government, a political elite, a college of philosopher-kings — the right to impose it on others? Could it be that by careful environmental conditioning mankind might be led to accept the loss of freedom and dignity — perhaps not even to miss them — in exchange for gains in happiness and peace of mind? What part has education, formal and informal, in the task of social and behavioural improvement? Two problems Mill himself seized upon as crucial: values and freedom (the latter both as a philosophical and a practical issue). Even more crucial are they today, when society is more complex, technology vastly more powerful and the consequences of its use (and misuse) more far-reaching. There is a third problem of which he is also aware: *quis custodiet ipsos custodes?*[25] — who will educate the educators? The answers to all three remain as elusive as ever; if Mill gives us no final solution, at least he provides clues and pointers for our guidance.

PHILOSOPHICAL ISSUES

It is assumed in the suggested reading, both here and later in the book, that students have access to one or more of the following journals: *Proceedings of the Philosophy of Education Society of Great Britain* (from vol. 12, 1978, entitled *Journal of Philosophy of Education*); *Educational Philosophy and Theory* (Philosophy of Education Society of Australasia); *Studies in Philosophy and Education* (San José State University, California, and Philosophy of Education Society, USA). These are abbreviated as, respectively: *J. Phil. Ed., Ed. Ph. and Th., SPE.*

Details of publication are given only when a book is first mentioned.

Numerous important issues arise from Mill's rejection of rationalism and intuitionism and his attempt to construct a theory of education on experiential foundations. The following are suggested for further exploration.

1.   *The nature and sources of knowledge*

Education is concerned partly with the acquisition of knowledge, and although it may not seem immediately obvious, different views of the origins and nature of knowledge do have clear implications for the methods and content of education (as will become apparent in Part III below).

An introduction to this area of philosophy (epistemology) can be found in: Chisholm, R. M., *Theory of Knowledge* (Prentice-Hall, 1966); Hamlyn, D. W., *The Theory of Knowledge* (Macmillan, 1970); and Pears, D., *What is Knowledge?* (Allen and Unwin, 1972). For a specifically educational orientation there is Israel Scheffler's *Conditions of Knowledge* (Scott, Foresman, 1965), which considers epistemology 'from the perspective of education'; and there are the essays in Part 2 of the volume edited by Dearden, R. F., Hirst, P. H., and Peters, R. S., *Education and the Development of Reason* (Routledge and Kegan Paul, 1972). Of particular interest is the ongoing debate on 'forms of knowledge' initiated by Professor P. H. Hirst; for this see his book of collected papers, *Knowledge and the Curriculum* (Routledge and Kegan Paul, 1974), chapters 3, 4 and 6. Epistemology and education are closely linked in Brent, A., *Philosophical Foundations for the Curriculum* (Allen and Unwin, 1978); chapter 3 is an extended critical discussion of Hirst's 'forms of knowledge'.

Plato's *Republic*, in which education is firmly based on his rationalist metaphysic of the Forms, affords a stimulating contrast to Mill's experientialism.

2. *Scientific method and theory*

Many important questions arise from Mill's attempt to provide a scientific basis for understanding and improving human beings. What kind of activity is science? How does it work? What confidence can we have in its conclusions? Are human beings proper subjects for scientific observation, experiment, prediction? What kind of activity is education, and how does it work? (For which see below, pp. 86ff.) What is a theory? What is an educational theory? How do educational theories differ from scientific theories?

Especially helpful here, because directly related to Mill, are the first five chapters of Ryan, A., *The Philosophy of John Stuart Mill* (Macmillan, 1970), and chapters 5 to 9 of Anschutz, P., *The Philosophy of J. S. Mill* (2nd edn, Oxford University Press, 1963). Ryan's *The Philosophy of the Social Sciences* (Macmillan, 1970) is an excellent introduction to scientific methodology, especially in its application to human behaviour and society; Louch, A. R., *Explanation and Human Behaviour* (University of California Press, 1969) is also helpful (it is reviewed in *SPE*, vol. 7, no. 4, 1972). See also, in the Oxford Readings in Philosophy series, Nidditch, P. N., ed., *The Philosophy of Science* (Oxford University Press, 1968), and Swinburne, R., ed., *The Justification of Induction* (Oxford University Press, 1974); the final article in the latter considers the possibility of necessary connections between successive events, which Mill rejects as inconsistent with free will (pp.38-9 above). Toulmin, S., *The Philosophy of Science* (Hutchinson, 1953 and repr.) is a useful introductory survey.

The meaning of 'theory' and of 'educational theory' is discussed in: O'Connor, D. J., *An Introduction to the Philosophy of Education* (Routledge and Kegan Paul, 1957), chapter 5; Hardie, C. D., *Truth and Fallacy in Educational Theory* (2nd edn, Teachers College Press, 1962); Moore, T. W., *Educational Theory: An Introduction* (Routledge and Kegan Paul, 1974); *J. Phil. Ed.,* vol. 6, no. 1, 1972 (O'Connor, D. J., Hirst, P. H.); *Ed. Ph. and Th.,* vol. 7, no. 1, 1975 (Naylor, F. D., Marshall, J. D.); *SPE*, vol. 7, no. 1, 1969 (Nagel, E.), no. 2, 1970 (Flower, E.).

3. *Freedom in a causal universe*

This is primarily a problem for general philosophy, but the educator cannot ignore it; for if human choice and activity are entirely predetermined, then his attempts to improve and develop individuality would seem unavailing: what happens must happen, so why bother? Belief in some scope for freedom of will would therefore seem a necessary justification for his efforts. There are many books on this issue, of which the following will serve for introductory study: Cranston, M., *Freedom: A New Analysis* (2nd edn, Longman, 1954) — mainly concerned with an analysis of the meaning of freedom, but Part 3 examines the problem of free will; Pears, D. F., ed., *Freedom and the Will* (Macmillan, 1963, and repr.); O'Connor, D. J., *Free Will* (Macmillan, 1972), which has a very full bibliography. Chapter 7 of Ryan's *The Philosophy of John Stuart Mill* is a critical exposition of Mill's case against determinism. The issue is brought into an educational context in Doyle, J. F., ed., *Educational Judgments* (Routledge and Kegan Paul, 1973) chapters 8 (Peters, R. S.) and 9 (Feinberg, J.).

4. *Selfhood and individuality*

The nature of the self and its relation to other selves and to the external world is another problem (or complex of problems) which the educator cannot ignore. For his work is essentially concerned with individual selves both as such (in their peculiar potential and growth) and in their interaction with the environment (which, of course, includes other selves). A useful entry into this area can be found in Ayer, A. J., *The Concept of a Person* (Macmillan, 1964), chapter 4, from which the book takes its title; he discusses the same problems in chapters 4, 5 and 6 of *The Central Questions of Philosophy* (2nd edn, Penguin Books, 1976). The mind-body relationship is examined in Malcolm, N., *Problems of Mind* (Allen and Unwin, 1972) and in greater depth and detail in what is now a philosophical classic, Ryle, G., *The Concept of Mind* (2nd edn, Penguin Books, 1963). Ryan's chapter 6 in *The Philosophy of John Stuart Mill* is a brief but helpful critical account of Mill's position.

We think of men and women (and children too) not only as individuals but as *persons*, a concept which brings us closer to the work of the educator; for this see Downie, R. S. and Telfer, E., *Respect for Persons* (Allen and Unwin, 1969).

5. *Fact and value*

Mill draws a sharp distinction between 'is' and 'ought', between indicative and imperative, between the statements of science and the recommendations of art (in his sense of the word — see above, p.67, note 1). The distinction is now a commonplace of philosophical discourse (though it is perhaps not quite so sharp as Mill and others since have assumed). Values, i.e. what we deem worthwhile or choice-worthy, are of fundamental importance in human life, both individual and social; philosophers have always been interested in them, and very much so during the present period of social change and ethical pluralism. For educational philosophers (and practitioners) they are of special significance in providing guidance for the determination of educational purposes (see also below, pp. 87ff).

Hudson, W. D., ed., *The Is/Ought Question* (Macmillan, 1969) brings together a number of papers on this 'central problem in moral philosophy' as the sub-title calls it. There are also two papers in Foot, P., ed., *Theories of Ethics* (Oxford Readings in Philosophy, Oxford University Press, 1967), chapters 3 and 7; and a number of others are cited in the bibliography. Warnock, M., *Ethics since 1900* (Oxford University Press, 1960) provides a useful background to this controversial issue. Essential reading in this area of values and moral choice is Hare, R. M., *The Language of Morals* (Oxford University Press, 1952); scarcely less valuable are two books by the American philosopher, C. L. Stevenson, *Ethics and Language* (Yale University Press, 1944) and its successor, *Facts and Values* (Yale University Press, 1963).

Values are discussed in: O'Connor, D. J., *An Introduction to the Philosophy of Education*, chapter 3; Phillips, D. C., *Theories, Values and Education* (Melbourne University Press, 1971); Langford, G. and O'Connor, D. J., eds, *New Essays in the Philosophy of Education* (Routledge and Kegan Paul, 1973), Part 2, especially chapters 7 (Langford, G.) and 8 (Peters, R. S.); *J. Phil. Ed.*, vol. 8, no. 1, 1974 (Burgess, J.); vol. 10, 1976 (Hare, R. M., Walsh, P.D.); vol. 12, 1978 (Nordenbo, S.E.); *Ed. Ph. and Th.* vol. 3, no. 2, 1971 (Gregory, I. M. M., Woods, R. G.).

On happiness as a (or the supreme) value Mill's *Utilitarianism* is obvious reading, together with Ryan's discussion of Mill's position in chapters 11 and 12 of *The Philosophy of John Stuart Mill*; Anschutz discusses Mill's utilitarianism in chapter 1 of his book, and there are two papers on it in Foot's collection of papers mentioned above. See also Barrow, R., *Plato, Utilitarianism and Education* (Routledge and Kegan Paul, 1975), and Feinberg, J., ed., *Moral Concepts* (Oxford Readings in Philosophy, Oxford University Press, 1969) chapters 1 (Ryle, G.), 2 (Hare, R. M.) and 3 (Kenny, A.). On happiness and education see *J. Phil. Ed.*, vol. 2, 1967-8 (Dearden, R. F.).

6.   *Sociology and behavioural engineering*

Mill believed that a scientific behavioural and social technology was essential to his overriding purpose of human improvement. Progress towards that end depended on understanding and applying the 'laws' which govern the behaviour of individuals and the activities and relationships of societies; only thus could control be exercised over and purpose imposed on individual and social development. The idea of such behavioural and social engineering has a venerable history going back at least to Plato; it has received fresh impetus from contemporary political ideologies and from the reinforcement psychology of B. F. Skinner. Among the many issues it raises are: the methodology of sociology and the validity of its conclusions and predictions; the use and efficacy of education as an instrument of social change; the ends to which that change should be directed (a problem of values, for which see above); freedom and authority (see below, pp. 165-7); indoctrination and censorship (below, pp. 138-9). The literature is vast and the suggestions here provide no more than a toehold.

Ryan's *The Philosophy of the Social Sciences* is again recommended, together with the collection of papers he has edited for the Oxford Readings in Philosophy series, *The Philosophy of Social Explanation* (Oxford University Press, 1973), and chapters 8, 9 and 10 of his *The Philosophy of John Stuart Mill*. The early chapters of John Dewey's *Democracy and Education* (1916), though written half a century ago, are still a thought-provoking statement of the role of education in society; compare with this the short essay by Peters, R. S., *Education as Initiation* (Evans, 1964). For additional contemporary writing the student could well turn to Hartnett, A. and Naish, M., eds, *Theory and the Practice of Education,* vol. 2 (Heinemann, 1976) and to its very full bibliography.

There is a great deal of relevant collateral reading, for instance: Plato's *Republic*; Aldous Huxley's *Brave New World*; Orwell's *1984*; B. F. Skinner's *Walden Two* and his justification of behavioural engineering in *Beyond Freedom and Dignity* (Cape, 1972); there is a review of this last, and a reply by Skinner, in *SPE*, vol. 9, nos. 1, 2, 1975. Passmore, J., *The Perfectibility of Man* (Duckworth, 1970) is a fascinating historical study of ideals of human perfectibility.

A severe critic of social engineering and its presuppositions (and of Mill in particular) is Sir Karl Popper in *The Poverty of Historicism* (2nd edn, Routledge and Kegan Paul, 1960).

PART III
The Educative Process

CHAPTER 1

Introductory

The word 'process' is here used as a collective term embracing all those activities which together constitute what might be called the mechanics of education, that is to say, all the multifarious means by which educational aims and objectives achieve (more or less successfully) their practical realisation. More is intended, however, than the mere sum of these practical activities; for process, in the sense here proposed, includes theory as well as practice, but theory specifically orientated towards practice as its justification and its recipe for success. To use the word thus may mislead if it suggests that there is only one process, an agreed pattern of educational theory-cum-practice which is adaptable to different goals but is fundamentally the same for all. This, of course, is not so: there are many possible conceptions of the educational process in this generalised sense; they differ according to the different psychological and epistemological assumptions that underlie them; they reflect diversity in value commitments and in the meanings assigned to 'education'; and these differences extend into the more specific instrumental activities which they embody. Provided this is understood, it is not inappropriate to speak of 'the process' as distinct from the particular 'sub-processes' which it embraces (for instance, skills of teaching, methods of control, pedagogical techniques peculiar to different curriculum subjects). In Part III we shall examine Mill's conception of the process of education (in the collective sense here defined, theory based and practice-orientated), including his views, in so far as they are ascertainable, on its constituent sub-processes; and this both for the school and for the wider education, formal and informal, which goes on outside the school. Inevitably the picture will be incomplete. Mill was not, nor did he claim to be, an expert on pedagogy; and his plans for a book on ethology, the science of the

formation of character, came to nothing (pp.60-1 above).
Nevertheless, the overall pattern of the process as he conceived it is
clear enough, as are many of the practical details within it.

   That education is wider than schooling is a conviction which
permeates Mill's thinking about both society and education. For us,
in an age of complex and sophisticated educational institutions,
there is a strong tendency to confine our notion of the educational
process to schools, colleges and universities; this is a mistake, of
course, and one that Mill does not make; to understand him it is
essential to broaden our perspective to include the whole compass of
influences which constitute the social environment. His clearest
statement of this conviction is in the opening paragraph of the
Inaugural Address:

> [Education includes] not only ... whatever we do for ourselves and
> whatever is done for us by others for the express purpose of
> bringing us somewhat nearer to the perfection of our nature; it
> does more: in its largest acceptation it comprehends even the
> indirect effects produced on character and on the human faculties
> by things of which the direct purposes are quite different; by laws,
> by forms of government, by the industrial arts, by modes of social
> life; nay, even by physical facts not dependent on human will, by
> climate, soil and local position. Whatever helps to shape the
> human being, to make the individual what he is or hinder him from
> being what he is not, is part of his education.[1]

He adds the comment, sadly obvious to us but less so to Mill's
contemporaries, that this education of total impact may equally well
be bad as good: 'And a very bad education it often is, requiring all
that can be done by cultivated intelligence and will to counteract its
tendencies.' There is a similar forthright statement in his second
review of de Tocqueville's *Democracy in America*:

> It has often been said, and requires to be repeated still oftener, that
> books and discourses alone are not education, that life is a problem,
> not a theorem, that action can only be learnt in action. . . . What can
> be learnt in schools is important, but not all-important. The main
> branch of the education of human beings is their habitual
> employment, which must be either their individual vocation or
> some matter of general concern in which they are called to take a
> part[2]

— and the former must be balanced by the latter to prevent an exclusive concentration on purely selfish interests. The same broad conception of education finds repeated expression in his writings; for instance, in the early 'Speech on Perfectibility' he points to 'the insensible influence of the world, of society, and public opinion' in contributing to moral education; he complains in *On Liberty* of the depressive impact of social custom and conformity upon individual development; in *Representative Government* he insists on the educative power of institutions and of participation.[3] In the *Autobiography* he tells us of the lasting impression left upon him by his visits to Ford Abbey in Somerset and by his first glimpse of the Pyrenees; and in *Political Economy* he claims that solitude and natural beauty are the cradle of noble thoughts and aspirations.[4] The message is clear: education goes on both within school and outside, and Mill would not have us forget it. It would be easy to multiply instances; however, others have already been noted, more will be found in later pages, and the role of environment in Mill's educational thinking will be examined at length in the following chapter.

Since conceptions of the educational process vary according to their psychological and other premises, it will be helpful to recall what these were for Mill. In fact, much that is pertinent to our present purpose can be inferred in advance from a consideration of his aims and value assumptions; much also indirectly from his criticisms of contemporary education (which embody, as it were, a negative statement of the same assumptions); much again from examining the scientific foundations which he establishes in the *Logic* and which are described in Part II above.

By means of his projected ethology and 'Doctrine of Ends' Mill firmly linked education (the practical art or instrument of ethology) to purpose and, by implication, since the one entails the other, to values. The relation between his theoretical science of behaviour and the practice of education he did not elaborate; nor did he systematically detail the aims, objectives and particular values to which he thought education should be committed. To remedy the former omission would be difficult and largely speculative, but not so the second. For education was so much a part of Mill's total thought that one can readily construct from his writings a coherent picture of what he believed its aims to be. Nor is there any doubt of his conviction that education is indeed a potent instrument of human purposes: in a letter to Harriet he writes of its 'omnipotence', and elsewhere he describes its power as 'almost boundless'.[5] The overriding goal to which he wished to direct education was clearly 'the improvement of mankind'; and if he may be said to have had *an* educational aim inclusive of all others, this was it. This distant ideal can be accomplished only by the improvement of particular societies, and to this too Mill was no less firmly wedded — not only Britain, but India, Ireland and others. Even this, however, is meaningful only as it is broken down into specific goals or values which give practical guidance to endeavour. Five principal goals of this kind can be distinguished in Mill's writings: happiness, altruism, individuality, freedom and truth.

To the first of these Mill is clearly committed by his utilitarianism; but he writes of the others in a manner which suggests that they too have intrinsic worth and are in some way constitutive of happiness. For instance, he insists in *Utilitarianism* on distinguishing happiness from hedonism; it is a certain *quality* of happiness he has in mind, a quality which requires the individual to sacrifice himself for the sake of others. Such sacrifice demands a nobility of character, a single-minded altruism, which Mill seems to regard, at least *for the individual*, as something valuable in its own right: the utilitarian doctrine, he asserts, 'maintains not only that virtue is to be desired, but that it is to be desired disinterestedly, for itself'.[6] He even links this ideal of virtue with the *agapé* of the New Testament: 'In the golden rule of Jesus of Nazareth we read the complete spirit of the ethics of utility.'[7] And in *Comte and Positivism* he goes so far as to declare that '. . . the direct cultivation of altruism, and the subordination of egoism to it, far beyond the point of absolute moral duty, should be one of the chief aims of education both individual and collective.'[8]

Individuality, too, emerges as a value with intrinsic status, as a goal to be pursued in its own right and as a criterion and constituent of human improvement. For Mill individuality is the freely chosen expression, in growth and development and in diversity of activity, of one's distinctiveness as a unique being; the crucial items of the concept are potentiality, development, distinctiveness (the uniqueness of one's own self in its differentiation and differences from other selves), variety in self-expression and choice. Certainly he writes of it as a means, for instance to economic enterprise, to the enrichment of society, to the testing of the worth of different forms of life: thus, in *Principles of Political Economy*, 'originality of mind and individuality of character . . . are the only source of any real progress' — a thought insistently echoed in *On Liberty*; and this is why it must be protected from government intrusion, from bureaucracy, from the pressures of 'collective mediocrity'.[9] But he writes of it, too, in a manner which seems to elevate it from something valuable as a means to something valuable in itself, as if he were hovering on the edge of commitment to belief in the essential worth of individuals as such. He complains in *On Liberty* that 'individual spontaneity is hardly recognised by the common modes of thinking as having any intrinsic worth or deserving any regard on its own account'; and he claims that, granted a 'tolerable amount of common sense and experience', a man's self-chosen mode of life is the best 'not because it is the best in itself, but because it is his own mode'.[10] Similar concern for individuality can be found in *Representative Government*, where 'the qualities of the human beings composing the society' is the principal criterion of good government, and in *The Subjection of Women*, where it contributes to his passionate plea for the equality of the sexes; it appears also in his admiration for the heroic (noted earlier) and in his championship of the underprivileged and the oppressed.[11] Whether or not Mill saw it as a rival to happiness in claiming intrinsic or ultimate status, he evidently regarded it as a value of the highest order of importance, an essential ingredient in his concept of improvement and an obvious goal, therefore, for the educator. (He was also aware, and makes abundantly clear in his essay 'Nature', that individuality has potential for evil as well as good; development must therefore be *selective*, and man's duty to his own nature is 'not to follow but to amend it'.)[12]

No one who has read *On Liberty* can doubt Mill's passionate commitment to freedom, conceived primarily, and negatively, as non-interference, but embodying more positive suggestions in serving as the soil (Mill's own metaphor) for the roots of individual growth and cultural progress. In this latter role he saw freedom as powerfully instrumental, but there are indications that it held for him a significance deeper than this. Many of these can be found in *On Liberty* itself; in chapter iii, for instance, he suggests that 'the free development of individuality is one of the leading essentials of well-being. . . it is not only a co-ordinate element with all that is designated by the terms civilisation, instruction, education, culture, but is itself a necessary part and condition of all those things. . . ."[13] Now, freedom and the free development of individuality are not identical;

nor is either the same as 'individual spontaneity' to which in the
following sentence he ascribes instrinsic worth; but in this passage
he comes close to equating all three and thus to bestowing on
freedom itself the same intrinsic value he gives to the last. Elsewhere,
in pleading for the equality of the sexes, he praises the 'life of rational
freedom', the attainment of which, if made possible by legal
independence of their husbands, would bring women 'an unspeakable
gain in private happiness'. Then, perhaps recalling his own restricted
childhood and the emotional release that terminated his mental
crisis, he continues:

> Let any man call to mind what he himself felt on emerging from
> boyhood — from the tutelage and control of even loved and
> affectionate elders — and entering upon the responsibilities of
> manhood. Was it not like the physical effect of taking off a heavy
> weight, or releasing him from obstructive, even if not otherwise
> painful, bonds? Did he not feel twice as much alive, twice as much
> a human being as before?[14]

Again, in comparing communism and socialism as forms of social
organisation the question he asks is, 'Which of the two systems is
consistent with the greatest amount of human liberty and spontaneity?'[15] For after the means of subsistence 'the next in strength of
the personal wants of human beings is liberty', and it is a want that
increases with the development of intelligence and the moral faculties.
Any form of education or social institution which encouraged the
exchange of freedom for comfort, affluence or even equality would
deprive its citizens 'of one of the most elevated characteristics of
human nature'. What Mill seems to be saying here and in similar
passages is not so much that freedom is instrumental to happiness
and well-being (though he would, of course, grant that it is), but
rather that it is *constitutive* of them; that freedom is among the
essential components of happiness, each of which, he states
elsewhere, is desirable *in itself* and as 'a part of the end'.[16]

Mill's concern for truth is apparent throughout his writings — and
not only for truth but for rationality and what he calls 'cultivated
intelligence',[17] between all of which there are close conceptual
connections. 'Truth and the general good,' he writes in 'Utility of
Religion', are 'the two noblest of all objects of pursuit.'[18]In his early
essay 'Civilisation' he asserts that 'an education intended to form
great minds' must 'call forth the greatest possible quantity of
intellectual *power* and . . . inspire the greatest *love of truth*';[19] but not
only 'great minds', for he was convinced that truth and a resolute

commitment to it by the whole body of citizens are fundamental to democracy — hence his conviction that universal education is essential as at least a step towards that ideal. Concern for truth is the basis of his plea for freedom of thought and discussion in *On Liberty* — and again, not only for the 'great thinker': 'it is as much and even more indispensable to enable average human beings to attain the mental stature which they are capable of.'[20] The same concern underlies his impassioned championing of the Platonic dialectic in its exposure of ignorance and falsehood and its endeavour to clarify such concepts as justice and virtue, good and evil. He writes of it with no less fervour in the *Inaugural Address*, commending both Plato and Aristotle for their 'noblest enthusiasm . . . for the search after truth and for applying it to its highest uses'; here too the value of truth forms part of his case for science education.[21] At a more personal level he writes to Florence Nightingale 'of the responsibility that lies upon each one of us to stand steadfastly and with all the boldness and all the humility that a deep sense of duty can inspire by what the experience of life and an honest use of our own intelligence has taught us to be the truth'.[22]This was a gospel he practised as well as preached; indeed, his transparent and undeviating honesty of intellect and intention is among the most conspicuous (and to our own age, wearied even more than his by evasive sophistries, refreshing) aspects of his character. Now, Mill was clearly aware that truth is important as a means — to happiness, to justice, to democracy, to personal stature and 'the dignity of thinking beings',[23] to the progress of science and other desirable ends — but here once again his concern seems at times to transcend the merely instrumental and become a passion for truth itself as an object worthy of pursuit in its own right

By pointing to these goals as desirable ends of human endeavour — indeed, more than this, as essential constituents of the good life — Mill fills out his concept of improvement with determinate content. Individual human beings, particular societies and mankind as a whole are changed for the better in so far as they approach and embody the ideals of happiness, altruism, individuality, freedom and truth. Now such a group of aims manifestly points to certain educational procedures, precludes others and calls for a distinguishable kind or quality of educational process. It will be an education which presents and demands high standards, which eschews an appeal to self-interested motives (and thus raises problems about competition, for which see below, p. 130); an education which seeks means of releasing individual potential, of encouraging creativity and imaginative divergence, and thus avoids imposing conformity or authority beyond that minimum which is indispensable for the child's own good and that of the community. It will be an education which promotes participation, because it is thus that men, women and children grow in responsible concern for their fellows, and which promotes self-help, thus imposing the onus of learning and choice upon the learner, stimulating thought and initiative and, once again, growth in responsibility as well as in personal maturity. It will be an education which encourages inquiry and discussion, since these kindle the desire for truth and at the same time assist its discovery, and which as a necessary corollary repudiates rote learning and the passive absorption of information from textbook or teacher. It will be a *situational* education in which the student (young or old) is encouraged to adapt to circumstances, work his own way through them and in so doing find that self-discipline (so much more effective than any imposed restraint) which is the essential counterpoise to freedom.

Such is the picture which emerges by implication from the values to which Mill is committed; a similar picture is reflected in his criticisms of contemporary education, in his comments on the impact of social environment and in his fears for state control. It can be found, for instance, in the essay 'On Genius', where he inveighs against an education in which things 'have *only* been taught and learned, but have *not* been *known*', in which other men's ideas are ground down to a convenient size and fed into the pupil, who mops them up but never truly absorbs them.[24] This is the education of passivity, of intellectual sterility, of inhibited growth; instead of releasing individuality into fulfilment it quells by the sheer weight of undigested cram and enervates the intellect into a mere knowledge box. This, together with the mortifying pressure of ecclesiastical control, is what has brought the English universities to their present state of scholastic impotence. Among the unwelcome consequences of civilisation, he writes in the essay of that title, is a relaxation of individual energy by increasing dependence on public provision, 'the general arrangements of society'. What energy remains (among the middle classes at least) is turned inwards towards the pursuit of financial gain; and in the scramble for self-advancement standards are perverted by false claims — 'any voice not pitched in an exaggerated key is lost in the hubbub'; success depends less on what a person is than on what he seems, and truth meanwhile becomes the victim of persuasion.[25] Among his principal fears for state control of education is, once more, the diminution of individuality by authority, by conformity, by mediocrity; and together with this is the loss, both to individual and society, of the educative force of private enterprise and participation, the loss too of that disclosure of truth which springs from experiment and diversity.

His epistemological and psychological premises also have their implications, which point in the same direction as those already inferred (thus suggesting interesting questions of priority and interdependence: which comes first and which determines the other, his epistemological or his axiological assumptions, and are they in fact dissociable?). Mill's epistemology is firmly based on experience: 'experiential' is the word used above to describe it; 'empirical' he eschewed as being, for him, restricted to the mere colligation of observational data. He rejects intuitionist epistemologies which find the origin of knowledge in truths either innate to the mind or apprehended independently of experience. The primary epistemological data are fed into the mind by sense perception, grouped and structured by association, conceptualised and generalised into systems of explanatory laws which, at their highest point of development, constitute *scientific* knowledge. This, as we have seen, raises important problems, not overlooked by Mill, of freedom, determinism and the extent to which human nature is explicable and predictable by causal laws. His not altogether convincing conclusion is that causal sequences can be diverted or initiated by a manipulation of environment effected by human volition, which is nevertheless still contained within, and therefore explicable by, causal uniformity. Such an epistemology led almost inevitably (in the existing state of psychological studies) to an associationist psychology; not that Mill, however, came to his associationism via his epistemology, for he was committed to both independently by his education and by other formative influences. The fundamental principle of associationism (to repeat a point made on p.49 above) is the tendency of 'ideas' or mental contents, produced in the mind by the impact of sensations on the nervous system, to form themselves into sequences or complexes; this linking of 'ideas' occurs principally as a result of similarity or contiguity in the original sensations, the intensity and duration of which are additional factors in effecting the association.

It would seem from various statements in his writings that Mill also accepted a version of the mind as possessed of certain faculties or powers which, it was supposed, could be trained in one activity of curricular area and the training then transferred to others; thus, powers of memorisation developed in the learning of Latin or French might be transferred, say, to the learning of historical facts. This so-called faculty psychology is not a necessary part of associationism, but it derives plausibility from the associationist conception of the mind, which approximates to physical and mechanical rather than organic models and is thus more readily accommodated to the notion of distinct faculties and transferrable mental packages. Its relevance to the process of education lies chiefly in the fact that Mill uses it to supply a justification for some curricular subjects (classics, for instance) as better suited than others to 'train the faculties', 'form the mind', promote 'a vigorous intellect' and so on.

What, we must now ask, are the educational implications suggested by Mill's experiential and associationist premises? A preliminary insight into these can be gained from considering briefly the intuitionist position which he rejects.[26] Its adherents claimed that certain truths and epistemological principles (for instance, causality, personal identity, the existence of God) are not discovered by empirical observation but are disclosed directly to the mind; in psychology they held that mental content is not solely the product of sense experience but derives in part from the mind's innate qualities or powers. The tendency of intuitionism, Mill believed, was towards a static conception of truth, not as something to be wrested from experience, created in the active exploration of phenomena, but rather as something to be passively accepted, ready-made, a pre-existing pattern to be absorbed or reflected. At best he thought it philosophically and scientifically untenable, at worst an oppressive source of prejudice, conformity and mental stagnation. Educationally he believed it to be a conservative and restraining force which encouraged an authoritarian and dogmatic pedagogy; for if truth is *revealed* rather than discovered, and *already* revealed as a result of previous intuition, the teacher's task is to mediate it, the pupil's to receive it, and if he be uninterested or recalcitrant, he must be 'disciplined' into acceptance. This is an education of submission, of enforced attention, contrived interest, rote learning and ultimate intellectual closure. (It is clear, too, from what he writes in the *Autobiography* that Mill regarded intuitionism and its insistence on the innate origins of human character as a major obstacle to social progress — 'one of the chief hindrances to the rational treatment of great social questions and one of the greatest stumbling-blocks to human improvement'. By contrast, the philosophies of experience and association are the natural allies of reform, 'full of practical consequences' and at the root 'of all the greatest differences of practical opinion in an age of progress'.)[27]

Contrast with this the consequences of experientialism: instead of a pattern to be absorbed, knowledge is a growing and flexibile edifice constantly supplied with new materials from experience; truth is open, progressive, not a finished product but a continuing adventure. Educationally there is a switch of focus from the teacher and his teaching to the pupil and his learning; since knowledge is the product of experience, it is in his experiencing that the pupil comes to know, in his immediate, individual response to and interaction with the sensory world (which here includes the books which present it to him and his fellow human beings who are part of it). This points, further, to an education of involvement, of participation, of experiment, of doing rather than memorising (though the latter is not dispensable); an education which, no less than the other, requires attention and motivation, but from *within*, from the pupil's own resources of interest and application. Restraint and discipline there will still be, but they too will come from within, from the acceptance, borne in upon the pupil by his direct dealings with the world around him, of the need for obedience to natural laws and for imposing upon himself the orderly and rule-governed procedures necessary to the attainment of his goals.

To the implications of experientialism must be added those of association psychology. Mental content is derived from experiential data which are structured within the mind according to associative links; but the data and the links which bind them are supplied by experience within an encompassing environment. From this there follow two conclusions of the greatest importance. First, mental content and structure vary and can be made to vary in accordance with the data presented to the recipient mind and with the manner, order, frequency, etc., of the presentation; change the data and their associative bonds, and the character and content of the mind are likewise changed; so too is the behaviour that flows from them.

Second, it follows that environment is the (or at least the *principal*) determining factor in forming mind and character; it is from this that the mind receives its experiential data, and what it receives, in what order and related to what, depends on the nature of the environment. This in turn depends at least in part on human agency; for men and women can choose the environment they and their children live in, giving it, for instance (as Mill would certainly wish), an extent and variety which will provide the widest range of data and thus promote a subtler and more complex 'mental chemistry' together with a greater potential for individuality and imaginative divergence. Here, then, we have the basic instrument of education, a potent means of shaping human beings. 'We are all,' wrote John Locke, 'a sort of camelions that still take a tincture from things near us'; and the control of 'things near us', he declares, is vital to children's upbringing and education.[28] Mill does not express himself so colourfully, but, as will be evident in the next section, he was no less convinced of the moulding power and educative importance of environment.

The educational implications of associationism suggest a number of questions, both interesting and perplexing. First, how far in fact does environment determine mental content and individual character? Associationism regards it as dominant, but what of hereditary and instinctual factors whose existence is undeniable and which must surely contribute something to the final product? And in allowing the dominance to environment, is there not a risk of exaggerating the power and importance of education, of naively exalting it into a panacea for human ills? Bentham and James Mill were strongly inclined to the Helvetian dictum, 'L'éducation peut *tout*', though the latter applied it to *classes* of men rather than to individuals and also took a wide-ranging view of education. John himself has been accused of the same error — Leslie Stephen, for instance, charges him with 'believing even to excess in the power of education' and another critic with being possessed by 'the educating mania'.[29] In 'Utility of Religion', at a time when his father's influence had lost its earlier compelling grip, he could still write that 'the power of education is almost boundless'.[30] Second, control of environment for educational ends implies selection and rejection of experiential data on the educand's behalf, whether he be child or adult; experience must be sifted, censored, in accordance with *a priori* value commitments. Now it would be stupid to deny the need for some such sifting of experience, at least for children (whose physical safety alone requires it); but pushed to extremes it leads to the kind of situation depicted in Huxley's *Brave New World* (and similarly but less obnoxiously in Plato's *Republic*) — a doctrinaire censorship, reinforced by a web of constricting regulations which confine the individual to pre-selected paths which he had no part in choosing. Such, needless to say, would be wholly alien to Mill's intention.

A further risk involved in associationism is that of obscuring the existence, and to that extent impeding the expression, of individual differences. For it is committed (or inclined, if the former is too strong a word) to a *tabula rasa* model of the mind such as Locke offers in his *Essay*.[31] On to this initially blank sheet are imprinted 'ideas' produced in the mind by the impact of sensory data; association links these ideas in the manner already described, and thus is built up our complex mental furniture. But does not this imply that all start equal and, further, that if all are subjected to the same environmental experiences, they will end up equal too? However, the facts suggest otherwise; for human difference is a commonplace of everyday observation — even within the family, where the experiential data approximate most nearly to the same for all. Moreover, to underplay or ignore such differences is surely to discourage and diminish individuality, divergence, variety; it is in *difference* of response, even to the *same* environment, that individuality largely consists. These again are consequences of associationism which Mill would wholeheartedly reject but of which he was too little aware; like other weaknesses in that psychology, they are due in no small measure to an over-mechanical conception of the experiencing mind.

Interestingly, Alexander Bain cites Mill's lack of awareness of this weakness, manifested in the form of 'his doctrine of the natural equality of all men', as one of his two chief errors as a scientific thinker: 'On this subject he was, in my opinion, blind to a whole region of facts. He inherited the mistake from his father, and could neither learn nor unlearn in regard to it.' The other error, which is also relevant to the present discussion, is his disregard of the physiological conditions of mental activity; not a total disregard, 'but he did not allow what every competent physiologist would now affirm to be the facts.'[32] What facts he does not specify, but no doubt he is referring to the hereditary, instinctual and emotive aspects of human nature and to the neurological basis of mental events. The criticisms are not wholly justified: Mill was not blind to differences of aptitude and intelligence (save in regard to his own intellectual superiority)[33] — his elitist tendencies are evidence enough of this; nor was he ignorant of or indifferent to the neurology of mental phenomena, indeed he expressly recognises both its importance and contemporary ignorance of it (p.50 above).

Finally, what of motivation? The associationist picture of education suggests passivity of response to a controlled set of experiential data. But what if the response is not forthcoming, or if it is one of rejection instead of acceptance? To present the data is not difficult, provided the teacher has sufficient knowledge, clarity of purpose and organisational skill; but to persuade children and students to apply themselves, to study the data, be involved in them, absorb them, digest them and finally use them, independently and constructively — that, as any teacher knows, is the crux of his task (and for some also their cross!). It has already been noted as a weakness of association psychology that it does not account satisfactorily for the volitional aspect of behaviour (pp. 56-7). Of this Mill was certainly aware. In his review of Bain's two volumes of psychology he points to 'the almost total absence in [its] analytical expositions of the recognition of any active element or spontaneity in the mind itself'. As a recipient of impressions the mind is passive; 'activity cannot possibly be generated from passive elements', therefore 'a primitive active element must be found somewhere.'[34] Hartley had found this in the relation between sensation and the muscular system, the former being somehow stored in the latter and available for recall as a stimulus to activity. Bain had improved on this (so Mill believed) by positing in addition a 'nervous influence . . . generated automatically in the brain itself . . . under the organic stimulus of nutrition' and providing the source of volition;[35] the ensuing activity was accepted or rejected according to the pleasure or displeasure that it offered.

Not only volition but attention too is necessary for the experiential data to make their impact; and the two are closely linked. On this there is a long and interesting note in Mill's edition of his father's *Analysis*, where the account of attention is (in John's view) instructive but inadequate.[36] He agrees with his father that attention requires an act of volition which is motivated by the prospect of something pleasurable; the anticipated pleasure attaches itself to the object of attention and thus induces volition. This, he adds, 'is the true account of all that we do when we fix our attention voluntarily'. However, although this may adequately explain a willing and easy act of attention, it does not explain *effortful* attention, where the will must be cajoled into attending. In this situation, John suggests, an additional element of desire is necessary; this is supplied indirectly by a dissatisfaction with oneself which creates the desire to strengthen the infirmity of one's desiring. 'There is thus called up, by our sense of the insufficiency of our attention in the particular case, the idea of another desirable end — greater vigour and certainty in our mental operations.' To the practising teacher, struggling with lower-stream, mixed-ability groups in state comprehensives, this may seem a sophisticated account of attention, suited only to intellectuals like Mill, already strongly motivated by high ideals of personal achievement. Yet the appeal to self-improvement and to standards higher than those yet attained has long been — and still is — a valuable pedagogic tool, which acquires further efficacy when it is related to pupils' vocational and leisure interests. It must be remembered too that psychology and popular education were in their infancy in Mill's day, and he must be allowed credit for recognising at that time both the importance of motivation and attention and their relevance to the practice of education. In two earlier notes he comments that an understanding of the role of pleasure and pain (or interest and aversion, in modern terms) is of great value 'both for the purposes of psychological science and for those of practical education', and herein 'consists the efficacy of education in giving a good or bad direction to the active powers'.[37] He regarded them as especially important, as will appear later (pp.195-6) in moral education.

A further problem emerges from a closer examination and comparison of the implications of experientialism and associationism — implications which Mill himself did not elaborate into a coherent theory of educational practice. That he understood the need to do so is clear from various comments. In the course of his review of Bain's psychological volumes he rebuts the charge that associationism, because it derives the nobler human attributes 'from the materials of our animal nature' is therefore a 'materialistic' doctrine. That mind has some physiological and material basis is, he argues, undeniable. This being so:

> If these nobler parts of our nature are not self-sown and original, but are built or build themselves up, out of no matter what materials, it must be highly important to the work of the education and improvement of human character to understand as much as possible of the process by which the materials are put together.[38]

Again, in his review of Grote's *Aristotle* he commends as still true his father's statement that 'the theory of education is far behind the progress of knowledge, and the practice lamentably behind even the theory.'[39] In yet another review, of Sedgwick's *Discourse*, he remarks on the ignorance of factors which contribute to an individual's moral judgements. Any philosophy of morals, he continues, must be preceded by 'clear and comprehensive views of education and human culture', in other words, by a 'philosophy of education'; otherwise morality and moral judgements cannot be understood, and for this, he adds, 'much yet remains to be done.'[40] Now if Mill had had the time and inclination to construct such a comprehensive educational theory, he would have become aware of a stress developing between his experiential epistemology and his association psychology, and perhaps even more between the latter and his commitment to individuality.

Experientialism, as we have seen, points to an educational practice which is centred on the inquiring mind, on learning not teaching, on individual response to experience; motivation, discipline, direction come, as far as possible, from *within*, and it is thus that individual potential is most effectively developed. Such an education has obvious affinities with the 'progressive' and 'child-centred' practices of today. Associationism, although it is an empirically based psychology, tends in another direction: it assumes, first, the malleability of human nature — mental content, character, behaviour; second, the possibility, indeed the desirability, of deliberately shaping human nature by feeding into it from experience pre-structured sensory data. This suggests a picture of the teacher not as one who sensitively tends the growing organism in its individual transaction with experience, but rather as one who imposes a set pattern of response aimed at goals determined for, not by, the individual in advance of his experiencing. Perhaps this is not an inevitable consequence of associationism, provided it keeps a firm hold on the principle of individuality; and education is impossible, whatever its theoretical basis, without some minimum pre-structuring of the environment. Yet although what is here suggested may be regarded as an abuse rather than a legitimate use of associationist theory, it is nevertheless an abuse inherent in the theory itself; for a psychology which, after a somewhat mechanical model, emphasises the manipulation of man and the means of manipulating him, lends itself to a mechanical concept of education in which the stress is on teaching rather than learning, on authority rather than freedom, on facts to be learnt instead of experience to be explored. The tendency is the greater, no doubt, when associationist theory is harnessed to urgent ideals of human improvement; for it may then be seized upon as a short cut to the millennium which conveniently by-passes the irritating anomalies and inconsistencies thrown up by individuals in the peculiarity of their experiential response. It is not altogether surprising, then, that James Mill and other utilitarians likewise committed to association psychology were so strongly attracted to the monitorial system of teaching introduced by Bell and Lancaster. Its appeal lay not only in its cheapness and its suitability, therefore, for mass popular instruction, but also in the fact that it lent itself to the associationist conception of education as the presentation of pre-structured experience, here in the form of 'programmed' information; this, once correctly ordered by a skilled teacher according to the laws of association, could be presented by any number of unskilled apprentices.

The strain between Mill's experientialism and individualism on the one hand and association psychology on the other is predictable from, though not apparent in, *Logic* VI. For what he writes there of ethology and its dependent art of education points away from the earlier Mill of 'On Genius' and 'Civilisation' in the direction of behavioural engineering and the subordination of individuality to carefully planned techniques of reinforcement (pp.75-7 above). Perhaps this is to extrapolate too far, but the possibility is certainly present as a logical practical outcome of the account of human nature he offers in the *Logic*, a nature susceptible to causal explanation and control by the laws of association. He would certainly have shrunk from such an outcome had he been clearly aware of it, and it may be that this did in fact happen and found expression, vehemently and decisively, in *On Liberty*. Here he rejects utterly the conception of human nature as 'a machine to be built after a model'; rather, it is like a tree which must develop 'according to the tendency of the inward forces which make it a living thing'.[41] There is perhaps some further indication of a revulsion from a mechanistic psychology in the *Autobiography*. Discussing the origins of his nervous crisis he complains that his father's application of associationism to his own (John's) education was superficial in its reliance on 'the old familiar instruments, praise and blame, reward and punishment'. Associations thus 'forcibly' produced are inevitably 'artificial and casual';

lacking any 'natural tie', they are incapable of resisting the corrosive effect of analysis.[42] What Mill seems to be attacking here is not associationism as such but a mechanical and insensitive use of association which disregards 'the inward forces' of spontaneous, affective human nature.

The strain or tension that we have been considering in the preceding paragraphs is not simply epistemological and psychological; it also reflects something in Mill's own character. His zeal as a reformer, his emphatic commitment to happiness and other primary values and his inclusion of human behaviour, no less than events in the material world, within the orbit of science all impelled him towards a policy of behavioural control, of using education as a means of wresting the actual into nearer conformity with the ideal. And, as we in this century know to our tragic cost, there is none so ruthless as the dedicated reformer who believes he has the means of manipulating humanity into the millennium. Mill was saved from such extremes by the restraints of reason, common sense and a deep-down respect for the integrity and individuality of other men and women. However, if we bear in mind this opposition of forces within him, it is easier to understand why some have seen him as an apostle of freedom and others as a moral totalitarian.[43] For himself he would welcome the tension, believing as he did that truth comes from dialogue and progress from the resolution of antagonisms (see below, pp.175-7).

Whatever the attractions of behavioural control, the dominant flow of Mill's thought is clearly towards a kind of education characterised by experience, inquiry and experiment; by freedom, activity, learning as against authority, passivity, teaching; by organic metaphors of nourishment, growth, development, response and interaction. As already suggested, this bears a strong resemblance to so-called 'progressive' theories of recent and present times; indeed, it is difficult in writing of Mill's educational thought to avoid borrowing the imagery and vocabulary of such theories — 'growth', 'response', 'interaction', 'involvement' are all instances of this. Moreover, there is much in Mill that shows a surprising congruity, sometimes almost word for word, with the ideas of educational philosophers and practitioners like John Dewey, Percy Nunn, A. S. Neill and, more recently, Ivan Illich and Paulo Freire, all of whom are regarded as 'progressives' of one kind or another (and the last two of whom are still, of course, very much with us).

What, we may well ask, were the sources of such seemingly

advanced views? There is no easy answer to this question, for Mill does not directly declare his indebtedness save in regard to his own education. Rousseau's *Emile* (1762) he must presumably have read; Rousseau himself he mentions a number of times, praising him in *On Liberty* for the 'salutary shock' of his paradoxical utterances, and in the essay on Bentham coupling him with Helvetius as among the few great French metaphysicians of the eighteenth century. Among much that he would disagree with in the *Emile* he would also find much that was acceptable — the appeal to sense experience, the emphasis on environment, on the importance of the family, on heuristic learning, on guidance rather than instruction. He was also familiar with the work and no doubt the writings of Pestalozzi. In *Leonard and Gertrude* (1781) and *How Gertrude Teaches her Children* (1801) he would again find much that was congenial — the importance of *Anschauung* (the child's immediate confrontation with experience), of observation, of activity (especially self-activity), of the home and its social context. It is difficult to believe that he had not read Locke's *Some Thoughts concerning Education* (1693; one of few educational classics in English), though he does not mention the book nor, so far as the present writer has discovered, does he acknowledge Locke as a contributor to educational thought. James Mill had evidently read it, for he commends Locke for his benevolence and democratic sentiments, while deprecating the limitation of his educational prescriptions to the role of the gentleman. It is a safe assumption, therefore, that John too had read it, the more so as he was thoroughly acquainted with the *Essay* from an early age and had a high regard for Locke as an eminent experientialist and one of the founders of association psychology. Certainly he would find himself in agreement with his experiential outlook, which is characteristic of *Thoughts* as well as central to the *Essay*, and with numerous items of educational principle and practice relating to environment, home, moral training, example, habit, language teaching and much more. Occasionally there are echoes in Mill not merely of Locke's ideas but of his words — for instance, in his strictures on classics teaching in the *Inaugural* and his recommendation that Latin and Greek should be learnt, like modern languages, 'by acquiring some familiarity with the vocabulary by practice and repetition before being troubled by grammatical rules'; with this compare Locke's injunction 'to trouble the child with no grammar at all, but to have Latin, as English has been, without the perplexity of rules talked into him'.[44]

In addition to these sources, whether actual or probable, there were many contemporary influences which may have made their impact on Mill directly or indirectly. Numerous novels drawing on the ideas of Rousseau's *Emile* were in circulation by the end of the eighteenth century, the most famous of them Thomas Day's *Sandford and Merton* (thirteen editions between 1789 and 1823). There were the voluminous writings of Maria Edgeworth, whose father, Richard Lovell Edgeworth, was an ardent follower of Rousseau. James Mill praises her in his 'Education'[45] and sent her a copy of Bentham's *Chrestomathia* in the hope of enlisting her support for a projected monitorial school in London. In addition to these and many other books proposing new forms and methods of education there were a number of 'experimental schools' in existence during the early part of the nineteenth century. Dr Charles Mayo founded a school at Cheam in 1826 based on Pestalozzi's principles. There was the Hills' school at Hazelwood in Birmingham, and a later offshoot at Bruce Castle in Tottenham, which among other innovations introduced a system of pupil self-government. Robert Owen's schools at New Lanark were well known and widely influential. James Mill knew Owen well and had frequent discussions with him, so John writes in a letter of 1873; but John himself was not altogether enamoured of his practices, mentioning in particular his (or the 'Owenites',) view of responsibility and punishment. Wordsworth was another likely influence; he and Coleridge were at one time much attracted to the company of Rousseau enthusiasts (including Lamb and Hazlitt), and although the later Wordsworth with whom Mill spent a few days in 1831 was not the younger man whose early poems had helped release him from his nervous crisis, something of the old spirit no doubt remained and was conveyed in their walks and talks among the Lakeland hills. Charles Dickens was yet another: Mill had met him in 1837 and commented in a letter on his shaggy appearance; his death in 1870 struck him 'like a personal loss'. He seems to have read most of his novels as they came into print and writes to Harriet that *Bleak House* is the only one he altogether disliked (Dickens had 'the vulgar impudence to ridicule the rights of women' and 'in the very vulgarest way'). The schoolroom of *Hard Times* (1854) depicts in its senseless disgorging of crammed information a pedagogy as repulsive to Mill as to the author himself.[46]

How far these sources brought new ideas to Mill and how far they merely reinforced what was already in his mind it is impossible to say. Of one influence, however, there can be no doubt, namely his father and the education he devised for John. Clearly there is much in that education and in the relationship between father and son that any progressivist would repudiate as 'unnatural', if not positively inhumane — the excessive rigour of Mill's intellectual studies, the emotional deprivation, the lack of practical activity (it was an education 'more fitted for training me to *know* than to *do*') and of play and companionship. Nevertheless, there was also much that was wholly in accord with progressive principles and whose value John later recognised and fully appreciated. Above all it was an education which forced him back upon his own resources, compelling him to 'find out everything for myself'; and despite its rigour and its enormous factual content, it was never a mere exercise of memory; his father 'strove to make the understanding not only go along with every step of the teaching, but, if possible, precede it. Anything which could be found out by thinking I never was told, until I had exhausted my efforts to find it out for myself.'[47] No wonder, then, that he could write in 'On Genius' that 'the end of education is not to *teach*, but to fit the mind for learning from its own consciousness and observation'[48] — a sentence that might well have been written by John Dewey or any other progressive educationist of our own time.

PHILOSOPHICAL ISSUES

1. *The concept of education*

Mill attempted no formal analysis of the concept of education, but indirectly he points to the need for it. For although he makes certain important distinctions, e.g. between schooling and the total impact of environment, between education by teachers and education by experience, between cram and growth, he leaves much of the concept obscure. Moreover, as has been noted in the text, his view of education contains ambiguities and tensions of which he was evidently unaware and which he made no attempt to resolve. Clarification of the concept and of its 'logical geography' has been one of the preoccupations of recent educational philosophy. Professor Peters has been a notable contributor to this; the first two chapters of his *Ethics and Education* (Allen and Unwin, 1966) are a good starting-point for study, together with his paper 'The Justification of Education', in the volume edited by him for the Oxford Readings in Philosophy series, *The Philosophy of Education* (Oxford University Press, 1973). There is also the volume of papers edited by him under the title *The Concept of Education* (Routledge and Kegan Paul, 1967); see his 'What is an Educational Process?' and various others. Further analyses of the concept are offered by Langford, G., in the volume edited by him and O'Connor, D. J., *New Essays in the Philosophy of Education*; and by Professor W. K. Frankena in Doyle, J. F., ed., *Educational Judgments*, chapter 1 (and for comment on this, see chapter 3). See too *J. Phil. Ed.,* vol. 4, 1970 (Peters, R. S.); vol. 6, no. 1, 1972 (Perry, L. R.); vol. 6, no. 2, 1972 (Reddiford, G., Telfer, E.); vol. 8, no. 1, 1974 (Smart, P.); and *Ed. Ph. and Th.,* vol. 4, no. 2, 1972 (Robinson, K.).

2. *Aims in education*

Closely related to the conceptual clarification of education is the elucidation of its aims; much has been written on this and many pronouncements made, from Plato to the present day. For recent contributions to this theme, see: Peters, R. S., ed., *The Philosophy of Education*, chapter 1, 'Aims of Education — A Conceptual Inquiry' (Peters, R. S., *et al.*); Dearden, R. F., Hirst, P. H., Peters, R. S., eds, *Education and the Development of Reason,* Part 1: A Critique of Current Educational Aims. It is interesting to compare Peters and Dewey on aims; both take the view, but for different reasons, that aims are constituents intrinsic to education, not goals external to it; see the paper by Peters *et al.* cited above and Dewey's *Democracy and Education,* chapter 8. A useful historical survey of educational aims can be found in Nash, P., Kazamias, A. M., and Perkinson, H. J., eds, *The Educated Man* (Wiley, 1965); it includes chapters on Plato, Locke, Marx, Dewey and Skinner.

3. *Progressive education*

It is suggested in the text that the implications of Mill's experientialism bear some resemblance to 'progressive' theories of education. 'Progressive' is a notion which is itself sadly in need of clarification, but the word is commonly attached to such writers and practitioners as Rousseau, Dewey, A. S. Neill and, more recently, John Holt, Ivan Illich and Paulo Freire. The following will provide an entry into this fascinating and controversial area of education: Rousseau, J. J., *Emile* (numerous editions; abbreviated in Boyd, W., ed., *Emile for Today,* Heinemann, 1956); Dewey, J., *Experience and Education* (Macmillan (New York), 1938, and later editions); Neill, A. S., *Summerhill* (Hart, 1960; Penguin Books, 1961); Freire, P., *Pedagogy of the Oppressed* (Penguin Books, 1972); Illich, I., *Deschooling Society* (Penguin Books, 1973); Holt, J., *Instead of Education* (Penguin Books, 1977). After reading some of these the student might then turn to Barrow, R., *Radical Education* (Martin Robertson, 1978), subtitled 'A Critique of Freeschooling and Deschooling'. See also the recent article in *J. Phil. Ed.,* vol. 12, 1978 (Darling, J.).

CHAPTER 2

Environmentalism

It has already been shown that both experientialism and association psychology point to the environment as a crucial determinant of mental content and character (though not necessarily the *sole* determinant). If the primary source of knowledge is in the data presented to the mind by sensory apprehension of the external world; if the bonds which link these data (and consequently predispose our thinking and our attitudes, likes and dislikes) are supplied from the same source; and if the external world and its sensory impact can be manipulated by human agency (as they obviously can), then the environment is inevitably an instrument of undeniable importance in the formation of human character, and must be recognised as such by the educator. It was certainly so recognised by Mill, not only, however, as a consequence of his epistemological and psychological premises, but as a result, too, of his own education and upbringing.

James Mill was himself a convinced associationist; this he makes abundantly clear in the article on education which he wrote for the *Encyclopaedia Britannica* and in his *Analysis of the Phenomena of the Human Mind.* 'The character of the human mind,' he asserts in the former, 'consists in the sequences of its ideas, . . . the object of education, therefore, is to provide for the constant production of certain sequences, rather than others'; and 'it is upon a knowledge of the sequences which take place in the human feelings or thoughts, that the structure of education must be reared.'[1] The two principal factors which determine these sequences are custom and pain-and-pleasure. It follows that 'the business of a skilful education' (which, like John, he takes in the extended sense of 'every thing which acts upon the being as it comes from the hand of nature, in such a manner as to modify the mind, to render the train of feelings different from what it would otherwise have been')[2] is so to arrange the circumstances of children, their total environment, that the desired associations are in fact produced by these two principal available means.

Inevitably he strove to establish the same doctrine in his son (at least as an intellectual commitment; much less certain is how far the attempt was extended to a detailed control of John's daily environment in order to secure the correct associations). In describing his nervous crisis of 1826 and seeking its explanation, John points both to the success and at the same time to the failure of associationism as applied to his own education:

> My course of study had led me to believe that all mental and moral feelings and qualities, whether of a good or of a bad kind, were the results of association; that we love one thing, and hate another, take pleasure in one sort of action or contemplation, and pain in another sort, through the clinging of pleasurable or painful ideas to those things, from the effect of education or of experience. As a corollary from this, I had always heard it maintained by my father, and was myself convinced, that the object of education should be to form the strongest possible associations of the salutary class; associations of pleasure with all things beneficial to the great whole, and of pain with all things hurtful to it. This doctrine appeared inexpugnable. . . .[3]

Intellectually John was convinced, and remained convinced, that association is indeed a powerful pedagogical and educational instrument if 'begun early and applied unremittingly';[4] to this extent James Mill was successful.

Where he failed, so it seemed to John, was in the superficiality of its application, by his placing too much confidence in 'the old familiar instruments, praise and blame, reward and punishment'; associations thus produced are 'artificial and casual'; 'pains and pleasures thus forcibly associated with things are not connected with them by any natural tie' and are therefore unable to withstand the 'dissolving force' of rational analysis when the subject is of an age to employ it.[5] This is cogent criticism — sufficient, one might think, to undermine belief in the efficacy of association as a practicable educational technique. Yet John did not withdraw his intellectual assent. Nor did the experience of his own upbringing and its consequences weaken his conviction of the practical implications of associationism for environmental control as an instrument of education; indeed, in some respects it was corroborated thereby, for he emphasises in the

Autobiography the permanent impact made on him by, for instance, his summer visits to Ford Abbey, his year-long stay in France and his first glimpse of high mountain scenery in the Pyrenees[6] (not all of which was part of his father's deliberate intention, but which nevertheless left him with indelible associations of interest and pleasure). The moulding force of environment and its value in furthering educational purposes are a constant theme in his writings; this will be illustrated and discussed later in the present section, but first we must consider a problem mentioned earlier (p.96), namely, the relationship between heredity and environment, nature and nurture, and their comparative importance in education.

Inherent in associationism is a tendency to ascribe the dominant role to nurture (including environment, of course); for its account of the formation of mind and character implies, or at least assumes, that the preponderant influence in shaping these is experience — which, ideally, is controlled by deliberate educational intent (though in practice *formative* experience may well be unpremeditated and unpredictable). This assumption leads readily to extreme views of the power of education, as in Helvetius' 'L'éducation peut *tout*'. James Mill had the greatest admiration for this French theorist; no one, he asserts in his *Encyclopaedia* article, 'has done so much towards perfecting the *theory* of education'. He goes on to expound his theory thus:

> If you take men who bring into the world with them the original constituents of their nature, their mental and bodily frame, in that ordinary state of goodness which is common to the great body of mankind, — leaving out of the account the comparatively small number of individuals who come into the world imperfect and manifestly below the ordinary standard, — you may regard the whole of this great mass of mankind as equally susceptible of mental excellence; and may trace the causes which make them to differ. If this be so, the power of education embraces everything between the lowest stage of intellectual and moral rudeness and the highest state, not only of actual, but of possible perfection. And if the power of education be so immense, the motive for perfecting it is great beyond expression.[7]

There is a good deal of unclarity here: what are these 'original constituents of their nature', what 'that ordinary state of goodness', and what 'the ordinary standard' which is the criterion of imperfection? However, James Mill is less interested in these theoretical considerations than in the practical importance of Helvetius' doctrine for education — *provided*, he is careful to emphasise, that education is taken in its broadest sense. Whether the differences between individuals are due 'wholly to the circumstances which have operated upon them since the first moment of their sensitive existence' or are 'in part produced by original peculiarities' he regards as less important than the need that 'these circumstances should, by careful and continued observation, be all ascertained, and placed in the order best adapted for drawing from them the most efficient practical rules.' He agrees with Helvetius at least to this extent: first, that 'enough is ascertained to prove, beyond a doubt, that if education does not perform everything, there is hardly anything which it does not perform'; second, that 'all the difference which exists, or can ever be made to exist, between one *class* of men and another is wholly owing to education'[8] (Mill's italics). To assign the difference to nature rather than to nurture is, he adds, based on supposition, not proof; yet he admits that there *is* a nature which at the very least contributes a potential which may be abnormal or below standard and thus impedes the work of the educator.

Controversy on this issue was not new to the nineteenth century; it is implicit in the social organisation of Plato's *Republic*, with its different classes innately distinguished as 'gold', 'silver', 'bronze' and 'iron', and in its educational recommendations, which include a rigid control both of human breeding (for the Guardian, i.e. 'gold' and 'silver', classes) and of environment. Nearer to the Mills' time it appears in Locke's *Thoughts concerning Education*; as an experientialist and an associationist himself, not surprisingly Locke comes down firmly on the side of nurture and education: 'I think I may say that of all the men we meet with nine parts of ten are what they are, good or evil, useful or not, by their education. 'Tis that which makes the great difference in mankind.'[9] Nevertheless, he accepts that natural endowment plays a part in human development — 'God has stamped certain characters upon men's minds, which, like their shapes, may perhaps be a little mended, but can hardly be totally altered'; and 'the bias will always hang on that side nature first placed it' (which reads almost like a contradiction of his earlier pronouncements, and perhaps suggests a certain ambivalence of view); hence the need for careful observation of children's 'natures and aptitudes'. And Locke, like both the Mills, attributes great importance to environment and to example as part of it — 'We are all a sort of camelions that still take a tincture from things near us'; for although by 'education' in *Thoughts* he means principally 'schooling' (or 'tutoring', to be more exact), he is not oblivious of its broader connotations. Controversy on the issue continued throughout the eighteenth century, fired afresh by Helvetius' emphatic stand on the side of nurture and by Rousseau's (often misunderstood and certainly ambiguous) appeal to 'nature', 'natural development' and education 'according to nature'. Even today the issue is disputed; there is disagreement still about the respective importance of endowment and environment in, for instance, the development of intelligence; and it has been further complicated by debate on the inheritance (or not) of acquired characteristics and by the claims made for the success of reinforcement techniques. However, we must leave the more general argument and turn now to J. S. Mill.

He allows the existence of 'nature' in the sense that every human being has a basic physiological, neurological and mental constitution which provides a necessary starting point for development, a potential for growth. For instance, there is innate in everyone a propensity for the association of ideas as a result of sensory experience; without this there would be no possibility of mental and intellectual growth. But how far this basic 'nature' may differ from one individual to another is far from certain; indeed, he seems reluctant to admit to any inborn differences at all save in those who are patently abnormal; such differences as are observable in the character of normal persons are, he thinks, more probably attributable to environmental circumstances than to natural capacity. However, in *The Subjection of Women*, where he discusses at some length (and, of course, rejects) the supposed inferiority of the 'weaker sex',[10] he grants that

> there is indeed a certain proportion of persons, in both sexes, in whom an unusual degree of nervous sensibility is constitutional, and of so marked a character as to be the feature of their organisation which exercises the greatest influence over the whole character of the vital phenomena. This constitution, like other physical conformations, is hereditary, and is transmitted to sons as well as daughters.

It is possible, he suggests, and even probable, that this 'nervous temperament' belongs naturally to more women than men. There are other qualities too which are generally regarded as especially characteristic of the female sex — a bent for the practical, intuitive perception, a sense of present reality which protects them from extravagant speculation ('a woman seldom runs wild after an abstraction'), and with these a certain mental 'mobility' which enables them to pass easily from one topic or activity to another without loss of concentration. (This last, he adds, though 'they perhaps have it from nature . . . they certainly have it by training and education.') He concludes, however, that it is impossible to judge the extent to which these and other differences between the sexes are natural or artificial, 'whether there are any natural differences at all; or, supposing all artificial causes of difference to be withdrawn, what natural character would be revealed'. The fact is, he rightly observes, a human being cannot be isolated from his circumstances in such a way as to discover experimentally what he might otherwise have been by nature.

In the same chapter of *The Subjection of Women* he concedes that national and racial characteristics are also due in part to 'nature': 'The French and the Italians are undoubtedly by nature more nervously excitable than the Teutonic races, and, compared at least with the English, they have a much greater habitual and daily emotional life.' No doubt the ancient Romans had the same temperament as their descendants of today, but in them it was overruled by 'the stern character of their national discipline'.[11] Thus, cultural factors, combined with education, may counteract and correct innate differences and infirmities. In his review of Tennyson's poems, published in 1835, he argues that the poet is possessed of two characteristics, for one of which he is indebted to nature, the other to cultivation:

> What he derives from nature is fine senses: a nervous organisation, not only adapted to make his outward impressions vivid and distinct (in which, however, practice does even more than nature), but so constituted as to be, more easily than common organisations, thrown either by physical or moral [i.e. psychological] causes, into *states* of enjoyment or suffering, especially of enjoyment: . . . This peculiar kind of nervous susceptibility seems to be the distinctive character of the poetic temperament. It constitutes the capacity for poetry; and not only produces . . . a predisposition to the poetic associations, but supplies the very materials out of which many of them are formed.[12]

It is also the source of imaginative power, which (he affirms in a footnote) is not itself 'a gift of nature' save in so far as it is a consequence of this same nervous susceptibility. Again, in referring to his own education he compares the immense amount of knowledge he absorbed in childhood and early youth with 'the wretched waste of so many precious years' characteristic of nineteenth-century schooling. The comparison would have less force, he comments, 'if I had been by nature extremely quick of apprehension, or had possessed a very accurate and retentive memory, or were of a remarkably active and energetic character'; but 'in all these natural gifts' he considered himself rather below than above average and (predictably) he assigns the success of his education — 'an advantage of a quarter of a century over my contemporaries' — to his early training.[13] This assessment of his own powers is surely a classic understatement, but the importance of the passage lies in its admission of an innate or 'natural' contribution to ability.

Some years later, in *Logic* VI, he feels compelled to address himself briefly to the problem of instincts — though he leaves it unresolved and, in the state of knowledge then obtaining, irresoluble. Although by far the greater part of character is attributable to education and environment and most of the remainder to differing individual reactions to sensory stimulus (but why do they differ? — he does not say), there are certain residual mental facts which seem to fall outside such explanation:

> Such . . . are the various instincts of animals, and the portion of human nature which corresponds to those instincts. No mode has been suggested, even by way of hypothesis, in which these can receive any satisfactory, or even plausible, explanation from psychological causes alone; and there is great reason to think that they have as positive, and even as direct and immediate, a connexion with physical conditions of the brain and nerves as any of our mere sensations have.[14]

In other words, there *may* be (and current rapid progress in the physiology of the nervous system suggests that proof, one way or the other, will ultimately be available) an innate basis for instinct which contributes *something* to differences in character. Only minimally, however, in Mill's view; for at the start and again at the conclusion of this paragraph in *Logic* VI he is at pains to stress the predominant role of education and environment in character formation. He adopts the same position in the essay 'Nature'; here he attacks the sentimentality 'which exalts instinct at the expense of reason' and bestows on every unreflecting impulse 'a kind of consecration'. The existence of instincts he does not deny — though he refuses to

theorise on what is or is not instinctive in human nature; what is
clear, he argues, is

> that nearly every respectable attribute of humanity is the result,
> not of instinct, but of a victory over instinct; and that there is
> hardly anything valuable in the natural man except capacities — a
> whole world of possibilities, all of them dependent upon eminently
> artificial discipline for being realised.[15]

Thus it can be seen that even where Mill does admit the existence
or the possibility of a hereditary or 'natural' contribution to character,
he regularly qualifies the admission by asserting that the extent of
the contribution is either indeterminable or greatly exceeded by that
of education and environment: the alleged differences between the
sexes 'may very well have been produced merely by circumstances';
without systematic cultivation the poetic gift will never achieve its
highest purpose of elevating humanity; instinct can be modified or
even wholly subdued by education.[16] There is an interesting passage
in a letter/article, 'The Negro Question', which he wrote for *Fraser's
Magazine* in January 1850. Here he vehemently combats the claim
made by Carlyle in the previous issue that negroes, because of
congenital inferiority to the white races, are born to be their servants.
Had the author troubled to investigate the laws of the formation of
character, Mill asserts, he would have 'escaped the vulgar error of
imputing every difference which he finds among human beings to an
original difference of nature':

> As well might it be said that of two trees sprung from the same
> stock one cannot be taller than another but from greater vigour in
> the original seedling. Is nothing to be attributed to soil, nothing to
> climate, nothing to difference of exposure — has no storm swept
> over the one and not the other, no lightning scathed it, no beast
> browsed on it, no insects preyed on it, no passing stranger stript
> off its leaves or its bark? If the trees grew near together, may not
> the one which, by whatever accident, grew up first, have retarded
> the other's development by its shade?

Human beings are not only subject to a far wider range of influences,
but they also have far greater opportunity to impede the growth of
their fellows; and those who start with an advantage regularly use
their strength to keep others weak. He concludes: 'What the original
differences are among human beings, I know no more than your
contributor, and no less; it is one of the questions not yet satisfactorily
answered in the natural history of the species.'[17]

Despite this disclaimer and his hesitancy elsewhere to proportion the roles of nature and nurture in the formation of character, there are passages in his writings where Mill declares himself uncompromisingly on the side of education and nurture. One such is in 'The Utility of Religion' (referred to above,p.96), where he is at pains to show that the moulding force often claimed for religion is due in fact to other influences, such as authority, public opinion and, not least, education.[18] 'Consider,' he writes, 'how tremendous is the power of education; how unspeakable is the effect of bringing people up from infancy in a belief and in habits founded on it.' Indeed, 'the power of education is almost boundless: there is not one natural inclination which it is not strong enough to coerce and, if needful, to destroy by disuse.' Especially powerful is *early* education, for impressions made in infancy and childhood have 'what it is so much more difficult for later convictions to obtain — command over the feelings' (which is why he felt able to assert many years earlier in 'Notes on the Newspapers' that while the state can *instruct*, only the family can *educate;*[19]but see below, pp.128-9). He goes on to cite the example of the Lycurgan institutions in ancient Sparta — 'the greatest recorded victory which education has ever achieved over a whole host of natural inclinations in an entire people'; all of which was due, not to religion, but to devotion to an ideal inculcated by early education. (What precisely he means by 'education' here Mill does not explain; but it can be assumed that in conformity with his normal usage he includes both formal institutions and the impact of the cultural environment.) Another such passage occurs in the *Autobiography*, during his comments on Sir William Hamilton's philosophy and his rejection of its intuitionism (see above, pp.50-1). Here he deplores

> the prevailing tendency to regard all the marked distinctions of human character as innate and in the main indelible, and to ignore the irresistible proofs that by far the greater part of those differences, whether between individuals, races or sexes, are such as not only might but naturally would be produced by differences in circumstances. . . .[20]

It is in the intuitional metaphysics, he adds, that this tendency has its source; and so agreeable is it to human indolence, and so inimical therefore to progress, that it must be 'attacked at the very root'.

It has already been noted that for holding such views (or for so expressing them) Mill has been charged with exaggeration. Interestingly, in a letter to Comte he himself writes of 'les exagérations d'Helvetius'; however, these 'exagérations'

> ont eu au moins l'avantage de donner une forte impulsion à la
> théorie difficile de l'éducation, théorie qu'aujourd'hui on néglige à
> tel point d'approfondir, que la plupart des penseurs ignorent
> jusqu'où les circonstances extérieures combinées avec le degré de
> sensibilité nerveuse générale peuvent d'après les lois physiolo-
> giques mentales, non seulement modifier le caractère mais
> quelquefois même en déterminer le type.[21]

The letter is mainly concerned with Franz Joseph Gall's phrenological
theories about the shape and structure of the brain; and in the
sentence previous to this quotation Mill has already expressed the
view that it is not only brain structure that requires investigation but
'l'ensemble de l'éducation (envisagée dans la plus grande extension
du mot)'. Even without this, and despite his complaint of the
inadequacy of research (and its implications of inconclusive evidence),
it is obvious where Mill's own commitment lies and what he expects
research to reveal.

There is a notable contribution to the nature/nurture debate and
its educational implications in his analysis of the concept of nature in
the essay of that name.[22] His principal purpose, he asserts, is to
examine the notion that 'the word Nature affords some external
criterion of what we should do' (p. 377) — in other words that it is
possible to derive from Nature (in some meaning or other) prescriptive
guidance for what ought to be done. Essential to this is a preliminary
examination of the meanings of 'nature', for 'language is as it were
the atmosphere of philosophical investigation, which must be made
transparent before anything can be seen through it in the true figure
and position' (p. 378) — a statement hardly to be bettered as an
expression of the value of linguistic clarification. First he distinguishes
the 'nature' of a particular object or animal from 'Nature' as the
totality of all that is. The former is the 'aggregate of its powers or
properties', 'its entire capacity of exhibiting phenomena' (p. 374),
including (in sentient beings) feeling and consciousness. These
properties and phenomena, since they display certain regularities,
can be generalised into 'laws' of the 'nature' of the particular thing.
The latter, 'Nature', is 'the aggregate of the powers and properties of
all things . . . the sum of all phenomena, together with the causes
which produce them, including not only all that happens, but all that
is capable of happening' (*ib.*); it is 'a collective noun for all facts
actual and possible'(*ib.*), suggesting the conception by an omniscient

mind of the existence of all things in their totality. Such, he asserts, is the correct scientific meaning of 'Nature' in this collective sense; and here too, of course, regularities are observed and generalised into 'laws'. Contrasted with it is the sense in which 'natural' is opposed to artificial, that is, to whatever is accomplished by human contrivance. This is a false opposition, since the artificial is itself encompassed within the totality of 'Nature' and its 'laws', which man can employ for his own ends but cannot evade. However, usage has thus established a second, though misleading, sense of 'Nature' as what occurs without man's 'voluntary and intentional agency' (p. 375).

So far, then, three meanings have been distinguished: 'nature' (of the particular thing), 'Nature' as totality and 'Nature' as not-man-made. Mill now returns to his initial point of departure, the notion that 'Nature' provides prescriptive guidance for what should be done. Which, if any, of these meanings is intended when 'Nature', 'natural', etc., are associated with commendation and obligation — as, for instance, in *naturam sequi* and *ius naturale* and in the 'naturalism' of Rousseau and his followers? And how does this emotive commendation come to be (pp. 375-6)? All three meanings refer to what *is*; it seems, therefore, that it may be necessary to distinguish a further meaning, one referring to what *ought* to be. But Mill rejects this: those who use the word in the prescriptive sense do so believing that what *is* constitutes an actually existing 'rule or standard for what ought to be' (p. 377); and when they use it thus they may be referring to any of the three meanings but usually to the second or third (which include the first). How, then, does the belief arise, and has it any justification?

The source of the belief lies principally in two ambiguities (pp. 377ff.). First, there is confusion between two uses of 'law': there are natural 'laws' (like gravitation and motion), which express observed uniformities in events; and there are man-made laws, whether statutory or merely customary, which impose legal and moral obligations. Failure to distinguish clearly between these leads to the error of supposing that each is obligatory in the same way; this is not so. Natural 'laws' *must* be obeyed; they can be utilised for human ends; their effects can be mitigated or averted; but there is no escape from them and they cannot be changed. The 'must' of human laws is very different; it is a 'must' not of necessity but of legal or moral injunction; it is not immutable and it can be disobeyed. Because the two 'musts' are not differentiated, the 'ought' of human law is transferred to natural 'law' and the latter invested with a spurious obligation-content. Second, there is confusion between *naturam sequi* and *naturam observare*, a confusion further confounded by the ambiguity of 'Nature' already noted (the totality of all that is, *or* not-man-made). Obedience (*sequi*) to 'Nature' in the totality sense is a necessity which cannot be avoided; to recommend it is therefore otiose. To *observe* 'Nature' in this sense is not the same as to obey (though commonly identified with it), but rather to study its phenomena and their laws in order to use them for human purposes — which is 'the first principle of all intelligent action' (pp. 379-80). Such study does not, indeed cannot, provide guidance for decisions about what *ought* to be done; all it can do is recommend what *must* be done (Nature and its 'laws' being what they are) *if* we wish to achieve certain objectives. To substitute 'ought' for 'must' here is a misuse of language; they are not synonymous, though they are commonly so regarded. (Implicit in Mill's argument is the existence of a logical gap — now a commonplace of philosophical discourse — between 'is' and 'ought'; he was clearly aware of a distinction between them: 'All inquiries are either into what is or into what ought to be, science and history belonging to the first division, art, morals and politics to the second' p.377; cf, *Logic* II, p.949) — though he is often accused of ignoring it in his attempt to establish happiness as the primary ethical principle.[23] However, he does not develop it here in logical terms to counter the derivation of ethical guidance from the 'is' of 'Nature' and natural 'laws'). Obedience to 'Nature' in the sense of not-man-made, 'the spontaneous course of things when left to themselves', is 'palpably absurd' (p. 380); for the very aim and object of action is to alter and improve Nature in this sense:

> If the artificial is not better than the natural, to what end are all the arts of life? To dig, to plough, to build, to wear clothes, are direct infringements of the injunction to follow nature. . . . All praise of Civilisation, or Art, or Contrivance, is so much dispraise of Nature; an admission of imperfection which it is man's business, and merit, to be always endeavouring to correct or mitigate. (p. 381)

At this point in the analysis there emerges a further possible source of confusion: by those who believe in a divine providence 'Nature' is often regarded as a model to imitate, and although this does not preclude control of natural phenomena for the conveniences of life, it suggests that in general we should 'be guided by the spirit and general conception of nature's own ways' (p. 382). Hence comes the belief, emotionally charged and readily exploited in rhetorical appeals, that 'Nature' offers us an example to follow in the conduct of our lives. This Mill rejects outright, opposing it with 'the undeniable fact that the order of nature, in so far as unmodified by man, is such as no being whose attributes are justice and benevolence would have made with the intention that his rational creatures should follow it as an example' (p. 383). The most obvious characteristic of 'Nature' (to anyone who is not blinded by prejudice) is its 'perfect and absolute recklessness . . . In sober truth, nearly all the things which men are hanged or imprisoned for doing to one another are nature's everyday performances' (pp. 384-5). He expresses himself no less forcibly elsewhere in the *Three Essays on Religion*. In the present essay he develops the theme in a digression which reveals a second but unstated purpose of his analysis (as well as intense personal conviction), namely, to refute the possibility of belief in a God who is both loving *and* omnipotent — the facts are overwhelmingly against it: 'If the maker of the world *can* all that he will, he wills misery, and there is no escape from the conclusion' (p. 388). However, there is no need to follow him along this line of thought.

Reverting to the main line of his analysis, he examines the view that distinguishes instinct from reason and places upon the former a stamp of divine approval. Instincts, it is argued, are 'positive stimuli' (p. 392) to action, implanted as such by 'the Author of Nature' (*ib.*) and intended therefore to be obeyed; reason, being the result of cultivation and training, more deliberate, less impulsive, less 'natural', belongs more appropriately to the human sphere of responsibility. Hence comes 'the vein of sentiment so common in the modern world' (*ib.*), which consecrates instinct into an imperative which must not be disobeyed — made worse by elevating every feeling or impulse to the status of instinct.[24] No doubt he has in mind here the educational romanticism which derives from Rousseau's *Emile* with its declaration that 'God makes all things good' and its injunction to 'fix your eyes on nature';[25] though impossible to apply consistently in practice and never formulated into a coherent theory, it nevertheless 'remains a standing prejudice' (*ib.*) against the authority of reason. As we have seen, Mill utterly rejects it: goodness is not natural; whatever instincts may or may not be, they are valuable only as potentialities whose realisation depends on strenuous 'artificial discipline' (p. 393). This assertion he exemplifies by pointing to a number of virtues —

courage, cleanliness, unselfishness, self-control, veracity, justice —
all of which are the products of careful and persistent cultivation;
veracity in particular he picks out as 'the virtue with which writers
like Rousseau delight in decorating savage life' in contrast with 'the
treachery and trickery of civilisation' (p. 395). But this is 'a mere
fancy picture contradicted by all the realities of savage life' (*ib.*). That
the *germs* of these virtues exist in human nature he is willing (with
due explanation) to admit; but their hold is tenuous and disputed by
luxuriant weeds; from these they must be protected and their own
growth carefully cherished:

> It is through such fostering, commenced early, and not counteracted
> by unfavourable influences, that, in some happily circumstanced
> specimens of the human race, the most elevated sentiments of
> which humanity is capable become a second nature, stronger than
> the first and not so much subduing the original nature as merging
> it into itself. . . This artificially created or at least artificially
> perfected nature of the best and noblest human beings is the only
> nature which it is ever commendable to follow. (pp. 396-7)

Even this, he adds significantly, is not itself the standard but rather
the visible embodiment of standards previously chosen and deliberately cultivated by education and training — that is to say, the
selection and growth of the germs are governed by *values*, values
which are presupposed in the choices made by the cultivator.

This analysis of 'Nature' and 'natural' has important educational
implications; some of these Mill is at pains to emphasise as central to
his purpose; others he mentions in passing or leaves to be inferred.
First, it follows that, as commonly used, such sloganised precepts as
'follow nature', 'conformity to nature', 'natural growth', 'natural
interests' have no place within serious educational purpose or
practice; they are expressions of unanalysed sentimentality, muddle-
headed romanticism, which falsify the reality of children's upbringing
and development. They are dangerous too: it may be argued, for
instance, that all 'natural' impulses have a purpose and must therefore
be allowed a degree of expression; some of them indeed have a
purpose, Mill admits, in preserving the species, but unless carefully
controlled they may become 'fetters which impede free action'
(p. 397), barriers to self-improvement and destructive of society;
others, like cruelty, have no place in civilised communities, and 'it
should be the aim of education not simply to regulate [them] but to
extirpate . . . or to starve them by disuse' (p. 398). No less dangerous

is the extenuation of guilt by equating 'natural' with 'non-culpable' (p. 401); since all action has a root somewhere in natural impulse, there is no wickedness which cannot thus be excused. The lesson for the educator is clear: from the given potentialities of human nature he must select, and then protect and nourish, those which he judges conducive to the well-being of the individual child and of the community (or communities) of which he is a member; it is a task, a *selective* task, of liberation — *from* the undifferentiated claims of natural impulse (which, as Mill rightly observed, are an impediment to free action) *into* the freedom of orderly, disciplined, choice-directed activity. There is no escape from this responsibility, nor from the necessity of education as a purposive, authoritative attempt to amend and improve the raw material of human potentiality; nature without nurture is a recipe for barbarism.[26]

But, second, this does not mean that the phrase 'follow nature' has no legitimate meaning. Interpreted as careful observation of what *is* — phenomena and their laws — and a resolve to work with this 'given' in order to utilise it for human ends, to 'follow nature' is, as Mill has said, the first principle of intelligent action and supplies us not with prescriptive guidance (ethical or otherwise), but with 'a rational rule of conduct' (p. 379) — 'to know and take heed of the properties of the things we have to deal with, so far as these properties are capable of forwarding or obstructing any given purpose' (*ib.*). For all successful enterprise depends on knowledge of and compliance with the facts and 'laws' of the particular area of activity — atomic physics, meteorology, medicine, psychology or whatever. For the educator this interpretation of 'follow nature' (and associated phrases like 'natural growth' and 'natural interests') points to the need for observation and understanding both of child nature in general and of the particular children with whom he is personally concerned. Normal bodily growth follows a course which is broadly predetermined but may differ from individual to individual; puberty and its earlier incidence in girls than boys is an obvious instance. If Piaget is right, moral and intellectual growth also follow predetermined patterns — again with individual variations. To disregard these patterns of development is to invite failure in the enterprise of education. So too with individual children: within the general patterns of child development each has his or her own nature distinguished from others by a peculiarity of endowment which the educator must observe and (*selectively*) foster. For each child in his care he must ask: What have I got here? What is the material given me to work with? And, the material being what it is, the laws of growth being what they are and my resources of skill and equipment being what they are, what can I reasonably aim at and hope to achieve? Thus interpreted, 'follow nature' has indeed a legitimate meaning for the educator and can offer him a rational rule of procedure.

But *not* prescriptive guidance: it does not tell him what he *ought* to aim at, what in the given nature of the child he *ought* to select and what to discard. Whence, then, comes this prescriptive guidance? In the present essay Mill does not tell us — he is more concerned with establishing where it does *not* come from; but the answer can be found in other writings and has been discussed above (pp. 88-92). Here he gives only a brief, but highly significant hint — though his very analysis of 'Nature', both in its purpose and in its results, firmly implies that an answer must be found. After his examination of various virtues and his insistence that each is the product of education he concludes that the only nature which it is commendable (in a prescriptive sense, as distinct from a rational rule) to follow is 'the artificially perfected nature of the best and noblest human beings' (p.120 above), and then: It is almost superfluous to say that even this cannot be erected into a standard of conduct, since it is itself the fruit of a training and culture the choice of which, if rational and not accidental, must have been determined by a standard already chosen' (pp. 396-7). In other words, the values which guide the educator are anterior to his work; his selection from the given potential of child nature and of the individual boy or girl, and the directions in which this potential is fostered, are guided by value choices already made, some of them issuing from his own personal commitment, others from the cultural context in which he is involved. The prescriptive value-content of the educational process cannot be derived from 'Nature'; 'follow nature' is not and cannot be a substitute for considered rational choice of the values injected into education; it is a *human* responsibility.

In his rejection of the notion that child growth can safely be left to its own unregulated spontaneity; in his insistence on human responsibility for choice, for purposive direction of education, for the deliberate injection of values into a neutral potentiality; in distinguishing freedom as disciplined activity from the unthwarted expression of impulse or instinct; in pointing to the need for observation of the given so that it may be better shaped towards human ends — in all this, Mill's analysis is a valuable contribution towards clarity of educational thinking and greater effectiveness of educational purpose. Perhaps of greatest significance at the present time is the importance he assigns to the value element in education (manifested in choice, purpose and the cultivation of specific virtues in 'untutored human nature' (p. 393).). Education, as Professor R. S. Peters has often reminded us, is not merely change, but change *for the better* (or what is so considered); it therefore embodies conceptions of what is worthwhile, of what is choice-worthy, to be preferred.[27] Only too frequently, however, educational endeavour is vitiated from the start by a disregard (whether through ignorance, laziness or flabby incompetence) of this essential prescriptive, valuational ingredient of education. Research has provided copious (and indispensable) information about the 'is' of human nature, but the 'ought' which is implicit in the attempt to improve it has not received its due share of attention. The analysis has also, of course, confirmed Mill's own commitment to the preponderant role of nurture in the process of education; further, it confirms the importance of education itself in both its broader and its more limited meanings, and supports associationism in pointing to environment as a vital factor in mental and moral growth. It is this last, environment as an instrument of education, that will occupy us for the remainder of this chapter.

Mill was not only committed to environmentalism as a theoretical deduction from experientialism and association psychology; he was also convinced of its truth as a practical reality — convinced that the environment is in fact a powerful moulding influence, assimilating to itself the plasticity of human nature, and because of this can be used with deliberate intent as an equally powerful instrument of educational purposes. The fact of environmental influence is a constant theme throughout his writings, from his earliest articles (written when he was most obviously in the grip of utilitarian orthodoxy) to the publications of his later years. In a speech 'On the Present State of Literature', made in 1827-8, he argues that the degeneracy (as he judges it) of contemporary prose writing is due to the malign influence of 'the spirit of the age':

> Every man is a man long before he is a poet or a philosopher. Thousands of impressions are made upon the mind from without before it acquires the power of originating a single one from within. Every man, long before he begins to think or to write, has imbibed more or less of the opinions, the sentiments, the modes of

thinking and acting, the habits and associations of that portion of mankind among whom his lot is cast. We all know the power of early impressions over the human mind and how often the direction which they give decides the whole character, the whole life of the man. The greatest men of every age generally bear a family likeness to their contemporaries. . . .

Inevitably, therefore, 'the majority of literary men take their colour from the age in which they live.'[28]

Some fifteen years later, in *Logic* VI, he finds it necessary, as a preliminary to formulating his ethology, or science of the formation of character, to explain first the difficulty of arriving at secure general laws of human nature by the normal procedure of inference from observation: one obvious reason is the ethical and practical impossibility of conclusive experiment; another — the significant one for our present purpose — is the sheer complexity of the influences impinging on any one individual and uniquely distinguishing him from every other, for 'it is certain that our mental states, and our mental capacities and susceptibilities, are modified, either for a time or permanently, by everything which happens to us in life.'[29] Later still, in *The Subjection of Women*, he complains of the common addiction to belief in the natural origin of characteristics which in fact (so he believes) are the result of environmental conditioning:

> Of all difficulties which impede the progress of thought and the formation of well-grounded opinions on life and social arrangements the greatest is now the unspeakable ignorance and in-attention of mankind in respect to the influences which form human character. Whatever any portion of the human species now are or seem to be, such, it is supposed, they have a natural tendency to be, even when the most elementary knowledge of the circumstances in which they have been placed clearly points out the causes that made them what they are.[30]

The study of history, where it is not prejudiced by conclusions presupposed, points to 'the extraordinary susceptibility of human nature to external influences' and the extreme variability of characteristics which are commonly regarded as universal.[31] Here, of course, he is arguing against the assumption that women are essentially and by nature different in character and capability from men; but the particular argument, as in the case of writers, is firmly derived from the general principle of environmental influence. In *Principles of Political Economy* he refers specifically to the Irish, rejecting the imputation that 'the backwardness of Irish industry, and the want of energy of the Irish people in improving their condition' is due to 'a peculiar indolence and *insouciance* in the Celtic race'. He then makes the same general point: 'Of all vulgar modes of escaping from the consideration of the effect of social and moral influences on the human mind, the most vulgar is that of attributing the diversities of conduct and character to inherent natural differences.'[32]

The same message comes from the *Inaugural Address* where, in a passage already referred to (p.86 above) he distinguishes education in the sense of schooling from the broader meaning of the total impact of experience and environment. It comes too from the essay 'Utility of Religion', where he argues that the powerful influence commonly thought to be intrinsic to religion is due rather to its association with three environmental forces, authority, education (in the narrower sense but including informal influences) and public opinion, whose efficacy in shaping mind and character is grossly underestimated.[33] Indeed, there can be no doubt that Mill's commitment to environmentalism, though initially derived from his father as part of associationist doctrine, became and remained a rooted conviction of his own. This conclusion is reinforced by the numerous particular instances, occurring throughout his writings, of the manner in which he thought environment exercised its formative power.

The human environment is both physical (that is to say, it embraces the animate and inanimate world of nature) and social. The influence of the former is not unimportant: it is the setting within which our lives are lived, and as such it imposes demands and limitations which it is perilous, if not impossible, to ignore. Moreover, response to it is reflected in attitude and character — in courage, initiative, inventiveness or, if the odds are too great, in apathy and resignation; thus, in so far as it is subject to human control, it can be used as a deliberate instrument of education. Mill was well aware of this: his own response to scenic beauty has been noted above, and he repeatedly recommends the protection of the natural environment for recreation and the satisfaction of deep human needs — he was in fact an early conservationist. To this we shall return later; meanwhile, what of the social environment? Here again a distinction must be made; for there is a more general context of social life and culture — traditions, customs, relationships and practices both commercial and private — which are mostly a matter of informal consensus or simple habit; there is also the formal context of law, government and political institutions. Each context exercises formative influences which are powerful and pervasive; of these too Mill was fully aware. Let us look first at the more general and informal.

His most vehement (and at times perhaps exaggerated) assertion of the impact of social influences is in the essay 'Civilisation'.[34] The progress of civilisation, he argues, has two principal effects, the relaxation of individual energy and the diminution of the individual by the growing power of the masses. A 'rude state' of society demands initiative, mental and physical, in defence of family, property and liberty. Civilisation, by the very protection which it provides, reduces the need for such initiative and the only inducements left for energy and enterprise are wealth, personal ambition, philanthropy and 'the love of active virtue'. Of these the most powerful and universal is the first; hence a contraction of energy and its diversion to this one object, not so much by the aristocracy (who already have enough and, lacking any other stimulus, are reduced to lethargy) as by the middle classes. A further result of advancing civilisation is the absence, save for a very few, of personal confrontation with the harsher aspects of life — 'violence . . . the struggle of one indomitable will against another . . . the alternate suffering and infliction of pain'. From this comes a reluctance to *accept* suffering and hardship as the price of enterprise — 'there is much more of the amiable and humane and much less of the heroic'; in the wealthier classes the result is 'a moral effeminacy, an inaptitude for every kind of struggle'. The second effect of civilisation is a contraction of the individual, of his power and importance, of his ability to establish himself, his character in contradistinction to that of the crowd. To compensate for this diminution of himself the individual is obliged to shout louder to make himself heard — 'any voice not pitched in an exaggerated key is lost in the hubbub'; hence comes a loss of openness and sincerity, and their place is taken by dishonesty, deception, salesmanship and the 'plausible pretence' that thrusts aside the claims of simple merit — all seen at their worst in 'commercialism'. Especially regrettable is the impact upon literature, since 'it corrupts the very fountain of the improvement of public opinion itself': mass literacy has created a demand for mass reading matter; quantity has ousted quality, and books, superficially scanned, are gulped down but not digested.

It may be objected that 'Civilisation' is an early work which shows its immaturity in overstatement and facile conclusion. (In fact, it is not so early; Mill was thirty when it was published, and one must remember his claim in the *Autobiography* that his education gave him an advantage of a quarter of a century over his contemporaries.)[35] It would be a mistake to dismiss it thus: whether or not one agrees with his analysis, the underlying message is clear, that human beings respond to and are shaped by their social and cultural environment, whose influence (educative or miseducative according to judgement) is powerful and inescapable. Nor should one lightly conclude that his analysis is at fault: the 1830s were very different from the 1970s, but anyone who honestly and reflectively considers the scene in Britain today must entertain at least the possibility that energy, initiative and the will to succeed have been sapped by over-protection and the diversion of responsibility from individuals to the state; and that one reason for resort to violence and subversion is the increasing sense of frustration as the individual finds himself more and more deeply enmeshed in the toils of a bureaucracy whose ears are deaf to his complaints. His remedies too are not without relevance for our own situation: first, greater and more effective co-operation to secure a co-ordination and concentration of effort whose impetus makes it irresistible; second, vastly improved education, including a national system and a fundamental reassessment of educational purposes; third, 'forms of polity calculated to invigorate the individual character'[36] — which, then as now, points among other things to the need for an electoral system which ensures a genuine representation of the will of the people.

Moreover, the views expressed in 'Civilisation' are confirmed repeatedly in other writings, not only in those of the same early period but also in his later and more mature works. In his speech on 'Perfectibility' (1828) he complains that public esteem is no longer the reward of 'high intellectual and moral excellence' but of wealth and private favour, and (he adds perceptively) it is the possessors of these latter 'whose actions are imitated, whose opinions are adopted, and the contagion of whose failings is caught by the mass of mankind'.[37] Thus are social values created and perpetuated. There is a similar complaint in a letter of 1829 to Gustave d'Eichthal: the Englishman's massive preoccupation with the pursuit of wealth has resulted in restriction of sympathy, moral insensitivity and a blind indifference to serious discussion.[38] In *Political Economy* Mill draws attention to the force of public opinion: to deny this is to display a profound ignorance of human nature and of the extent to which conduct is regulated by deference to public approval or displeasure. For example, in the public mind procreation is closely associated with power and virility; the result is too much sex and consequent over-population; change public attitudes, he suggests, and the birth rate will fall.[39] Another obvious example is the social and political inferiority of women: this, he argues in *The Subjection of Women,* is due not to any natural deficiency, but to convention, prejudice and the male desire for dominance. The family, of course, is a potent influence for good or ill: at its best it can be 'a school of sympathy, tenderness and loving forgetfulness of self'; more often it is 'a school of despotism' nourishing 'wilfulness, overbearingness, unbounded self-indulgence, and a double-dyed and idealised selfishness' — an inevitable result of the husband's unlimited power over his wife.[40]

In March 1850 Mill wrote an article for the *Morning Chronicle* whose main purpose was to complain of the inadequacy of the law in cases of violence against the person, mostly women and children. He concludes with a paragraph which stresses the moral impact on children of living amid violence in the overcrowded homes of the labouring classes; the passage is worthy of quotation in full, not only for its illustration of environmental influence, but also for its aptness to our own situation of increasing violence and, as many believe, the lack of firm response from the law:

> Let anyone consider the degrading moral effect, in the midst of these crowded dwellings, of scenes of physical violence, repeated day after day — the debased, spirit-broken, down-trodden condition of the unfortunate woman, the most constant sufferer from domestic brutality in the poorer classes, unaffectedly believing herself to be out of the protection of the law — the children born and bred in this moral atmosphere — with the unchecked indulgence of the most odious passions, the tyranny of physical force in its coarsest manifestations, constantly exhibited as the most familiar facts of their daily life — can it be wondered if they grow up without any of the ideas and feelings which it is the purpose of moral education to infuse, without any sense of justice or affection, any conception of self-restraint — incapable in their turn of governing their children by any other means than blows? The law, whose utmost exertions would not be more than enough to withstand this mass of depraving influences, makes so little use of its powers and opportunities, measures out its reproofs and punishments by such a scale, that the culprits believe almost the worst of these brutalities to be venial, and all minor ones to be actually permitted — while their victims regard their suffering and debasement as the regular course of things, which the law sanctions

and the world allows; and when not crushed entirely, they seek a wretched compensation by tyrannising in their turn, when any hapless fellow-creature comes within their power.[41]

His claim in 'Civilisation' for the invigorating challenge of difficulty and hardship is echoed in *Political Economy*: 'it is difficulties, not facilities, that nourish bodily and mental energy'; again:

> The business of life is an essential part of the practical education of a people, without which book and school instruction, though most necessary and salutary, does not suffice to qualify them for conduct and for the adaptation of means to ends. Instruction is only one of the desiderata of mental improvement; another, almost as indispensable, is a vigorous exercise of the active faculties, labour, contrivance, judgement, self-control; and the natural stimulus to these is the difficulties of life.[42]

Not that adversity should be deliberately induced for the sake of the response it evokes — indeed, it is our duty to diminish the ills of human existence; but to make life too easy is to rob it of stimulus and to leave potential undeveloped. No less essential to growth, and especially the growth of higher talents, is an environment of freedom and variety. This is a prominent theme of *On Liberty* — 'Genius can only breathe freely in an *atmosphere* of freedom'; human differences require differences in experience and opportunity — 'the same mode of life is a healthy excitement to one . . . to another it is a distracting burthen' and 'unless there is a corresponding diversity in their modes of life, they neither obtain their fair share of happiness nor grow up to the mental, moral and aesthetic stature of which their nature is capable.'[43] The criterion he proposes in *Political Economy* for assessing the respective merits of socialism and private ownership is which of them allows 'the greatest amount of human liberty and spontaneity'; communism, he suspects, would fail this test as it is inconsistent with that 'multiform development of human nature, those manifold unlikenesses, that diversity of tastes and talents' and variety of view which, by the stimulus of intellectual 'collision' and novelty of idea 'are the mainspring of mental and moral progression'.[44] It is the combination of freedom and diversity, he argues in his review of Grote's *History of Greece*, that distinguished Athens among the states of ancient Greece and were the foundation of her greatness.[45]

It may be as well at this point to interpose two cautions. First, though Mill objects to much in his contemporary environment and is vehement in his condemnation of it, yet he is also aware of its merits and of the fact that, in general, the environment can serve to invigorate and improve as well as diminish human potential. This should be clear from what has already been said, but the point is worth emphasising. Commerce, for instance: this brings us into contact with persons dissimilar to ourselves, facilitates the exchange of ideas and encourages tolerance; it is even, because of the personal interests involved, 'rapidly rendering war obsolete'; it is thus both 'the principal guarantee of the peace of the world' and 'the great permanent security for the uninterrupted progress of the ideas, the institutions and the character of the human race'.[46] It is when commerce degenerates into 'commercialism' that Mill rejects it; by the latter he means an immoderate addiction to the pursuit of wealth, with all its accompaniments of salesmanship, 'puffing' (extravagant and specious advertising) and cutthroat competition — not that competition as such is necessarily harmful for, despite certain moral objections, it has economic advantages and can promote healthy rivalry in service to the community.[47] The Press too is of enormous benefit as a 'great diffuser of information, of mental excitement, and mental exercise', carrying the public 'into a region of ideas and interests beyond its own limited horizon'; abused, however, it contributes to the superficiality of contemporary culture and the decay of literature.[48] In short, the environment can both elevate and depress, educate and miseducate; civilisation is purchased at the price of risks which must be clearly seen and firmly withstood. The second caution is this: Mill's emphasis on environment may lead to suspicions of determinism, that we are simply and inevitably the product of circumstances. This is certainly not Mill's position, though he was acutely conscious of the problem and argues it out in *Logic* VI, chapter ii and in chapter xxvi of *Sir William Hamilton's Philosophy*. The core of his argument is that, though we live in a universe of causal uniformity which applies no less to human actions than to physical events, men and women are able to introduce 'a new antecedent'[49] into the causal sequence and thus change the course of events; they are able, therefore, by modifying circumstances to modify themselves, to *use* the environment in promoting their own self-improvement. Thus, character is not wholly and irrevocably formed by environment: 'Ideas are not always the mere signs and effects of social circumstances; they are themselves a power in history'[50] (see above, pp. 39-40).

Of particular interest, especially in relation to modern controversy, is Mill's belief that environment influences intelligence. What intelligence is and whether it owes more to nature or to nurture are still matters for argument. In the 1930s and 1940s the weight of opinion was on the side of nature, and education in England and Wales was directed towards a tripartite organisation reflecting, in the euphemistic phraseology of the Norwood Report, a 'diversity of human endowment' but corresponding in practice to differences in general intelligence as shown (or supposedly shown) by the 11 + examination.[51] Since then research has shown conclusively that intelligence, measured by performance in formal tests, is diminished or increased in response to environment (a fact which is used both to justify and condemn comprehensive schools and mixed-ability classes). There is little doubt that Mill would allow nature, innate ability, a significant part in general intelligence; but he was convinced too of the contribution of environment. For instance, in urban societies 'the mere collision of man with man, the keenness of competition, the habits of society and discussion, the easy access to reading . . . produce of themselves a certain development of intelligence.'[52] A woman's household responsibilities, demanding as they do a frequent switch of attention from one detail to another, give her an advantage over men in intellectual mobility and concentration.[53] In a *Morning Chronicle* article of 1846 he attributes the energetic and intelligent agriculture of the Palatinate to 'the possession of a property in the soil'; he continues:

> A day-labourer who earns his wages by mere obedience to orders may become a good artificer in his particular manual operation, but his mind stagnates. He is not paid for thinking and contriving but for executing. He may be a better peg in some vast machine, though even that is not true in an unqualified sense. But in sagacity, in thoughtfulness, in power to judge of consequences and connect means with ends, in all which constitutes the practical talent of a human being, in every intellectual faculty which it ought to be the object of popular education to cherish and improve, which of these men is likely to bear off the palm — the one who drudges through a stated task for daily wages, or the one whose task is the agreeable one of finding every way of improving and making valuable a small farm, of which the produce is his own and which is the permanent inheritance of his children?[54]

— a passage which is strikingly relevant to our own contemporary problems, particularly in the motor and other manufacturing industries. He makes the same claim in opposing the cottier system of agricultural tenancy prevalent in Ireland.[55] Political institutions also have their influence on intellect and intelligence: 'Among the foremost benefits of free government is that education of the intelligence and of the sentiments which is carried down to the very lowest ranks of the people when they are called to take a part in acts which directly affect the great interests of their country.'[56]

The last example brings us to the second of the two areas of social environment distinguished earlier, namely, the more formal institutional context (pp.125-6). This too is powerfully influential;it is also more readily amenable to deliberate control and therefore to educational purposes. Such clearly was Mill's view, expressed repeatedly and with confident conviction. For instance, there is a lengthy discussion of the influence of political constitutions on national character in chapters ii and iii of *Representative Government*, where he is trying to establish the criteria of a good form of government.[57] The principal test, he decides, is the degree to which a particular form of constitution promotes 'the virtue and intelligence of the people themselves'. Government is more than a machinery of administration (though this is obviously important); it is also 'a great influence acting on the human mind', 'an agency of national education', and it is to be judged not only by its organisational efficiency but also 'by what it makes of the citizens . . . its tendency to improve or deteriorate the people themselves'. Despotism may well be the appropriate form of government for a nation as yet uncivilised and undisciplined, 'as a means of gradually training the people to walk alone'; but its influence is depressive, conducive in the population at large to passivity, mental inertia and stunted morality. Only representative democracy fulfils the essential criterion of good government by promoting 'a better and higher form of national character than any other polity whatsoever'; and this in numerous ways. By widespread diffusion of responsibility, by allowing its citizens a voice in the management of their own affairs, by encouraging active participation at local and national levels (and all this on a foundation of freedom), it promotes self-reliance and self-discipline, mental vigour, initiative, resolution in the face of difficulties and a responsible concern for the general good. It is not simply that forms of government and political constitution *are* formative of character and conducive (or not) to human improvement; in Mill's view they *ought* to be so regarded, and those forms deliberately sought and fostered which contribute most to the education of their citizens into a mature and responsible humanity. There is a positive duty to regard and to use forms of government as instruments serving educational ends. (To correct possible misunderstanding it needs to be said that Mill did not regard representative democracy as an infallible source of intellectual and moral improvement; like those of the general social environment, its benefits, he believed, were accompanied by risks which it required perpetual vigilance to avert. The will of the majority could become a deadly tyranny, imposing a uniform mediocrity which stifled individuality.)[58]

The views expressed in *Representative Government* are confirmed elsewhere. In the *Autobiography*, describing the development of his political thinking in the 1830s, he remarks that he 'ceased to consider representative democracy as an absolute principle and regarded it as a question of time, place and circumstance' (which is entirely consistent with his conclusion in *Representative Government* that democracy, though the best form of polity according to the criteria he adopts, is not necessarily the one best suited to a nation's particular condition). He continues:

> I now looked upon the choice of political institutions as a moral and educational question more than one of material interests, thinking that it ought to be decided mainly by the consideration, what great improvement in life and culture stands next in order for the people concerned as the condition of their further progress, and what institutions are most likely to promote that.[59]

His review (1837) of Carlyle's *French Revolution* criticises the author for underestimating 'what constitutions and forms of government can do' towards the acceptance of beliefs and principles.[60] In his 1840 review of de Tocqueville's *Democracy in America* he agrees that it is participation in the business of society that stimulates and maintains political interest among the people and counteracts the debasing tendencies of commercialism:

> Whatever might be the case in some other constitutions of society, the spirit of a commercial people will be . . . essentially mean and slavish wherever public spirit is not cultivated by an extensive participation of the people in the business of government in detail, nor will the desideratum of a general diffusion of intelligence among either the middle or lower classes be realised but by a

corresponding dissemination of public functions and a voice in public affairs.[61]

He criticises Bentham for virtually ignoring one of the most important aspects of law, its educative function: the laws of a country are 'an instrument of national culture' and, like political constitutions, must be adapted to circumstances, just as 'a tutor gives his pupil different lessons according to the progress already made in his education' (the imagery is significant of Mill's constant underlying educational purpose).[62] In *Political Economy* he emphasises the moral influence of law; ostensibly it upholds honesty and good faith, and these are the lessons it teaches; but

> if there are ways and means by which persons may attain the ends of roguery under the apparent sanction of the law, to that extent the law is demoralising. . . If, again, the law, by a misplaced indulgence, protects idleness or prodigality against their natural consequences or dismisses crime with inadequate penalties, the effect both on the prudential and on the social virtues is unfavourable.[63]

And such, he comments, is too often the case in contemporary England. The *Morning Chronicle* article referred to above (p.128) makes the same point — bad or ineffective law results not only in human suffering but in moral degradation. Even a just system of taxation, he asserts in *Representative Government*, 'tends in an eminent degree to educate the moral sentiments of the community'.[64]

A distinction was made earlier between the physical and the social aspects of environment (the latter further distinguished as the general cultural and the formal institutional). Consideration of the physical environment was there postponed as the less important of the two — but by no means *un*important — and we must look briefly at this before moving on to some concluding comments on environmentalism in education. Reference has already been made (p.109) to Mill's recognition of the impact of the physical environment upon himself. This is confirmed by a reading of the letters he wrote to Harriet during his tour in 1855 of Italy, Sicily and Greece; for these reveal an extreme sensitivity both to natural beauty and to the architectural splendours of the Acropolis and other ancient sites (also, at an earlier stage of the tour, to the artistic treasures of the Italian churches and museums).[65] There are several passages in his other writings which underline this response, to nature especially but to man-made beauty too. In 'The Claims of Labour' he applauds the creation of parks and gardens for the enjoyment of the labouring classes and deplores the 'counter-progress of stopping up paths and enclosing commons' and the erosion of wilderness by encroaching agriculture.[66] Though he does not say so here, it is clear from a similar passage in *Political Economy* that he thought of nature as an educative influence, refreshing to the spirit and a stimulus to the imagination: 'Solitude, in the sense of being often alone, is essential to any depth of meditation or of character; and solitude in the presence of natural beauty and grandeur is the cradle of thoughts and aspirations which are not only good for the individual, but which society could ill do without.' He hopes, therefore, that growth in population will not destroy what is left of untamed nature; there is little satisfaction

> in contemplating the world with nothing left to the spontaneous activity of nature; with every rood of land brought into cultivation, which is capable of growing food for human beings; every flowery waste or natural pasture ploughed up, all quadrupeds or birds which are not domesticated for man's use exterminated as his rivals for food, every hedgerow or superfluous tree rooted out, and scarcely a place left where a wild shrub or flower could grow without being eradicated as a weed in the name of improved agriculture.[67]

In a speech on land tenure reform, delivered late in his life in 1871, there is even a hint of the concept of national parks to protect 'the really wild lands which are still as nature left them'; whether or not any attempt be made to cultivate them (and some, then as now, were virtually uncultivable), they should 'belong to the nation'.[68]

Railways are another threat to the English countryside. In an article written in 1836 for the *London and Westminster Review* he welcomes the prospect of cheap and rapid transport but deplores the proliferation of lines for the sake of profit and calls for a rational policy (including an element of nationalisation) which will be economically viable and will also protect the countryside from being 'levelled and torn up in a hundred unnecessary directions by those deformities'. It is disgraceful, he adds, that no consideration should be given to 'the character of the natural scenery which is threatened with destruction' — for instance, the proposed routes for the London to Brighton line with their threat to the Vale of Norbury at the foot of Box Hill. Contrast with this Parliament's vote of £11,000 for two Corregios and its boasted concern for the fine arts; the truth is that

MPs value by cost not worth, and they have neither taste themselves nor any 'real wish to cultivate in the people the capacity of enjoying beauty'.[69]

In all this there is much that modern conservationists can both recognise and applaud as akin to their own purposes. No less notable for its conservationist tendencies (and its foresight) is a passage in a letter of 1866 to a friend in New Zealand who had written describing the beauty of the Middle (i.e. South) Island and its impassable mountain barrier. Mill comments thus:

> The very idea of anything impassable and impenetrable is almost too charming, now when every nook and corner of our planet has got or is getting opened to the full light of day. One of the many causes which make the age we are living in so very important in the life of the human race — almost, indeed, the turning point of it — is that so many things combine to make it the era of a great change in the conceptions and feelings of mankind as to the world of which they form a part. There is now almost no place left on our planet that is mysterious to us, and we are brought within sight of the practical questions which will have to be faced when the multiplied human race shall have taken full possession of the earth (and exhausted its principal fuel). Meanwhile we are also acquiring scientific convictions as to the future destination of suns and stars, and the whole visible universe. These things must have ultimately a very great effect on human character.[70]

Conservation means different things to different people — enjoyment of the countryside, protection of threatened species, control of population, prudent exploitation of resources. Mill was concerned for all of these, not excluding the second (and seemingly least likely). In January 1864 he wrote from Avignon to the *Gardeners' Chronicle* complaining of a competition organised by the Royal Horticultural Society and offering prizes for the three best herbaria of every English county and three further prizes for the best of all these winners, a competition, he thought, which was likely to denude the countryside of all its rarer species.[71] In addition, however, he believed that the natural environment had an educative function which alone was sufficient to justify protecting it from human despoliation. At the root of this belief, no doubt, was his own delight in natural beauty, touched off in childhood by the country walks with his father 'in the country lanes towards Hornsey' and by the grounds of Ford Abbey, '*riant* and secluded, umbrageous and full of the sound of falling waters'; it was constantly replenished by his travels in Britain and Europe, and in the months of his nervous crisis it was reinforced by the poetry of Wordsworth, which appealed with such deep solace 'to one of the strongest of [his] pleasurable susceptibilities, the love of rural objects and natural scenery'.[72] Certainly man must attempt to improve nature — of this Mill had no doubt; and her resources must be utilised for his own good. But he must also learn from nature, establish with her a relationship not of exploitation but of mutuality involving, on his side, respect, understanding and obedience and contributing to the enrichment of his being.

Although the nature/nurture argument is by no means concluded (witness, for example, recent controversy on Professor Eysenck's pronouncements on heredity),[73] the potency of environment, both as an influence on human development and as an educational instrument, is now taken for granted. (There is also an increasing recognition of the *complexity* of environment as a system of interacting and interdependent factors, damage to one of which — for example, the ozone layer as a result of supersonic flying — may throw into imbalance a whole set of delicate relationships.) Moreover, the distinction between education *inside* and education *outside* school has become increasingly blurred: national parks and nature reserves, the physical aspect of towns, villages and individual buildings, industrial relations, politics, the media, the entire social environment are now seen, far more than ever before, as contributing to education in the broad sense that Mill consistently distinguishes: 'Through a thousand voices these speak to the young: ultimately the whole community is the educator of its young and it cannot divest itself of this responsibility by devising the most perfect scheme of schooling to be contained safely within the four walls of a school building'[74] — so writes a modern educationist in words that might have been Mill's. Hence has come a greater emphasis on the educative importance of the home, of the local community, of nursery schools to enlarge, enrich (and *correct*) children's early environment; and within the statutory system of education environmental arguments are adduced in support of comprehensive schools, mixed-ability groupings, co-education, school journeys and the inclusion of parents, pupils and non-teaching staff in governing bodies (the last on the grounds that extension of responsible participation promotes an educationally supportive environment within the local community).

Association psychology is no longer acceptable in the crude form proposed by its nineteenth-century advocates (though it has affinities with modern reinforcement techniques — see above, pp.75-6); but the environmentalism to which it pointed has lost none of its force. It is undeniable that human beings *are* malleable, responsive to environmental influences, shaped (or coloured, like Locke's camelions) by the context of daily living; indeed, on this depend their survival and the larger processes of natural selection and evolution. It is no less true that environment *can* be so structured or manipulated as to elicit certain responses (and exclude others), and thus to induce conformity with selected values and purposes. It is on these two facts that the possibility of education depends — assisted, of course, by pedagogical expertise, technology and a supporting administration. For in so far as it is *deliberate*, education, in its narrower and broader meanings, is basically a manipulation of environment for the purpose of imparting specific knowledge, skills and values, and of promoting specific behavioural attitudes and practices. So used, environment is an especially powerful educational instrument, because for the most part it operates by suggestion rather than by inculcation, by the unconscious or barely conscious formation of habits rather than by explicit instruction. Absorbed imperceptibly, it becomes 'second nature', controlling thought and behaviour in ways unsuspected and often undetectable. (Even philosophers, a species supposedly immune from any solicitation save that of pure reason, are demonstrably men of their time and society.)

Herein lies not only its potency but also its danger, and though the former was obvious to Mill, the latter was not. Rousseau writes in the *Emile* of 'well-regulated liberty', by which he means an environmental situation devised to induce attitudes and practices believed by the educator to be desirable yet leaving children with the illusion of freedom because they are unaware of the (to them) unobtrusive environmental pressures to which they are being subjected; and, as Rousseau comments on a later page, 'There is no subjection so complete as that which preserves the forms of freedom.'[75] In other words, environment can be (and is regularly used as) a subtly powerful instrument not simply of education but of *indoctrination* (the distinction between the two is far from clear, and it is not here assumed that the latter is necessarily objectionable). It should be noted too that such educational (or indoctrinational) use of environment is *ex*clusive as well as *in*clusive: not only are desired elements included (for instance, approved curricular content and ethical practices) but the undesired are excluded (pornography from the school library and aggressive discourtesy from personal relations). Environmentalism thus involves a censorship of experience which imposes a restriction of freedom and individuality and is contrary to the doctrines of *On Liberty*. Again, Mill is unaware of the danger — at least as it arises from the educational use of environment — though he does of course argue against restriction of thought and discussion in chapter ii of that essay. If it were possible to question him on this, he would perhaps resort, as he does in *On Liberty* and *Utilitarianism,* to reliance on the informed opinion of those best qualified to judge — 'the wisest of mankind', whose authority 'should be submitted to by that miscellaneous collection of a few wise and many foolish individuals called the public'.[76]

Environmentalism gives rise to another problem, urgent for ourselves at the present time, but of which Mill was only partially aware, and then as a social and political rather than an educational issue. To serve educational purposes environment must be amenable to deliberate manipulation. Much of our environment is not — for instance, the structure and forces of the physical universe, the 'laws' of organic life and the limitations they impose. These in general must be accepted as they are; we can (and must) learn to live with them and avoid their dangers, and to some extent we can utilise them to our own ends; but radically alter them, this we cannot do. Not so the social environment: here too there are 'laws' — man's sociality, his need for security, order, communication — but of a kind more flexible than those of the physical and organic world; however, within these general 'laws' man can and does manipulate his social environment to create distinctive cultures, patterns of value, of behaviour, of interrelationships. Some areas of the social environment lend themselves more readily than others to manipulative control; such are the health, security and educational services, and within this last, schools especially (as currently conceived) permit a high degree of environmental manipulation, inclusive and exclusive, in accordance with chosen purposes. Contrast with this the almost total lack of deliberate educational control (in *democratic* societies — it can be very different in totalitarian regimes) over other areas of the social environment: radio and TV, films, books, the Press, advertisements, public opinion — all of them highly formative and often hostile to the purposes structured into the environment of schools.

Hence comes a conflict — a conflict between two environments, the one (schools) highly structured and highly purposive, the other scarcely at all; a conflict between the values and purposes deliberately embodied in the former and those prevalent in the latter. By some it is seen (erroneously, so the present writer believes) as a conflict of cultures, middle-class *versus* working-class, the liberal-literary tradition *versus* grass-roots, popular, pragmatic self-expression. However interpreted, the conflict is perplexing and intractable — even for Plato so long ago: how, he asks in the *Republic*, can a young man remain untarnished by the impact of popular values?

> Won't he be swamped by the flood of popular praise and blame, and carried away with the stream till he finds himself agreeing with popular ideas of what is admirable or disgraceful, behaving like the crowd and becoming one of them?. . . Make no mistake, to escape harm and grow up on the right lines in our present society is something that can fairly be attributed to divine providence.[77]

Nor was Mill wholly unaware of it: the total impact of environment is often, he remarks in the *Inaugural*, 'a very bad education . . . requiring all that can be done by cultivated intelligence and will to counteract its tendencies'.[78] In our time the conflict shows itself in the resistance of pupils to learning, to authority, to discipline, to such traditional virtues as diligence, honesty, self-control and respect for others; not only is it frustrating the endeavours of teachers, but currently it is prejudicing the success of comprehensive education which, it is now increasingly recognised, cannot prosper without a supportive social environment. Mill, at a time when the concept of universal education was still in its infancy and that of compulsory state education scarcely conceived, could hardly have foreseen the urgency of our problems. Were he able to advise us now, he would point us in the direction of the 'educative society' in which formal education and the informal impact of environment work in harmony (or at least in creative tension, instead of outright conflict), committed to the same fundamental values and mutually supporting each other in a common educational enterprise.

PHILOSOPHICAL ISSUES

1. *Language and education*

The nature/nurture controversy is not basically philosophical but scientific — a matter of fact which calls for patient research using scientific techniques of investigation. However, Mill's analysis of 'nature' points to an area of philosophical inquiry which has engrossed the attention of philosophers for half a century, namely, language, meaning and the uses of language in various kinds of discourse (educational, political, religious, etc.). For those who are not familiar with this it would be well to read Warnock, G. J., *English Philosophy since 1900* (Oxford University Press, 1958) and a simple introduction to Wittgenstein, such as Hudson, W. D., *Ludwig Wittgenstein* (Lutterworth, 1968). At a more advanced level, but lucid and readable, is Hospers, J., *An Introduction to Philosophical Analysis* (Prentice-Hall, 1953; 2nd edn, 1967; Routledge and Kegan Paul paperback, 1973); and there are two useful collections of papers, Lyas, C., ed., *Philosophy and Linguistics* (Controversies in Philosophy, Macmillan, 1971), and Parkinson, G. H. R., ed., *The Theory of Meaning* (Oxford Readings in Philosophy, Oxford University Press, 1968).

Educational philosophers have also devoted much of their efforts for the past twenty years to clarification of meaning and the uses of language; for instance, Professor Peters's *Ethics and Education* and, with Professor P. H. Hirst, *The Logic of Education* (Routledge and Kegan Paul, 1970); and there is the collection of papers edited by Professor Peters for the Oxford Readings in Philosophy series (cited above). Professor Israel Scheffler's *The Language of Education* is an important book in this field (C. C. Thomas, 1960); of particular interest are his chapters 'Educational Slogans' and 'Educational Metaphors', for these tie up closely with Mill's strictures on the prescriptive use of sloganised expressions like *naturam sequi* and of metaphors like 'law of nature'. For a critical assessment of analysis in educational philosophy, see Professor Edel's article in Doyle, J.F., ed., *Educational Judgments.*

2. *Indoctrination and censorship*

The use of environment as an instrument of education requires the deliberate inclusion within it of experiences considered valuable and the exclusion of those thought harmful; it is a *selective* process, as Mill was well aware. It is arguable whether such selective manipulation of environmental influence is *education* or *indoctrination* (with censorship as its negative arm) or both. Much depends on the meaning assigned to 'indoctrination', and this is a topic which has attracted a great deal of attention from educational philosophers — indeed, there would seem little left to say about it! As so often, the argument begins with Plato's *Republic* and continues in the other Utopian exercises mentioned on p. 81. For critical analysis of indoctrination in education, see: Snook, I. A., *Indoctrination and Education* (Routledge and Kegan Paul, 1972) and the volume of papers edited by him, *Concepts of Indoctrination* (Routledge and Kegan Paul, 1972); Doyle, J.F., ed., *Educational Judgments*, chapters 4 and 5; Langford, G. and O'Connor, D.J., eds, *New Essays in the Philosophy of Education,* chapter 2; *Ed. Ph. and Th.,* vol. 5, no. 1, 1973 (Cooper, D.E.); and *SPE,* vol. 7, no. 2, 1970 (Snook, I.A.); no. 3, 1972 (Rosemont, H.); vol. 8, no. 1, 1973 (Snook, I.A.).

CHAPTER 3

Method

In the first of the two previous chapters we considered the implications for educational practice which derive from Mill's value commitments, from his criticisms of contemporary education and society and from his epistemological and psychological premises; reference was made to certain tensions which manifest themselves between different directions of his thought and character — individuality and experientialism on the one hand and associative behavioural manipulation on the other, between freedom and his zeal for improvement; finally, it was claimed that Mill belonged to a 'progressive' current of educational thought, in which he is linked with such earlier writers as Locke, Rousseau and Pestalozzi and with twentieth-century educationists like Dewey and A. S. Neill. Among the major implications of Mill's experientialist/associationist position was his conviction that environment is a powerful educative force — indeed, *the* fundamental instrument of education — both within formal schooling and in the informal context of daily life; this environmentalism was examined at length in the second chapter, and with it Mill's contribution to the nature/nurture controversy as expressed particularly in his analysis of 'nature'. The present chapter and the next pursue these implications further into the method and content of schooling, the actual processes of instruction and the varieties of knowledge they are contrived to impart. It must be remembered, of course, that Mill wrote no treatise on education apart from the *Inaugural*, which is limited in scope and intention by the purpose for which it was composed and which, while offering a protracted survey of what he conceived to be a liberal education, includes no account of method. However, by bringing together numerous passages and comments in his other writings it is possible to piece together a view of the proper methods, skills and content of instruction which, though not as complete as one would wish, is coherent in itself, consistent with the rest of Mill's educational thought and also valuable in its anticipation of much that is now normal practice. A further aspect of his educational thought, his concept of liberal education, will be examined separately in a final chapter.

Experientialism, environmentalism and association psychology gave Mill the governing principles of the educational process, the general framework in which the many subsidiary elements of the process found their place and their cohesion. Enough has already been said about each of them to make this plain; in what follows, therefore, the framework is assumed and will not be further discussed. On the details of their practical implementation in school and classroom he has, in fact, little to say (and perhaps we should not expect more from basic principles, whose function is not to *serve as* practical procedures but to *suggest* them); however, their influence is obvious in many of his explicit recommendations such as habit formation, discovery methods and the force of example. Look first at habit. Mill does not press its importance with the insistence of Locke in his *Thoughts concerning Education* (where it occurs like a refrain throughout the book), but he is aware of it nonetheless. The efficacy of association as an instrument of education depends essentially on the formation of habitual 'mental trains', whether of thought or feeling; this was orthodox associationism as expressed, for instance, in James Mill's 'Education': 'The mental trains . . . are that upon which every thing depends, and . . . the mental trains depend essentially upon those sequences among our sensations which have been so frequently experienced as to create a habit of passing from the idea of the one to that of the other. . . .'[1] Though deviating somewhat from his father's general position (pp. 51-2 above), John agreed that repetition (frequency) is essential to the formation of associations. In a note on motivation in James's *Analysis of the Phenomena of the Human Mind* he argues that a motive to perform or to abstain from an act depends on associations of pleasure and pain, and these in turn depend partly on the intensity of pleasure or pain and partly on 'the frequency of repetition of their past conjunction with the act, either in experience or in thought. In the latter of these two consists the efficacy of education in giving a good or bad direction to the active powers.'[2] The word 'habit' is not used here, but the implication is clear and it is made explicit elsewhere.

Disciplined co-operation, essential to the protection of society from the enervating effects of civilisation, is learnt by acting habitually in concert with others, and 'habits of discipline, once acquired, qualify human beings to accomplish all other things for which discipline is needed.'[3] Habit is the basis of moral education: a course of action initially motivated by pleasurable association is eventually, by constant repetition, so firmly established as habit that it is performed without reference to the pleasure — 'the action itself becomes an object of desire, and is performed without reference to any motive beyond itself.' Such, indeed, is the objective of moral education, and it is 'only when our purposes have become independent of the feelings of pain or pleasure from which they originally took their rise, that we are said to have a confirmed character'. (It is this 'habit of willing', divested of its pleasurable association, that enables 'the moral hero' to persist in his course of action in the face of suffering.)[4] Habit resulting from constant repetition is the basis of facility in both physical and mental skills — so he argues in *Principles of Political Economy*; it is not the case that oftener means *better* (intelligence is an important factor here), but repetition does produce increasing facility of performance, whether in the workman at his bench or in the child at his books — and 'what can be done easily has at least a better chance of being done well.' It is such mental skill, the product of repetition and habit, that enables a child to tot up 'a column of figures with a rapidity which resembles intuition'.[5] Langauge, too, he asserts in 'Professor Sedgwick's Discourse', is learnt not by 'a rational instinct' (as Sedgwick had claimed) but as a result of habits established by constant practice: 'A child learns a language by the ordinary laws of association; by hearing the word spoken on the various occasions on which the meaning denoted by it has to be conveyed.'[6] Hence he recommends in the *Inaugural* that French and German be learnt not from books and masters in school but by sharing the daily life of native speakers (which is how Mill himself learnt French, but not German).[7]

Mill's experientialism, it was suggested above has clear implications for education and instruction: it points to experience, inquiry, observation, experiment as crucial factors in learning; to activity and involvement in the discovery (or *re*discovery) of truth; to procedures which, as far as possible, are learner-centred, self-motivated, self-disciplined. His writings provide ample illustration of this conception of the educational process. In his essay 'The Spirit of the Age' he warns that 'there are things which books cannot teach'; wisdom comes only from experience, without which there can be no genuine knowledge of life or of people.[8] 'There are many truths,' he asserts in *On Liberty*, 'of which the full meaning *cannot* be realised until personal experience has brought it home' — though some illumination even of such truths may come in the to and fro of discussion.[9] Theoretical knowledge, essential though it is for guidance and prediction, is insufficient on its own: 'No one who attempts to lay down propositions for the guidance of mankind, however perfect his scientific acquirements, can dispense with a practical knowledge of the actual modes in which the affairs of the world are carried on. . [10] In the same vein he stresses the importance for his own work 'as a theoretical reformer' of his direct experience at India House of the practical conduct of public affairs.[11]

In these passages Mill is using 'experience' in a broad sense extending beyond the confines of school; it also, of course, has specific application to the classroom. Here it manifests itself in 'discovery' methods involving active inquiry by the pupil and a shift of pedagogic focus from teacher to learner; the latter now assumes responsibility for his own instruction, while the former assists as guide and partner in the search for truth. And truth, he argues in the essay 'On Genius', is not something discovered once for all and then passively accepted, generation by generation; rather, it is a possession which must be claimed afresh for himself by every person born into the world. How does he claim it? 'There is only one way; and nobody has ever hit upon more than one — by *discovery*.' Genuine knowledge can never be vicarious:

> Those who have no eyesight of their own, or who are so placed that they cannot conveniently use it, must believe upon trust; they cannot *know*. A man who knows may tell me what he knows, as far as words go, and I may learn to parrot it after him; but if I would *know* it, I must place my mind in the same state in which he has placed his; I must make the thought my own thought; I must verify the fact by my own observation, or by interrogating my own consciousness.[12]

The same message is proclaimed in 'Civilisation'. Attacking current conceptions of university education, Mill firmly rejects the notion that to educate is to *inculcate*; the business of education is to create not disciples but thinkers, inquirers 'determined and qualified to seek truth ardently, vigorously and disinterestedly'; it must furnish the pupil 'with the needful aids and facilities, the needful materials and instruments' and then leave him 'to the unshackled use of them'.[13] His review, written for the *Globe* in 1835, of Horace Grant's two books, *Arithmetic for Young Children* and *Exercises for the Improvement of the Senses, for Young Children*, welcomes enthusiastically a method of teaching which encourages in a pupil 'the habit of really discovering truths for himself', leading him to mathematical rules *only* through acquaintance with particular facts on which he has employed 'his eyes, his hands, all his perceptive faculties, and his first nascent powers of judgement and reasoning'.[14] It is no wonder that in the *Autobiography* he picks out, as 'the one cardinal point' which was the principal cause of whatever good he derived from his education, his father's insistence on thrusting the onus of learning upon himself: 'Anything which could be found out by thinking I never was told, until I had exhausted my efforts to find it out for myself.'[15] Here he found the educational implications of his experientialism corroborated in himself and his own achievement. Nor is it surprising that he found fault with his father's habit 'of trusting too much to the intelligibleness of the abstract, when not embodied in the concrete' — for instance, in requiring him to read aloud by *rule* instead of showing him how it should be done; nor, again, that he regretted learning science *theoretically*, 'not trying experiments . . . nor even seeing, but merely reading about them'.[16]

Discovery implies doing, activity — mental, physical or both; it requires initiative in the learner, a positive venturing forth (under appropriate guidance) to explore experience. The contrast between activity and passivity and his decisive rejection of the latter are a recurrent theme in Mill; himself evidently a man of enormous energy, he deplored inertia and its concomitant moral and intellectual enervation. Hence, in part, came his admiration for heroic achievement, for the great *doers* and for the ancient Greeks: 'Bred to action, and passing their lives in the midst of it, all the speculations of the Greeks were for the sake of action, all their conceptions of excellence had a direct reference to it'; and their education was imbued with the same spirit and purpose.[17] However, it was not simply a matter of personal inclination: activity in discovery enables the learner to recognise his own powers, to develop them by exercising appropriate skills and disciplines, and thus to achieve independence of his teachers (a major educational objective). In *Principles of Political*

Economy, defending the principle of peasant ownership of land, he asserts categorically: 'If there is a first principle in intellectual education, it is this — that the discipline which does good to the mind is that in which the mind is active, not that in which it is passive'[18] (see above, pp.131-2). Similarly, in 'Civilisation' he writes that 'it holds universally, that the one only mode of learning to do anything, is actually doing something of the same kind under easier circumstances.'[19] Again, while arguing in *On Liberty* for a person's right to defy custom and 'to use and interpret experience in his own way', he writes:

> The mental and moral, like the muscular powers, are improved only by being used. The faculties are called into no exercise by doing a thing merely because others do it, no more than by believing a thing because others believe it. . . He who lets the world, or his own portion of it, choose his plan of life for him has no need of any other faculty than the ape-like one of imitation. He who chooses his plan for himself employs all his faculties[20]

— and 'choosing his plan for himself' is an essential ingredient of discovery activity.

Believing so enthusiastically in active learning harnessed to experience and discovery, Mill was appalled at the methods common in the schools of his day, and there were few things against which he protested with such powerful and persistent condemnation. In his review of Grant's *Arithmetic* and *Exercises*[21] he distinguishes two kinds of instruction 'which are as remote from each other as light from darkness'. He goes on to describe them thus:

> One of these is the system of *cram*; the other is the system of cultivating mental *power*. One proposes to stuff a child's memory with the results which have been got at by other people; the other aims at qualifying its mind to get at results by its own observation, experience and reflection. One treats a child like a creature that has nothing but a memory, and loads that memory with words, trusting to Providence for enabling the child some time or other to put a meaning into those words; the other considers the child as possessing intelligence as well as memory, and believes it to be the main object of instruction to strengthen that intelligence by judicious exercise.

For illustration he takes the teaching of Latin, which still followed the centuries-old procedure of making children 'learn by rote rules of syntax written in the very language which they are to help him to learn'. With this he contrasts the method which gives no rules until the pupil has sufficient knowledge of the language to understand them. Theory is learnt by seeing it at work; instead of beginning with abstractions, the pupil is led to them gradually through an accurate knowledge of the facts from which the rules are generalised. (In some such way, it seems, Mill himself learnt Latin; and the new Latin courses of the 1970s follow a similar procedure.) It was, of course, the special virtue of Grant's book, in Mill's view, that it applied this method to the teaching of arithmetic.

In the essay 'On Genius', published three years earlier, he had made the same distinction with more elaboration.[22] 'Modern education,' he complains,

> is all *cram* — Latin cram, mathematical cram, literary cram, political cram, theological cram, moral cram. The world already knows everything, and has only to tell it to its children, who, on their part, have only to hear, and lay it to rote (not to *heart*). Any purpose, any idea of training the mind itself, has gone out of the world.

'Is it any wonder,' he adds, 'that thus educated we should decline in genius?' Again there is a contrast, here with education in ancient Greece, which consisted not in 'grinding down other men's ideas to a convenient size and administering them in the form of *cram*' but in exercises aimed at training the mind, at developing mental *power*; and that 'was the education to form great statesmen, orators, warriors, poets, architects, sculptors, philosophers, 'because it formed *men*'. He seems in this essay to suggest that there is a degeneracy incorporate in the very process of civilisation whereby men turn from things themselves to opinions about them, from objects to their images reflected in other men's minds; imitation takes the place of action, memorisation becomes a substitute for thought — an appropriation of the results of mental power without the possession of it. In this spirit nature was studied not in nature but in Plato and Aristotle, the Christian Gospel was surrendered to 'grammarians and language-grinders' and the spirituality of Jesus buried under ethical formulae and casuistry. If educators would help stem the decline, then 'Let all *cram* be ruthlessly discarded.' He attacks cram again in the *Autobiography*, contrasting it here with the merits of his own education. Most boys, he complains, 'are crammed with mere facts, and with the opinions or phrases of other people, and these are accepted as a substitute for the power to form opinions of their own';

as a result they grow up 'mere parroters . . . incapable of using their minds except in the furrows traced for them'.[23] Such an education, he argues in *On Liberty*, lacks balance and intellectual stimulus; a pupil whose instruction comes solely from teachers and books hears only one side of a case; he is never jerked from mental complacency by the discipline of reasoned controversy (which was a principal virtue, he believed, of the ancient Socratic dialectics and even of the medieval disputations).[24]

It is obvious from these passages (and numerous others which could be quoted) that Mill had strong feelings on the subject of 'cram'. Why was this so, and with what justification? But first, what did he mean by it? The basic meaning of the verb is to fill a receptacle to excess by force or compression. It came to refer to the over-feeding of poultry to fatten them for the table; then by analogy the meaning was extended to instruction specifically aimed at preparation for examinations and thence to any instruction or learning hastily undertaken (as the Oxford Dictionary puts it) 'not so much with a view to real learning as to the temporary object aimed at' and 'without regard to its permanent retention or educative influence'. This is very much in line with Mill's thinking, but his usage (both of noun and verb) can be particularised into a number of distinct and educationally significant notions. For him cram is rote learning, facts and ideas docketed in memory for later retrieval — not that memorisation is in itself undesirable (there is much that all of us, at school and after, must simply memorise and hold in readiness) but cram *stops* at memorisation; what it stores is *inert*, and this in two senses: it is not for *use* (save artificially, to demonstrate that it has been remembered), and it is not *understood*. Cram is verbalised learning in which words are mortified into mere sounds and shapes 'to which the children affix either no idea at all or ideas too indistinct to have any hold on their minds or influence on their conduct'.[25] This absence of understanding is central in Mill's rejection of cram: where information is memorised but not understood there is no genuine knowledge, no *possession* of truth — only a spurious appropriation of ideas to which the pupil has no rightful claim because he has not made them his own. Thus, cram is second-hand, imitative not creative, a step removed from the reality of knowledge and experience; parasitic on the efforts of others, it encourages in the pupil neither self-reliance nor the spirit of inquiry.

The divorce between cram and understanding is an objection he emphasises in his review of Mrs Austin's translation of the Cousin Report on public education in Prussia. Here he argues that state grants, endowments and voluntary contributions are sufficient, if *quantity* were the only consideration, to provide the means for a national education in England; what is grievously lacking is *quality* in the existing teaching.[26] To prove his point he quotes Sir William Molesworth (see the previous paragraph, note 25) and then at great length from a series of lectures by a Dr Biber on the teaching he had observed in certain National and Lancasterian schools. Arithmetic, religious knowledge, reading, writing, moral education — in all these the teaching is vitiated by verbalised instruction which by-passes the children's understanding. In the first of them they are taught to *cipher* but remain in absolute ignorance about *number*; and without knowledge of number they cannot even be efficient cipherers. It is the same in religious teaching: after a pupil had read the parable of the Prodigal Son, Dr Biber asked the class for the meaning of 'riotous living' and received as answers only synonymous phrases which they understood as little as the original. And in their writing exercises: a boy had written half a dozen times on his slate, 'Live in love': ' "What are you writing here?" I asked. "Live in love." "And what does that mean?" "I don't know." "You don't know! But don't you know what *'love'* means?" "No!" "Or do you know what *'live'* means?" "No!" "What must you do to live in love?" "I don't know!" '[27] 'The most frightful perversion of all,' writes Mill, commenting, is in the infant schools: places where children should learn to live, 'designed exclusively for the culture of the kindly affections . . . are converted into places for parroting gibberish'.[28]

Clearly, cram as Mill conceives it violates both the spirit and the procedures of experientialism; it is also an affront to truth and intellectual honesty. Instead of using facts to create knowledge, it stores them, pretending that knowledge has already been attained; it reverses the proper logic of inquiry by making rules, i.e. generalised principles, the start instead of the finish of the learning process. Moreover, it contradicts the experience and the beneficial conse-quences of his own education, and it ignores the genuine educational needs of English society — not least of the working classes, who must be taught not to imbibe words but to develop their minds and so become 'rational beings . . . capable of foresight, accessible to reasons and motives addressed to their understanding'.[29] Yet again, cram implies a perverse conception of learning and of the teacher-pupil relationship, reducing the child to the status of a mere receptacle — a jug-mug model of the instructional process — instead of regarding him as a living and growing intelligence. In all this there are strong enough reasons, intellectual and emotional, for Mill's vehement antipathy to cram.

There is still another, however, which finds expression (as in the paragraph quoted above from his review of Grant's *Arithmetic*) in his contrast between the two methods of instruction 'as remote from each other as light from darkness'. What cram does *not* do, and what all instruction *should* do, is cultivate 'mental power'. The phrase (or its equivalent) occurs repeatedly: the fundamental purpose of 'an education intended to form great minds . . . is to call forth the greatest possible quantity of intellectual *power'*; those who followed the 'gigantic' minds of Plato and Aristotle found it easier to remember than to think and abandoned 'the pursuit of intellectual power'; the wretched education of Mill's time does not elicit 'mental powers' (except, he adds, in a few).[30] Akin to 'mental power' is the similarly recurrent notion of 'mental training' and its equivalents: in contemporary society 'any idea of training the mind itself' has disappeared; contemporary education provides no 'mental training' adequate to resist the impostures of the time; no scientific teaching was ever better suited for 'training the faculties' than that which he received from his father; 'mental cultivation' is desirable for its enlargement and elevation of human worth.[31] Cram contributes nothing to mental power. True, it exercises memory, but mechanically in a manner which facilitates only mental *storage*; its accumulated data atrophy for lack of the skills to employ them; it is a dead-end kind of instruction.

This insistence on mental power as a criterion of successful teaching is not simply a device to sharpen the contrast between the two methods, the one benighted, the other enlightened. It is also a corollary of Mill's demand for activity and discovery in learning, and of the consequent shift of focus from teacher to learner. For if the mind is to be active in discovery, it must know *how* to discover; it must acquire and develop the skills which enable it to find out for itself. It is these skills, indispensable to the experiential pursuit of knowledge, that constitute what Mill understood by mental power. What did he suppose them to be? He offers us no systematic clarification of his conception of mental power, but its main ingredients can be determined readily enough from scattered passages. It should be noted that not all these ingredients are intellectual; some, and not the least important, are affective or attitudinal. The learner must have a commitment to truth, to seek it, as he advises the students at St Andrews, 'at all hazards'; it is for this, for their 'noblest enthusiasm both for the search after truth and for applying it to its highest uses', that he commends the ancient dialecticians earlier in his *Address*.[32] With this goes a consciousness of ignorance, humility in acknowledging it and a consequent unease which acts as 'a pungent internal stimulus' in dispelling it.[33] Important, too, is an attitude of independence, of resistance to intellectual conformity, to prejudice, to dogma, of determination to form and to defend one's own beliefs.[34] None of these comes naturally or easily; they are a slow growth, the product of patient fostering. The example of others is vital (see below, p. 177ff), and so too, as we have seen, is habit; difficulties and responsibilities encourage effort of will and intelligence.[35] Mental power requires this firm affective basis, and Mill does not lose sight of it; but it is its component intellectual skills that he has principally in mind. Experientialism points to the importance of what may be called 'inductive skills': accurate observation, careful assessment of evidence, valid inference from particular to general, 'a wholesome scepticism' in assenting to conclusions. It is for these that Mill specially commends the sciences in the *Inaugural Address*. They exemplify 'what the process of interpreting experience really is', and by submitting himself to their training and discipline the student identifies himself with these procedures.[36] (He praises Horace Grant's two books for teaching similar skills at a simpler level — p.146 above). However, mental power is broader than this; it comprises skills which belong to the traditional deductive logic ('ratiocinative' is Mill's word) — accurate inference from given premises, detection of fallacy, the capacity to weigh both sides of an argument ('the principal lesson of Plato's writings') — and others of more general intellectual application.[37] Among the latter are classification and analysis (to which the classical languages, he believes, are a valuable introduction), conceptual clarification (which digs beneath 'the loose and vague generalities' of popular parlance to the ideas, if any, which lie beneath), and precision in language and thought.[38]

No doubt present-day psychologists and philosophers will question whether 'mental power' has any meaning clear enough to allow it a useful part in educational discourse, but the phrase was certainly meaningful for Mill. To him it signified the resource of the man who, possessed of these intellectual skills, was able to recognise problems and attack them with vigour and expertise; the man capable of 'methodising knowledge' by relating its parts to each other and to the whole; the exact thinker disciplined to rational procedures and able to formulate and express his ideas with sensitive precision; the man dedicated to truth, who, refusing to rely on the thoughts of others, insists on 'interrogating his own consciousness', searching for truth within himself in his own response to experience, which is, indeed, the end of education — 'not to *teach*, but to fit the mind for learning from its own consciousness and observation'.[39] It was an ideal, of course, the culmination of what he envisaged as the best course of education, and as yet, he would freely admit, available only to a privileged few (though even the most elementary education could contribute to it by proper methods of instruction); and it was a *worthy* ideal, too little in evidence in his own time and still, alas, in our own. It came close to realisation, if we accept what he writes in the *Autobiography*, in his own education: he praises the drilling he received in logic and the detection of fallacy, the practice (required by his father) of analysing the speeches of Demosthenes, his close study of Plato's dialogues and their 'searching *elenchus*' (inestimable 'as an education for precise thinking'), the daily *compte rendu* of his father's exposition of political economy written and rewritten to the point of complete clarity, his abstracts of Locke's *Essay* and Helvetius' *de l'Esprit*, read to his father and criticised by him. He acknowledges too the effect of his editing of Bentham's *Rationale*, which not only made him a clearer thinker but also 'gave a great start' to his powers of composition, eliminating the 'jejuneness' of his earlier writing.[40] If all this seems immodest, pointing to Mill himself as the embodiment of mental power, there is no hint of conceit in his account of it (a fault from which his father took great pains to protect him); and he warns of the dangers, manifested in his nervous crisis, of an over-intellectualised education and an excessive practice of analytical skills.

The strength of Mill's feeling against cram and its associated methods is obvious from the preceding paragraphs. The principal reasons for it are also clear: cram contradicts fundamentally not only his own attitude to life — energetic, critical, creative, autonomous — but also his account of knowledge, science and truth, reversing (as we have noted) the logic of inquiry as Mill understood it, suppressing mental power and promoting a kind of intellectual dishonesty. Further, it denied the experience of his own education which, despite its defects, he judged to have been highly successful. Yet another reason, which will be apparent later, is its conflict with what Mill deemed a proper relationship between teacher and pupil. However, it should not be supposed that he wholly rejected verbalised and memorised learning or authoritative teaching: words are essential for communication and for conceptualisation, but they must be *live* words with a potential for growth, not mortified fossils shelved in the brain and bereft of understanding. Memory too is an essential tool of scholarship, providing (where properly used) a solid basis of relevant fact which, far from restricting the mind, liberates it into new freedoms. (In this, Mill does not make the mistake of certain 'progressives' who have supposed that children pick up and retain the basic facts in any area of knowledge simply by repeated exposure to or employment of them. He would accept their plea for investigation, for the creation rather than the absorption of knowledge, for understanding at a conceptual, not a merely mechanical, level; he would nevertheless insist on that solid basis of memorised fact which frees the mind for its own explorations.) As for authority, he states plainly in his review of Grant's books 'that many truths must be taken upon trust from others'; but though a child must be told many things by his teacher, he insists that

> those things which he can investigate he should be taught to investigate: those things which are level to his faculties — to all our faculties — he should be accustomed not to get by rote without understanding, but to understand, and not merely to understand, but whenever possible to find out for himself.[41]

Justification for Mill's attack on cram can certainly be found in his own educational and epistemological premises; but other questions remain. Was cram, in practice in the schools of his time, the arch-enemy he thought it? And is it as pedagogically damaging as he supposed? These are large issues, which cannot be dealt with satisfactorily here. The rote learning of material, which remains inert because it is neither understood nor utilisable, has been an unhappy feature of European education at least from the time of Horace — and no doubt earlier, in Alexandrian and classical Greece.[42] It appeals to teachers because it is easier, superficially more effective and more assessable than any other methods of instruction; it is a ready tool of the classroom, especially welcome (even, sadly, inevitable) when books are few, resources scarce, classes large and psychology primitive. In the early nineteenth century, at the beginnings of mass education in England, there was further reason for its popularity in the pressure for cheap education for large numbers through the monitorial system: such a system, dependent on 'teachers' whose task was to impart what had been selected and arranged by their superiors, received readily a method which economised skill and lent itself to mechanical imitation. That rote methods were common in the early and mid-nineteenth century is a fair inference from Dickens's *Hard Times* (1854) which caricatures them in the classroom of Mr Gradgrind.[43] As for pedagogical justification, it can fairly be said that Mill's principal charges against cram are supported by the general movement of educational thought and practice during the present century: activity, learning by doing, by application, by practice, pupil participation in the process of instruction, his autonomy in learning, his interaction with teachers, with fellow pupils, with the materials of instruction, understanding and conceptualisation as proper goals of intellectual education — all these, together with a growing respect for the pupil's own personality, point away from the mechanisation of learning implied in the system of cram (*not*, however, from memorisation as such — a point too often overlooked by 'progressives' in classroom and syllabus reform, but not, as already noted, by Mill).

Despite the vehemence of Mill's attack on cram, he expresses elsewhere views which may be interpreted as at least implying, if not positively requiring, teaching methods of the cram variety. We have already noted that in his review of Bain's *Psychology* he is at pains to rebut the charge that associationism is a materialistic doctrine; and, further, that there is a tension between associationism and the experientialism which is the foundation of his epistemology (pp.99-102). Assuming human malleability and the consequent possibility of shaping human nature by associative techniques, associationism points towards (to put it no more strongly) predetermined, imposed and reinforced response as the basic pedagogic instrument and towards the mind as essentially a storage-retrieval system; such is not so very distant from the notion of cram. His 'faculty psychology' (pp.151-3) points in the same direction; and if memory is included among the 'faculties', cram may even be defended as a means of exercising it. In *Representative Government* and *On Liberty* he insists on the need for examinations, in the former as a test for receiving the franchise, in the latter to enforce a law on compulsory educational attainment; and they must, he further insists in *On Liberty*, be 'confined to facts and positive science'.[44] Here again one suspects that such examinations, of limited but powerful motivation and predominantly factual, would lend themselves to cramming. So too, even more obviously, would his suggestion of payment by results in his 'Endowments' article of 1869: 'Where is the necessity that the teacher's pay should bear no relation to the number and proficiency of his pupils? . . . The real principle of efficiency in teaching, payment by results, is easily applied to public teaching. . .'[45] Evidently Mill had not thought through to the pedagogical implications of these suggestions (and lacked the practical knowledge to do so); had he made the attempt, his epistemological and intellectual principles would presumably have warned him of these implications in time to reject their premises.

Leaving aside these apparently discrepant elements, it seems clear that Mill's view of the proper methods of instruction carries with it certain consequences for the learning situation and for classroom relationships. Instruction which emphasises experience, discovery, understanding and the release of mental power, shifting the focus of activity from teacher to pupil, must give due heed to children's mental state and stage of growth. This is now a commonplace of educational theory (though less conspicuous in practice), especially since the work of Piaget; it is important also, of course, for traditional methods — which have too often been vitiated by ignoring it; for child-centred instruction it is crucial. In Mill's time psychology had scarcely achieved standing as an independent science and child psychology was virtually unborn, but there was some recognition, perceptible in Mill himself, of an order of unfolding of children's capacities which the educator must acknowledge and with which his scheme of instruction must accord. There are hints of it in Mill's review of Grant's books, where he writes of withholding linguistic rules until children are able to understand them, of encouraging them to 'rise gradually' to such generalisations, of presenting material 'in such an order' that their minds accompany the teaching, and of allowing them to investigate 'those things which are level to [their] faculties'.[46] In his review of Bain's *Psychology* he admits that we have only limited powers of apprehending what goes on in children's minds, but by observing their behaviour 'we have some means of ascertaining what, in their minds, precedes what. We can often, by sufficiently close observation, perceive a mental faculty forming itself by gradual growth.'[47] (Bain himself in his *Education as a Science* (1878) has a chapter entitled 'Sequence of Subjects — Psychological' and comments: 'It is important for us to grasp, if we can, not merely the leading components of our intellectual structure, but also the order of their unfolding.')[48] There is a similar passage in the *Autobiography* where, within his indebtedness to European thinkers whom he was reading about 1830, Mill includes the idea 'that the human mind has a certain order of possible progress, in which some things must precede others, an order which governments and public instructors can modify to some, but not to an unlimited extent'.[49] He is perhaps thinking here more particularly of political development (as in the early chapters of *Representative Government*), but his mention of 'public instructors' suggests that he had psychological growth also in mind.

If the recognition of 'an order of unfolding' (to borrow Bain's phrase), of stages of mental growth which admit certain methods and curricular content while prohibiting others, is one important aspect of the learning situation that Mill's views require, another is the teacher's assumptions concerning the nature of knowledge and learning. These, of course, must be in line with Mill's own pronouncements as surveyed above, and on most teachers of Mill's time (and many still of our own) these assumptions would impose a Copernican revolution of attitude. For knowledge in Mill's classroom is not something the teacher imparts but something the child acquires or, better, *creates* or *re-creates* in the course of his own investigations; it is alive with a potential for growth, not only by factual expansion resulting from further exploration but within the child's own consciousness in his reflection upon it, in his application of it to relevant use, in his conceptualising of it into a generalised structure which augments his capacity for still further exploration of greater range and depth. It is not a gift bestowed by others but a personal stake to be claimed, justified, defended, if necessary abandoned. Knowledge is *authentic*: 'those who have no eyesight of their own, or who are so placed that they cannot conveniently use it, must believe upon trust; they cannot *know*.' Knowledge, he continues, 'comes only from within; all that comes from without is but *questioning*, or else it is mere *authority*.'[50] Correspondingly, learning is not an open-mouthed passivity of ready receptacles storing inert, pre-selected, pre-digested information, but an active search, guided under loose rein and largely self-motivated by interest and the very desire to know. 'Instruction, when it is really such,' he writes in *Political Economy*, 'does not enervate but strengthens as well as enlarges the active faculties.'[51] Thus conceived, knowledge and learning demand not only different attitudes in the teacher but a transformation of the classroom — away from chalk, talk and desks in rows to the flexibility of individual tasks, group work and resource centres; but Mill was unable to carry the argument as far as this.

However, he understood clearly enough that his conception of knowledge and learning required a very different teacher-pupil relationship from that which was prevalent in the schools of his time. Instruction can no longer be a one-sided affair of donor and recipient, dominie and *discipulus*; it becomes a co-operative enterprise in the search for truth, wherein the teacher, though having the advantage of greater skill and knowledge, is nevertheless essentially a fellow explorer. It is a situation of interaction: 'it is not brick walls nor instruments nor books' that constitute instruction, 'mind must be taught by mind'; or, as he quotes approvingly in a letter of 1867, 'real education depends on "the contact of human living soul with human living soul".'[52] The teacher's function is to make ignorance aware of itself, to guide along the path of inquiry, to develop skills and judgement and a grasp of principles; and all this not 'in the spirit of dogmatism'[53] but by suggestion, by reasoned argument, by stimulating the desire for knowledge, by his own example and attitude. His goal as teacher is to make the pupil independent of instruction:

> An enlightened instructor . . . by strengthening [his pupils'] intellects, storing their minds with ideas, and directing their attention to the sources of evidence not only on every doubtful, but on every undisputed point, at once qualifies and stimulates them to find the truth for themselves.[54]

Impartiality and intellectual honesty are therefore among his essential qualities; granted these, it matters not what his own opinions are, for he will state them fairly and balance them with opposing views. His classroom will be characterised by friendliness and an air of freedom: for the former Mill especially commends Thomas Arnold of Rugby and 'the example he set of friendly intercourse between master and scholars'; the latter, he believes, beneficially distinguishes English schools from French, whose more rigid control ensures a greater quantity of learning but at the expense of educational quality.[55]

(Interestingly, Mill sees implications in all this for the size of schools: genuine interaction of mind and character between teacher and pupil he thinks unlikely in a school of more than two to three hundred; but in too small a school the teacher's energies and attention are diffused by the need to teach too many things at too many different levels of attainment.)[56]

This change of relationship does not mean an easy time for the pupil nor (as we shall see later) any lack of discipline: a teacher who does too much for his pupils may achieve popularity but he will teach them little. Commenting on the rigours of his own education, he writes: 'A pupil from whom nothing is ever demanded which he cannot do, never does all he can.'[57] And in *On Liberty*, defending the sceptical questioning of established doctrine: 'Both teachers and learners go to sleep at their post as soon as there is no enemy in the field.'[58] Mill did not intend the classroom to be a place of lax habits or effortless surrender to inclination. Nor did he wish to detract from the legitimate role and authority of the teacher: 'When we desire to have a good school, we do not eliminate the teacher';[59] he is by no means a dispensable element in the process of instruction. In schools the teacher's authority derives from his practical expertise, from his greater knowledge and experience and from his position as a representative of social and academic traditions; this is very different from (nor, of course, does it justify) 'the old notion of education that it consists in the dogmatic inculcation from authority of what the teacher deems true'.[60] Indoctrination is not part of the teacher's function; on this Mill is emphatic. Not dogmatism but inquiry is the teacher's proper function, he tells his university audience at St Andrews, repeating the view he had expressed years earlier in the *Monthly Repository* that not only religion but *every* subject should be taught 'in an inquiring, not a dogmatic spirit — so as to call forth, not so as to supersede, the freedom of the individual mind'.[61] Indoctrination is a gross abuse of the teacher's position; instead of liberating the intellectual powers, it enslaves and paralyses them; indeed, 'it is a total misunderstanding of all the objects of teaching to suppose that it has anything to do with impressing the teacher's opinions'[62] — or, of course, anyone else's.

It is not surprising that Mill was critical of schools and teachers as he saw them at that time, and thought their deficiencies a powerful argument for state intervention in education. Among his strictures were the poor quality of the teaching, the ignorance of students going up to university, the verbalised, mechanical instruction of the elementary schools (many of whose teachers were 'as ignorant as the most untaught of their scholars'),[63] the obsession with cram, the lack of mental interaction — these have already been noted. In a letter to T. H. Huxley he writes of the need for 'improvements in the *mode* of teaching': 'It is disgraceful to human nature and society that the whole of boyhood should be spent in pretending to learn certain things without learning them'; granted 'proper methods and good teachers', Latin and Greek could be thoroughly learnt and still leave ample time for science and modern languages; in any case, if science were as badly taught as classics, 'it would not do their minds any more good'.[64] (He makes the same point in the *Inaugural*, arguing that 'if the two classical languages were properly taught', there would be room enough in the curriculum for anything else that needed to be included; and in the *Autobiography*, where he claims that the success of his own education, at least in the sheer quantity of knowledge amassed, 'places in a strong light the wretched waste of so many precious years as are spent in acquiring the modicum of Latin and Greek commonly taught to schoolboys'.)[65] He shares the dismay of a Liverpool headmaster, an enthusiast for spelling reform, that the number of children who leave school 'able to read a newspaper with understanding' is smaller than the number of teachers in the schools; no doubt a simplification of orthography would help, but even without this 'there certainly is no necessity that it should take "seven years of the best learning period of a child's life" to teach him to read. So great a waste of time only proves the wretchedness of the teaching.'[66]

Nor is it surprising that Mill was not greatly enamoured of the monitorial system, which was widely adopted during the nineteenth century as a cheap means of extending education to the masses, and was strongly supported by the early utilitarians, including Bentham and James Mill. The structure and operation of the system lent themselves to mechanical, memorised instruction; moreover, a monitor's repertoire of knowledge and of the methods of imparting it was strictly limited, and this implied the assimilation of any one school to a common curriculum and a common method of learning. In these respects the system was clearly at variance with the learner-centred tendency of Mill's experientialism and its implications of open-ended, inquiry-based, interactive methods of instruction, and no less incompatible with his condemnation of cram. He was subjected to a form of it in his own education, for his father required him to teach in turn to his younger sisters and brothers what he had learnt himself, and this task, he tells us, constituted 'a considerable part of my day's work'. Although he acquired from the exercise a more thorough knowledge and a more lasting retention of what he taught, and perhaps also a greater facility in explanation, he concludes that:

> in other respects, the experience of my boyhood is not favourable to the plan of teaching children by means of one another. The teaching, I am sure, is very inefficient as teaching, and I well know that the relation between teacher and taught is not a good moral discipline to either.[67]

He says little more on the subject, but in his review of the Cousin Report he quotes at length in evident disapproval of the monitorial system as practised in the National and Lancasterian schools. Apart from repudiating the methods of instruction (see above, p. 150), he took exception to the means commonly employed of rewarding good behaviour by issuing tickets of a specific pecuniary value (eight a penny) and penalising bad behaviour by their forfeiture; thus children learn that duty is done for reward's sake and that 'past good conduct amounts to a licence for the commission of sin'.[68]

In fairness to the teachers it must be added that Mill recognised other sources of deficiency in the demands of parents, managers and others. Parents, he asserted in his article 'Endowments', are determined by two considerations in regard to their children's instruction: first, pecuniary profit — and most of them, seeing little connection between this and what their children study at school, decry the latter as useless; second, the customs of their class, which, no less than the former, cramp both the content and the purposes of instruction.[69] (Mill uses this as an argument for endowed schools, which, he believes, could offer 'models of good education' independent of such restrictive interests.) Managers too impair the efficiency of instruction, especially in denominational schools, where too often their concern is for the religious teaching at the expense of any other:

> A teacher whose heart is in the work, and who attempts any enlargement of the instruction, often finds his greatest obstacle in the fears of the patrons and managers lest the poor should be 'over-educated'; and is driven to the most absolute evasions to obtain leave to teach the common rudiments of knowledge. The four rules of arithmetic are often only tolerated through ridiculous questions

about Jacob's lambs, or the number of the Apostles or of the Patriarchs; and geography can only be taught through maps of Palestine, to children who have yet to learn that the earth consists of Europe, Asia, Africa and America.[70]

Clearly, an essential remedy for the imperfect state of instruction, to whomever due, was an effective training of teachers; this he recommends as 'the most important step towards a national system' as well as being of inestimable value in itself.[71] But not an easy remedy: the reform of schools is slower even than the reform of governments and Churches, 'for there is the great preliminary difficulty of fashioning the instruments — of teaching the teachers'.[72] Universal education is essential, he writes in a diary entry of 22 January 1854, but 'who will educate the educators?'[73]

Consideration of teacher-pupil relationships leads inevitably to the question of 'discipline'; this is an untidy concept which needs some preliminary elucidation. Today it commonly refers to control in the classroom, a well-regulated situation in which children conduct themselves in an orderly manner and the teaching proceeds acording to plan. Less often it is used as a synonym for punishment, the consequence which befalls those who defy control. Different, but with features in common with the former, is the discipline of a field of knowledge (mathematics, physics, Latin or whatever), the skills and procedures requisite for its study and the necessary response which these demand from the student. Again, the word is frequently used with a dominantly moral flavour, referring to the self-restraint and effort necessary for the attainment of an ideal, for the accomplishment of a task or for obedience to rules of conduct. Now Mill was not immediately concerned, as is the practising teacher, with problems of classroom control, but his use of the word carries something of this meaning; far more, however, it leans towards the academic and moral; occasionally it has overtones of punishment. It signifies for him an educational regime which encourages persistence of application, perseverance in the face of difficulties, the subduing of immediate inclination to more distant and worthwhile purposes; which produces in pupil and student a certain strength, determination and resilience of character that facilitate achievement; which trains in intellectual skills and procedures, both those specific to particular studies and those (like analysis, deduction and imaginative theorising) of more general application; which, for the sake of social cohesion and accord, encourages (but not uncritically) the acceptance of established cultural values and commitment to basic norms of behaviour. Implicit in all this, as became apparent in Mill's analysis of 'nature' (pp.116-123 above), is a *selective* development of human potential (an 'artificial discipline') within a value structure at first imposed but later freely accepted (or possibly rejected). This final point should be especially noted, for discipline in Mill's meaning is not essentially (though initially, for young children, it must be) a prescribed order; nor is there any intrinsic value in restraint as such. Discipline is *for the sake of* more effective, more worthwhile achievement, whether in the development of personal potential or in social progress; and ultimately and at its best it comes from *within*, by the individual's own choice and effort.

The social need for discipline is firmly asserted in a passage in the essay on Coleridge. Among the indispensable conditions of social permanence is a lifelong education whose 'main and incessant ingredient is *restraining discipline*', which he particularises thus:

> to train the human being in the habit, and thence the power, of subordinating his personal impulses and aims to what are considered the ends of society; of adhering, against all temptation, to the course of conduct which those ends prescribe; of controlling in himself all the feelings which are liable to militate against those ends, and encouraging all such as tend towards them. [Tenses changed from original][74]

Without this there will be conflict, a neutralising of energy and consequent decline. The moral aspect of discipline is emphasised in Part II of *Comte and Positivism*, where he advocates 'the direct cultivation of altruism and the subordination of egoism to it'; this, he thinks should be a principal aim of education, including an element of 'ascetic discipline'; and he hopes that 'children and young persons will one day be again systematically disciplined in self-mortification; that they will be taught, as in antiquity, to control their appetites, to brave dangers, and submit voluntarily to pain, as simple exercises in education'.[75] All that he says on mental power and mental training contributes to the intellectual content of his concept of discipline — the value of logic, of analysis, of the Platonic *elenchus*, of scientific, linguistic, historical and aesthetic studies, all of them in their various ways promoting the skilful, orderly, economic (and thus *disciplined*) employment of the faculties.

He comes closest to the classroom situation in a remarkable passage in the *Autobiography* where he is commenting on his father's character and his demeanour towards his children. Tenderness, he writes, was the moral quality most lacking in his relationship with them, and the response of the older children, including John, was one of fear and loyalty rather than love. (Later in life and towards his younger children his attitude was very different; so too was the response — 'They loved him tenderly.')[76] John is uncertain whether for himself there was gain or loss in his father's severity; at least it did not prevent him from having a happy childhood. Then, generalising, he continues:

> I do not believe that boys can be induced to apply themselves with vigour and, what is so much more difficult, perseverance, to dry and irksome studies by the sole force of persuasion and soft words. Much must be done, and much must be learnt, by children, for which rigid discipline and known liability to punishment are indispensable as means. It is, no doubt, a very laudable effort in modern teaching to render as much as possible of what the young are required to learn easy and interesting to them. But when this principle is pushed to the length of not requiring them to learn anything *but* what has been made easy and interesting, one of the chief objects of education is sacrificed. I rejoice in the decline of the old brutal and tyrannical system of teaching, which, however, did succeed in enforcing habits of application; but the new, as it seems to me, is training up a race of men who will be incapable of doing anything which is disagreeable to them.

He concludes, then, that 'fear as an element in education' cannot be dispensed with,

> but I am sure that it ought not to be the main element; and when it predominates so much as to preclude love and confidence on the part of the child to those who should be the unreservedly trusted advisers of after years, and perhaps to seal up the fountains of frank and spontaneous communicativeness in the child's nature, it is an evil for which a large abatement must be made from the benefits, moral and intellectual, which may flow from any other part of the education.[77]

Quite apart from its significance for John's own educational experience and his attitude to his father, the passage raises numerous questions which penetrate controversially to the very core of the educational process: the role, if any, of fear in our dealings with children; the role of interest in learning; the relationship between freedom and authority; the role of punishment and what kind of punishment (Mill nowhere mentions that he was beaten by his father). One's first reaction, no doubt, is to disagree with Mill as contradicting the mood at least, not to say some of the central principles, of present-day educational theory. Fear, it may be said, is surely unacceptable as an educative tool, apart from the elemental protective fear of physical injury; yet, on second thoughts, is it so wrong that children should *fear* the consequences of their actions in, say, drugs or sexual intercourse or even disobedience of the school rules? Of course, it depends partly on what one means by fear: a fear which cowes and subdues, which 'seals up the fountains of frank and spontaneous communicativeness', is clearly counter-productive; but fear interpreted as a healthy respect for authority, for standards, for failure to achieve one's best — this is not so obviously alien to our cherished educational beliefs. Nor is Mill evidently wrong in what he says about interest. Certainly it is 'laudable' to facilitate learning, whether through interest or improved technique; but if in so doing we discourage children from effort, persistence and the resolve to master difficulties, then it may well be that 'one of the chief objects of education is sacrificed' — and there is perhaps some danger of this in modern educational practice. However, whether or not one agrees with Mill on fear and interest, there is surely no disputing the conspicuous good sense of his concluding observations on children's love and trust.

The relationship of freedom and authority is another of the controversial issues raised by Mill's comments, quoted above, on the role of interest, discipline and fear in education. Though freedom is among his principal values, he never subjected the concept to the rigorous and detailed analysis one might expect; the same is true of authority and of the relation between the two. Genuine freedom, he asserts in the introduction to *On Liberty*, means 'pursuing our own good in our own way' — with the proviso that we allow others to do the same; later in the essay freedom is 'doing what one desires'.[78] These descriptions are akin to what is commonly known as 'positive freedom' — freedom *to* or *for*; but in much of his argument he virtually equates freedom with non-interference or 'negative freedom' (which, in the present writer's view, is the correct account of the concept). There is inconsistency, even muddle, here. On the other hand, he makes it plain — as others have not always been careful to do — that freedom, whether as non-interference or as doing what you like, does not properly belong to children, whose immaturity requires that they 'must be protected against their own actions'.[79] Nor does it escape him that children must be initiated (though he does not use the word) into a culture, and that this too imposes limitations on their freedom: education, in the narrower sense which he adopts for his *Inaugural Address*, is 'the culture which each generation purposely gives to those who are to be its successors'[80] to enable them to maintain and improve upon the existing level of attainment. Such an account of education is incompatible with a policy of strict non-interference.

Clearly, this points to the need for authority in the sense of a respected locus of rules, propriety, correctness (whether in law, morals, art or some other area of particular expertise); and in education it points to the need for disciplined control by a person or persons in whom authority is vested. This was obvious to Mill, champion though he was of individuality and freedom. Without authority civilised life was impossible, and he saw as the 'three great questions in government': 'To what authority is it for the good of the people that they should be subject?' 'How are they to be induced to obey that authority?' 'By what means are the abuses of this authority to be checked?'[81] A further question which constantly perplexed him was where the boundary should be drawn between the authority of the individual over himself and that of the state to interfere. Politically the ultimate authority must be the will of the majority, but this is fraught with danger, and it is essential, he thought, for there to be 'a perpetual and standing Opposition to the will of the majority' to ensure that intellectual and moral advance is not crushed beneath a mean and prejudiced uniformity; hence his partiality towards an educated elite to whose 'superiority of cultivated intelligence' the majority would show due deference.[82]

The need for authority is no less in other spheres — the intellect, morality, the arts. In an early essay he writes:

> It is right that [every man] should follow his reason as far as his reason will carry him, and cultivate the faculty as highly as possible. But reason itself will teach most men that they must, in the last resort, fall back upon the authority of still more cultivated minds, as the ultimate sanction of the convictions of their reason itself.[83]

A few years later, in 'Professor Sedgwick's Discourse', he expresses the view that the function of a university is to provide 'the education by which great minds are formed', minds whose superior qualities will lead the mass of their countrymen 'to greater achievements in virtue, intelligence and social well-being' and inspire the leisured classes to appreciate and emulate this very superiority.[84] This claim that there must be deference to intellectual authority was one he never relinquished; even in *On Liberty* he does not reject outright the suggestion (posed as an objection to free discussion) that 'simple minds', having reached the limit of their capacities, must 'trust to authority for the rest'.[85] So too in morals, Mill argues, there must be a supreme ethical principle, 'some standard by which to determine the goodness or badness, absolute and comparative, of ends or objects of desire'; and this standard is, of course, 'the happiness of mankind, or rather of all sentient beings'.[86] The authority of this ultimate principle is backed by secondary rules whose justification is derived from it, but which are normally sufficient in themselves for ethical guidance without further appeal — for instance, honesty, fair dealing, impartiality, tolerance. And in the arts there is the authority of an ideal beauty exemplified in the great masters; for art is 'the endeavour after perfection in execution', a perfection which is evidenced in all great poetry, music, painting, and even in the mundane products of daily life if they are infused with the earnest desire for this same perfection *and* obedient to its authority.[87]

In education authority manifests itself in the teacher as an expert in a particular area of knowledge and the means of imparting it, as a representative of the school community, its rules and manner of life, and as a representative of the laws and culture of society as a whole. Mill does not explicitly distinguish these three aspects of the teacher's authority, but it is obvious from what has already been said that he was aware of the first and last (and of their importance), and the second (since the school is a society in miniature) could hardly have escaped his notice. Of crucial importance is a proper balance between this authority and children's freedom to develop, to discover, to choose, to express themselves in expanding individuality — and this not just for development's sake but as essential also to efficient pedagogy. For Mill well knew, as has already been shown, that teaching, rightly conceived, is not *instruction* or 'dogmatic inculcation' but *enabling to learn* — by guidance and motivation, by provision of resources, by interaction of mind with mind; and this demands a constant and sensitive adjustment of authority to freedom, the former relaxed as children learn (and learn by) a disciplined use of the latter.

His views on punishment are mainly expressed in discussion of other issues rather than in direct analysis: in chapter v of *Utili-tarianism* they emerge from his examination of the meaning of justice and of the nature and origin of the sentiments attached to it; in *Sir William Hamilton* the topic is the freedom of the will leading to a consideration of Robert Owen's 'necessitarianism' and its implica-tions for moral responsibility; in his edition of James Mill's *Analysis* the context is psychological and the need is to explain, whether by association or otherwise, the 'animal' or affective element in moral attitudes and the origin of the notion of obligation. What he writes here is augmented and supported by brief references in a number of letters and articles; there is also his speech in Parliament opposing the abolition of capital punishment (a speech which, contrary to what might be supposed, is notable for the deep humanity of its argument). Evidently he gave considerable thought to punishment, principally, of course, within the socio-political adult context; however, his conclusions in this sphere have relevance also for education, and in occasional passages Mill himself shows that he has not excluded children from his consideration.

The idea (indeed, the actuality) of punishment is integral to his account of justice and obligation and of the sentiments attached to them. In *Utilitarianism* he argues that 'the generating idea of the notion of justice' is 'the idea of legal constraint' or 'penal sanction'; it is also essential to the notions of right and wrong: 'We do not call anything wrong, unless we mean to imply that a person ought to be punished in some way or other for doing it; if not by law, by the opinion of his fellow-creatures; if not by opinion, by the reproaches of his own conscience.' (Herein, he adds, lies the crucial distinction between 'right' and 'expedient', the former implying deserving or not deserving to be punished, in one or other of these three ways, the latter implying no more than distaste or disagreement and liking or approval.) This is not to equate justice with morality, for the former includes (as the latter does not) the idea of a due or debt which must be paid, non-payment of which carries with it a recognised penalty. So much for the notion of justice, but what of the sentiment which accompanies it? In this, Mill affirms, there are 'two essential ingredients . . . , the desire to punish a person who has done harm', together with the belief that someone has in fact been wronged. The former ingredient is itself composed of two affective elements, 'both in the highest degree natural'; these are 'the impulse of self-defence, and the feeling of sympathy'. It is common to all animals 'to resent and to repel or retaliate' harm done or attempted against themselves or those with whom they sympathise; human beings differ only in their greater capacity for sympathy and the wider range (consequent on superior cognitive ability) of its application. The sentiment of justice, he concludes, 'in that one of its elements which consists of the desire to punish, is . . . the natural feeling of retaliation or vengeance, rendered by intellect and sympathy applicable to those injuries . . . which wound us through, or in common with, society at large'.[88] In itself the sentiment is non-moral; it is moralised by its socialisation to accord not simply with personal whim or pleasure but with the general good.

The notion of justice thus includes a rule of conduct (implied in legal sanction against breach of it) and a sentiment which supports the rule; the idea of punishment plays a crucial role in regard to both. The justification for the rule lies in 'the general utility', and the power of the sentiment derives both from its naturalness and from 'the extraordinarily important and impressive kind of utility which is concerned'.[89] In this way Mill interprets the concept of justice consistently with his utilitarian premises. He argues similarly, but very briefly, in a footnote to James Mill's *Analysis*: association theory cannot alone account for the feeling of duty or obligation; in addition there is required the idea of punishment, affectively rooted in our animal nature and including the various ingredients mentioned above.[90] In a letter of 1859 to W. G. Ward (author of a theological treatise, *On Nature and Grace*) he argues that to persons of normal moral feeling the word 'ought' means that if they act contrary to a certain rule they will be punished; here too he rejects his father's associationism as inadequate and attributes the notion of obligation and its accompanying sentiment to man's sociality and 'the indispensable condition of all society' that each should respect the happiness of his fellows and be punished (legally or otherwise) if he does not: hence, 'on this basis, combined with a human creature's capacity of *fellow-feeling*, the feelings of morality properly so called seem to me to be grounded, and their main constituent to be the idea of punishment.'[91] (In this passage Mill allows a more significant role to conscience and to religious or humanistic ideals.)

In *Sir William Hamilton*[92] the immediate issue (within the chapter on the freedom of the will) is the 'necessitarians'' denial of human responsibility on the grounds that 'a man's actions . . . are the result of his character, and he is not the author of his own character. It is made *for* him not *by* him.' It follows, they argue, that 'there is no justice in punishing him for what he cannot help'; persuasion and education are admissible, but not punishment. But what, Mill asks, is meant by moral responsibility? 'Responsibility means punishment. When we are said to have the feeling of being morally responsible for our actions, the idea of being punished for them is uppermost in the speaker's mind.' This feeling, he further explains, consists either in the expectation that we *shall* be punished *if* we act so, or simply that we shall *deserve* punishment; the former is the result of parental, educational or cultural conditioning, or of rational reflection on experience, and is therefore readily explicable. The latter, the feeling of desert, is more problematic; though due in part to the expectation of punishment, the root of it lies in the knowledge that punishment *justly* follows the violation of 'the rule of right', that is, the rules which society imposes for its own security and the general good and which are recognised as binding by all persons of normal moral outlook — which is close to the position he argues in *Utilitarianism* and the letter to W. G. Ward. (It will be noted that he is greatly complicating his argument by adding to the initial simple notion of punishment the further ideas of 'right' and 'just'.) However, the question raised by the 'necessitarians'' denial of responsibility is still unanswered: is it just to punish a man for what he cannot help? Mill's answer is that he *can* help it: causation (to which he is committed — on this see above, pp. 38-42) is not the same as determinism; it does not follow that because actions are caused they could not happen otherwise than they do; the criminal *can* be deterred from his intent by the more powerful motive of avoiding the certainty of punishment; only if it had *no* power of influencing the will would punishment be unjust, for it would then be no more than a mere retrospective retaliation for wrong done (which view, as we shall see, Mill rejects).

So far we have been mainly concerned with Mill's account of the conceptual relationship of punishment with justice, obligation and responsibility, and of its affective origin in the desire, augmented by natural sympathies, for protection of self and society. This is not the place to attempt a critique of his views (which seem to the present writer to contain ambiguities of language, inconsistencies of argument and dubious psychological assertions which might have been corrected by a fuller and more determined analysis). Rather, we must turn to the justification and purpose of punishment (closely interrelated and both partly implied in the preceding paragraphs), and to the educational implications of his position. He names three principal objectives for punishment (each of which can also constitute a justification); they are retribution, reform and deterrence. His attitude to the first is not wholly unambiguous: in *Sir William Hamilton* he repudiates emphatically the belief

> that there is a natural affinity between the two ideas of guilt and punishment, which makes it intrinsically fitting that whenever there has been guilt, pain should be inflicted by way of retribution. . . The merely retributive view of punishment derives no justification from the doctrine I support.[93]

Yet in this very passage he allows that feelings of indignation and resentment at wrong done are salutary in themselves and that their satisfaction may 'in certain cases' (but only as a means to this end) permit retribution. In *Utilitarianism* he admits that there is a natural hankering after the *lex talionis*, a proportionate vengeance for wrong done, and that this is 'universally included' in the idea of justice; in the notes to *Analysis* and in *On Liberty* he uses the words 'retaliate' and 'retaliatory' in a way which suggests acceptance of retribution in this sense;[94] and his approval of flogging for crimes of brutality again carries overtones of 'an eye for an eye' (see below). Perhaps Mill was caught here indecisively between head and heart, impelled by the former towards a rational humanity, by the latter towards recognition of deep emotional presures.

However it may be, there is no doubt that he thought reform and deterrence to be the chief purposes of punishment, justified by their effects on the wrongdoer and the benefits accruing to society and wholly consistent with the principles of association psychology. He says little to suggest positive recommendation of the former, but seems rather, on the occasions when he mentions it, to assume that it has a rightful place in the rationale of punishment. For instance, in his review of proposals for changes in the criminal law he writes sympathetically of a plan for rehabilitation of criminals 'as one among many systems of reformatory discipline . . . worthy to be tried by way of experiment upon the less corrupted of the persons convicted of minor offences'.[95] However, to extend it to all would not only be an affront to the honest but would also, and more significantly, remove or seriously diminish the incentive to refrain from crime. Again, in a letter to Florence Nightingale he expresses the belief that some minds are impervious to any consequences of their crimes except punishment; this is, therefore, 'the sole means available for beginning the reformation of the criminal', and fear of similar punishment is the only inducement which deters others from wrongdoing.[96] These passages give the clue to his real position, which is that deterrence is the dominant purpose of punishment, with reform as a highly desirable but secondary objective. This is confirmed by his constant emphasis on self-defence and the security of society as justification for punishment: *because* punishment deters, it protects both the individual and the general good.[97] Indeed, this is the only justification for restraining personal liberty — not simply the reform of the offender — and once granted, it permits any degree of coercion necessary to secure its effect.[98] Deterrence is a major theme in his speech against the abolition of capital punishment: 'To deter by suffering from inflicting suffering is not only possible, but the very purpose of penal justice', and death is 'beyond comparison the least cruel mode in which it is possible adequately to deter from the crime'.[99] 'The great purpose of punishment,' he writes in an *Examiner* article, 'is *example*'; and the force of example, he explains elsewhere, lies not in the punishment itself but in the expectation of incurring it for a similar offence — which is why '*certainty* in punishments has a greater effect than severity'.[100]

What application has this account of punishment to the education of children? Much of the answer must be supplied by inference, for Mill himself gives little help; having no practical involvement in schooling and no family of his own, he lacked occasion for serious consideration of the role of punishment in children's upbringing. That he had given it thought, however, and felt deeply about some aspects of it is obvious from various passages and brief comments. If the idea of punishment is a necessary part of the concepts of justice, obligation and responsibility, then children must acquire the idea; this is possible only if the actuality of punishment is a part of their environment — that is, if children are in fact punished, and are known to be punished, for breaking the rules of the community. (Whether Mill is right in this is a different matter — and, indeed, dubious; but our concern here is not the accuracy but the implications of his views.) At a more practical level punishment is necessary both as a deterrent or disincentive to the would-be transgressor and also as a positive incentive towards disciplined effort; this is clearly his intention in the passage quoted above from the *Autobiography* where he asserts the need for 'known liability to punishment'. (Interestingly, he welcomed the extension of deterrence to parents as a means of combating juvenile delinquency — Mill's words — commending the suggestion that they, not their children, should be legally responsible for the latter's wrongdoing.)[101] Punishment also has a part to play in the wider process of moral education. Association theory requires the conjunction of pleasure and pain, respectively, with good (desirable, approved) and bad (undesirable, disapproved) behaviour; and Mill seems to regard pain as more effective to this end — 'everyone knows . . . that pain is a stronger thing than pleasure, and punishment vastly more efficacious than reward.'[102] As association becomes habitual, it gives rise to a disinterested liking for good and aversion from bad which develop further into moral ideals; punishment alone, Mill writes, can

> produce the associations which make the conduct that incurs it ultimately hateful in itself, and which, by rendering that which is injurious to society sincerely distasteful to its individual members, produces the fellowship of feeling which gives them a sense of common interest and enables them to sympathise and co-operate as creatures of one kin.

Of the three purposes of punishment named by Mill, retribution he would surely reject as having no place in education; deterrence, however, is important both for the child's good and for that of the school; so too is reform, to which he seems here to attach prior importance — 'in the case of children [their] own improvement, as long as their education lasts, is the main end to be considered.'

In two passages, one a brief letter, the other in an article in the *Sunday Times*, he speaks directly on the punishment of children and on one aspect in particular; these are of sufficient interest to quote fully. The letter is a reply to a schoolboy who wished to compete for an essay prize offered by the *Boys' Own Magazine* and who had written to Mill for his views on flogging ('a few lines, written in your usual clear, lucid manner'). He obliged thus:

> To give a proper answer to your question would be to write the essay which you are intending to write. But if you wish for a mere opinion, expressed in a few words, I would say,
>
> 1. Severe punishments of some kind are often necessary for boys, but only when they have been negligently or ill brought up and allowed to acquire bad habits.
> 2. Assuming severe punishment to be necessary, any other mode of punishment that would be effectual is preferable to

flogging. In the case, however, of certain grave moral delinquencies, chiefly those which are either of a cowardly or of a brutal character, corporal punishment in that or some equivalent form may be admissible.[103]

There is much here that one wish to question. What kind of 'severe' punishment has he in mind other than corporal? Should boys be punished for the negligence of their parents? What 'grave moral delinquencies' justify flogging? And is flogging the best cure (or cure at all) for brutality and, more particularly, cowardice? But we must pass on to the second passage, which seems to the present writer to display much accurate and sensitive insight into the problem of corporal punishment.

The occasion of the article[104] was a court case in which a judge, sentencing a man for immoderate beating of his illegitimate child, had remarked almost apologetically that 'no serious stain' would attach to the defendant's character. Mill refers also to a recent decision of Parliament that boys might be beaten at the discretion of two magistrates but men might not ('boy' and 'man' being distinguished by the difference between thirteen years and fourteen). Why, he asks, should flogging have been almost abolished for adults but not for children? Why is it assumed that a punishment thought brutalising and degrading for grown men is 'quite fit and proper for helpless infancy'? If it is degrading to the former, it is no less to the latter; and children are as amenable to control without it as are their elders: 'A parent or teacher who cannot rule without the lash shows as much incapacity as brutality.' The familiar argument that everyone is flogged in youth and is 'much the better for it' reflects discreditably on the intelligence and moral sense of those who offer it. He concludes thus:

> Take any naturally sensitive boy who has been habitually flogged and one who has never suffered that indignity; compare them, observe the difference in self-respect, and in all that depends on self-respect, which will mark those two human beings throughout life. On a boy of dull, hard nature its effect is to render him ten times harder than he would be without it — to qualify and prepare him for being a bully and a tyrant. He will feel none of that respect for the personality of other human beings which has not been shown towards his own. The object of his respect will be power. He will crouch to power in others, and will have nothing in his own nature to prevent him from trampling on those whom he has power over. If he does not do so, it will be from nothing better than fear of opinion or fear of punishment.

There are two methods of instruction and education to which Mill attaches special importance, discussion and example. The first of these, he asserts in the *Autobiography,* contributed notably to his own intellectual development. In the winter of 1822-3 he had brought together a small group of contemporaries to discuss the basic principles of utility; this Utilitarian Society, as he called it, broke up after three years and was replaced by a group which met twice weekly for several years to study works in political economy, logic and psychology, and to thrash out the issues arising in them 'until we had untied every knot which we found'. He writes thus of its impact on himself:

> I have always dated from these conversations my own real inauguration as an original and independent thinker. It was also through them that I acquired, or very much strengthened, a mental habit to which I attribute all that I have ever done, or ever shall do, in speculation; that of never accepting half-solutions of difficulties as complete; never abandoning a puzzle, but again and again returning to it until it was cleared up; never allowing obscure corners of a subject to remain unexplored, because they did not appear important; never thinking that I perfectly understood any part of a subject until I understood the whole.[105]

In his review of Grote's *Aristotle* he refers (impersonally) to the same experience, expanding his comments into a general educational recommendation:

> There would be nothing impracticable in making exercises of this kind a standing element of the course of instruction in the higher branches of knowledge, if the teachers had any perception of the want which such discussions would supply, or thought it any part of their business to form thinkers, instead of 'principling' their pupils (as Locke expresses it) with ready-made knowledge.[106]

What did he believe to be the special value of such discussions? Part of the answer is in the above description of its impact on himself: intellectual habits of dogged persistence in exploring problems to their full extent and depth, of dissatisfaction with any incompleteness of analysis or understanding (both of which he repeats in different words in his review of Grote). The rest can be supplied from what he writes elsewhere: it assists in distinguishing truth from error, in revealing fallacies and inconsistencies ('All the inconsistencies of an opinion with itself, with obvious facts, or even with other prejudices, discussion evolves and makes manifest'),[107] in eliciting new ideas or new facets of old (thus contributing, so he tells us in the *Autobiography,* to his own theories of international values and of profits). In all this, discussion promotes intellectual clarity and the discovery of truth; without it, without the open clash of opinion in searching argument, there can be no 'rational assurance of being right'.[108] Moreover, it promotes the discovery of truth *for oneself* — not at second-hand, passively accepted as fact or doctrine, but by personal involvement (interaction, in Dewey's terminology) and therefore alive with potential for growth.

Discussion can take place at different levels: there is the informal, spontaneous discussion of the dinner party or railway compartment; there is the still informal but organised and purposeful discussion of the kind that Mill took part in; and beyond these there is a sophisticated level of discussion where it has become a formal technique of argument or disputation aimed directly at dispelling ignorance and establishing truth. Of the last kind are the Socratic discussions or dialectic (exemplified in the Platonic dialogues) on which Mill lavishes high praise in his review of Grote's *Plato* and elsewhere; they are unsurpassed, he believes, 'as a discipline for correcting the errors and clearing up the confusions incident to the *intellectus sibi permissus'* — this in the *Autobiography.* In 'Grote's *Plato'* he traces the development of dialectic from Zeno of Elea to Socrates and Plato, who refined its techniques 'to a perfection never since surpassed' both as 'negative scrutiny', or *elenchus,* and as positive search for meaning, definition and classification.[109] At this level discussion has epistemological and metaphysical ramifications; for there is, Mill suggests, an 'antagonist principle' whereby truth is disclosed in the conflict of opposing views, an 'antagonism of influence' which is the only guarantee of progress. 'Antagonist modes of thought' are as necessary in speculation as are mutually checking powers in a constitution.[110] The idea is not original to Mill — nor did he so claim; it is prominent, as he well knew, in the Greek pre-Socratic philosophers and in Hegel, and it is essential to his own argument in *On Liberty* and his essay on Coleridge. In his own thinking the antagonism appears under various guises, some of which have been noted — for instance, freedom and authority, progression and permanence, nature and discipline, individuality and behavioural control; and much of his intellectual endeavour was given to resolving these oppositions into an acceptable pattern of truth. He applies the principle to education in his claim that the abstract analytical procedures of science must be balanced by activities which present objects 'clothed in properties and circumstances, real life in its most varied forms'.[111] 'When,' he asks in 'Two Kinds of Poetry', will education consist, not in repressing any mental faculty or power, from the uncontrolled action of which danger is apprehended, but in training up to its proper strength the corrective and antagonist power?'[112] (He was later to elaborate this claim in the programme of liberal education set forth in his *Inaugural Address.*)

Whatever one may think of 'antagonism' and its metaphysical and epistemological overtones, one can hardly dissent from Mill's conclusions as to the educational value of discussion at its various levels, even the most informal. Indeed, here again he anticipates modern practice, both in educational institutions as such and in the media. For it has come to be increasingly recognised that discussion not only contributes to clear thinking, the discovery of truth and intellectual habits of persistence and completeness; it has further educative value in encouraging participation, in resolving emotional stresses and in promoting, if not community of view, at least an agreement to differ which provides a basis for mutual respect and collaboration. For all these reasons it is also, in the wider meaning of education, a potent instrument for democracy. Of course, discussion requires leadership, guidance and obedience to rule — in other words, technique and discipline; to learn this is itself a lesson of great importance — and difficulty, as any teacher knows who has successfully led a group of obstreperous adolescents from initial clamour to an orderly and fruitful interchange of view. Mill had no illusions about this; nor about the need for fact and access to fact, without which discussion becomes a charade of insubstantial posturing, as tedious as it is unproductive — which is one reason for his insisting on the diffusion of information as one of the prime duties of government.[113]

The use of example as an instrument of education is an obvious deduction from Mill's environmentalism. Human beings are shaped by all the influences which surround them, most of all by those which emanate, directly or indirectly, from other human beings; the more notable and impressive these persons are, the more powerful their impact; to place children in their company thus becomes a matter of deliberate educational policy. ('Directly' refers to the

actual presence of living persons, 'indirectly' to persons alive or
dead whom children encounter in history, literature or, nowadays,
in the media.) In addition to logical inference, this conclusion
derives support from the known imitativeness of children, which is
a principal means of their learning, and also from association
theory, which points to the importance in shaping character of what
they like, admire or respect (on the latter see also below, pp. 196-7).
From childhood Mill had always been impressed by greatness —
partly as a result of his father's deliberate educational intent, for he
tells how James gave him books to read 'which exhibited men of
energy and resource in unusual circumstances struggling against
difficulties and overcoming them'. He mentions his 'reverential
admiration for the lives and characters of heroic persons, especially
the heroes of philosophy': there was Socrates, of course, that 'model
of ideal excellence'; and Plato ('others can instruct, but Plato is of
those who form great men'); and Pericles, whose 'lofty spirit and
practical wisdom' were 'a course of education' for the Athenian
demos; and Jeremy Bentham, whose *Principles of the Penal Code*
(in Dumont's French translation) made of him 'a different being';
James Mill, too, by his passionate concern for the general good
'warmed into life and activity every germ of similar virtue that
existed in the minds he came into contact with' — including evidently,
John's.[114]

What was good for himself must also, he believed, be good for
others; thus personal experience, with the support of theoretical
justification, shaped itself into educational precept. Of this there are
numerous expressions in Mill's writings. In a review of William
Hare's *Letters from Palmyra* he complains that contemporary
literature no longer portrays men and women of 'a more generous
and loftier order' than that of everyday: 'nature and probability are
thought to be violated if there be shown to the reader. . . characters
on a larger scale than himself.' He continues:

> Yet from such representations, familiar from early youth, have
> not only the noblest minds in modern Europe derived what made
> them noble, but even the commoner spirits what made them
> understand and respond to nobleness. And *this* is Education. . .
> Not what a boy or girl can repeat by rote, but what they have
> learnt to love and admire is what forms their character.

Educational books in particular have lost 'the chivalrous spirit',
while 'the popular novels of the day teach nothing but. . . lessons of

worldliness' (the results of which are yet to be seen in the next generation); in contrast, the old romances 'filled the youthful imagination with pictures of heroic men and, of what are at least as much wanted, heroic women'.[115] Similar views appeared in an earlier review of books written under the pseudonym of Junius Redivivus. The educative force of literature lies in its portrayal of elevated character: 'the beginning of all nobleness and strength is the faith that such nobleness and strength have existed and do exist in others, how few soever and how scattered.' The eternal value of the writings of a Plato or a Milton lies in their assurance that Plato and Milton have indeed existed and that we, 'according to the measure of our opportunities, may, if we will, be the like'. So too the 'goodness' of the Gospels consists not in their doctrines but in their record of the life of Christ.[116] There is also a powerful passage at the end of his translation of Plato's *Gorgias* (written in the same period of his life as these two reviews):

> The love of virtue, and every other noble feeling, is not communicated by reasoning, but caught by inspiration or sympathy from those who already have it; and its nurse and foster-mother is Admiration. We acquire it from those we love and reverence, especially from those whom we earliest love and reverence; from our ideal of those, whether in past or in present times, whose lives and characters have been the mirrors of all noble qualities; and lastly, from those who, as poets or artists, can clothe those feelings in the most beautiful forms, and breathe them into us through our imagination and our sensations.[117]

Plato, of course, is one of these, and Christ is another.

Thus far Mill has in mind the indirect influence of historical and literary characters, whose impact on the young, he argues, is a principal justification for the inclusion of history and literature (especially those of the ancient world)in the curricula of schools and universities.[118] But there is also the direct impact of living persons. The home is of crucial importance here, but the example of teachers can also have incalculable consequences for good upon the lives of pupils and students: 'There is nothing which spreads more contagiously from teacher to pupil than elevation of sentiment'; and he goes on to assert (somewhat optimistically) that students have often 'caught from the living example of a professor a contempt for mean and selfish objects and a noble ambition to leave the world better than they found it.'[119] Be this as it may, the educational importance of example, whether of the living, the dead or even the fictional, cannot be denied. Teachers, Mill rightly claims, 'cannot make their scholars what they themselves are not';[120] the same is true, *mutatis mutandis,* of parents. Yet the power of example and its instrumental use present the educator with awkward problems. Careful and pointed selection of books or teachers can make of example a potent means of indoctrination; thus, a course in history or literature can easily be slanted towards a particular religion, ideology or political creed, and a teacher can manipulate the presentation of *himself* with the same effect, using his authority, charismatic or otherwise, to impress on his pupils his personal attitudes and opinions. Mill was aware of this problem, as we have seen (p.159 above), and he insists that teaching must be impartial, 'in the spirit of free inquiry, not of dogmatic imposition'.[121] Moreover, example can be powerful for evil as well as for good; there must therefore be selection, by inclusion and exclusion, of books and teachers just as of the environment generally; but by what criteria, and whose, and how rigorously should this censorship of experience be applied? The first of these questions Mill would answer by pointing to happiness, freedom, individuality, truth and altruism as primary values. For the other two — who shall decide and how rigorous the censorship — he offers no adequate answer; just as he was more aware of the potency of environment than of its dangers, so too it seems that he was more alive to the positive power of good example than the detrimental effects of bad.

PHILOSOPHICAL ISSUES

1. *Teaching and learning*

The traditional notions of teaching and learning as, respectively, the imparting and the imbibing of information have been greatly modified during the last century — the result not so much of theory as of enlightened practice. However, theory has made its contribution from the work of psychologists and sociologists and from philosophical analysis of 'teaching' and 'learning'. It is the last which concerns us here, for which see: Peters, R. S., ed., *The Philosophy of Education*, chapters 8, 9 and 10, and *The Concept of Education*, chapters 2, 3, 7, 8, 9 and 10; Hirst, P. H. and Peters, R. S., *The Logic of Education*, chapter 5; Dearden, R. F., *Problems in Primary Education* (Routledge and Kegan Paul, 1976), chapters 5 and 6; and Scheffler, I., *The Language of Education,* chapters 4 and 5. There are also numerous articles in the journals, e.g., *J. Phil. Ed.,* vol. 7, no. 1, 1973 (Freeman, H.); vol. 9,

1975 (Marshall, J. D.); vol. 12, 1978 (Langford, G.); *Ed. Ph. and Th.,* vol. 6, no. 1, 1974 (Kerr, D. H.); *SPE,* vol. 9, no. 3, 1976 (Liveritti, R. H.).

2. Child-centred education

Mill's recommendation of discovery methods and, by implication, a 'child-centred' pedagogy brings him very near to twentieth-century educational practice. Inevitably, this concept of 'child-centredness', which is closely allied to the changed notions of teaching and learning, has not escaped philosophical scrutiny. A useful introduction to the subject (though not wholly philosophical in its approach) is Entwistle, H., *Child-centred Education* (Methuen, 1970); Professor Dearden offers a brief analysis of the concept in chapter 4 of his *Problems in Primary Education.*

Closely related are the various considerations of children's 'interests', 'needs', 'wants', 'growth'; see, for instance, Wilson, P. S., *Interest and Discipline in Education* (Routledge and Kegan Paul, 1971) chapters 1 and 2; Professor Dearden's two chapters (3 and 4) in Dearden, R. F., Hirst, P. H. and Peters, R. S., eds, *Education and the Development of Reason*; Professor White's chapter, 'Dewey's Theory of Interest', in Peters, R. S., ed., *John Dewey Reconsidered* (Routledge and Kegan Paul, 1977); and the articles in *J. Phil. Ed.,* vol. 8, no. 2, 1974 (White, A. R., Wilson, P. S.); vol. 9, 1975 (Freeman, H.); vol. 10, 1976 (Wilson, P. S.); and vol. 12, 1978 (Straughan, R.).

Among the classic expositions of child-centred education are Rousseau's *Emile* (1762), Froebel's *The Education of Man* (1826), Dewey's *Experience and Education* (1938), Sir Percy Nunn's *Education: Its Data and First Principles* (Arnold, 1920; 3rd edn, 1945) and the various writings of A. S. Neill.

3. Freedom and authority

Issues concerning freedom, authority and their relationship constantly emerge from Mill's account of the educational process — for instance, in his insistence that education is selective (which implies authoritative imposition of values and consequent curtailment of freedom of choice) and, in the present chapter, in his emphasis on the need for obedience to justifiable authority and for discipline and punishment. The issues are political and moral as well as educational — indeed, they enter into virtually every aspect of life. A major work in this field (but sociological and political rather than educational) is Benn, S. I. and Peters, R. S., *Social Principles and the Democratic State* (Allen and Unwin, 1959). Professor Peters's *Ethics and Education* covers some of the same ground from an educational slant. Another major work is Nash, P., *Authority and Freedom in Education* (Wiley, 1966). Downey, M.E. and Kelly, A. V., *Theory and Practice of Education* (Harper and Row, 1975) has a chapter on authority, and Dr P. S. Wilson's *Interest and Discipline in Education* has chapters on discipline and punishment (and an extensive bibliography). Also relevant are chapters 8 and 9 in Doyle, J.F., ed , *Educational Judgments,* Barrow, R., *Moral Philosophy for Education*

(Allen and Unwin, 1975) and Bridges, D. and Scrimshaw, P., eds, *Values and Authority in Schools* (Hodder and Stoughton, 1975), which also has an extensive bibliography.

Honderich, T., *Punishment: The Supposed Justification* (Hutchinson, 1969; rev. edn Penguin Books, 1976) includes a critical assessment of Mill on punishment (chapter 7).

CHAPTER 4

Content

In considering Mill's views on the content of education we shall be concerned more with curricular principles, that is, with criteria of selection, justification, purpose and structure, than with details of particular subjects, though some of these must also be included. Mill himself distinguishes between liberal, vocational and elementary education (see also below, pp.205-6). The first is an education characterised by breadth, balance, generality and intellectual freedom; it liberates potential, is non-specialised, non-vocational and serves as a basis both for fullness of personal living, including responsible citizenship, and for professional studies. It is examined at length in the next chapter and no more need be said of it meanwhile than is necessary to elucidate his comments on other aspects of the curriculum. On vocational education he has little to say: he recognises the need for specific training for such professions as law, medicine and engineering, as well as for skilled occupations in industry; but always he insists that vocational training should proceed from a broader basis of general or liberal education and should itself be aimed not simply at the acquisition of specific skills but at the understanding of principles. Thus, in writing of one Indian college he expresses pleasure that instruction is not confined to 'technical details of engineering and surveying, but embraces the elements of a general scientific education'.[1] As for England, he complains that middle-class parents 'set no value on any instruction not strictly professional' (as often he is careful to point out that things are different in Scotland); the purpose of universities, he claims in the *Inaugural*, is not to prepare students for earning a living, but to make them 'capable and cultivated human beings'; elsewhere he welcomes industrial schools for the poorer classes, 'not to improve them as workmen merely, but as human beings' by teaching them to use their minds as well as, and in the service of, their hands and to acquire habits of order, regularity and rational behaviour.[2] For Mill, what a man is, his character and conduct, weighs more than specific skills in this or that occupation; it is to the former that educational effort must chiefly be directed.

However, there are 'certain primary elements and means of knowledge' which all members of the community should acquire during childhood;[3] these it is the task of elementary education to impart. ('Elementary', it should be noted, had not yet, when Mill wrote these words, the formal statutory meaning it received later in the century and held until the 1944 Act. It refers in this passage to fundamental skills and information which he believed necessary in nineteenth-century Britain; he has in mind principally 'the labouring classes' but not a particular age range.) Among these 'primary elements' are literacy and numeracy, without which an individual can neither conduct his own affairs nor participate effectively in the work and life of the nation. This is true anywhere, and so we find Mill agreeing, in a draft letter to India, with the statement that 'the grand attention of government should, in the first instance, be directed to affording means to their subjects at large to acquire simply the elementary parts of literature, reading, writing and arithmetic'.[4] He says little about writing, regarding it, no doubt, as a mechanical skill to be taught as expeditiously as possible, how to do so being a practical decision best left to the teacher's expertise. However, he allies himself to the views of Dr Biber (p.150 above), who condemns the practice of making children write on their slates words they do not understand and of selecting words 'merely from a regard to the number of their syllables'; as a result 'the children are so stupified that they lose the habit of thinking altogether.'[5] Practice in writing should not be a mindless exercise but part of the children's growth in understanding and power of intelligent communication.

Reading he regards as vitally important, not simply as a skill to be acquired for its obvious utility value, but as a means both to enjoyment and to education of mind and character. His complaint against the ineffectiveness of teaching it was noted earlier (p.160); he had made a similar complaint many years before in the *Monthly Repository* of 17 April 1834, attacking Lord Brougham's speech of the previous day against a national education. It is not simply enough, Mill argues, to have schools and teaching; no less important is their quality:

What, in itself, is it, to be merely able to read? But the children do not at present even learn to read. What proportion of those who have been taught reading can read *fluently*? or have had the meaning of half the words they laboriously spell out explained to them? Put a book into their hands, and see how many of them will answer that they can only read in the book they are accustomed to.[6]

Once fluency *is* established, children should be encouraged to read as widely as possible; what they need is 'the most miscellaneous information and the most varied exercise of their faculties':

They cannot read too much. Quantity is of more importance than quality, especially all reading which relates to human life and the ways of mankind; geography, voyages and travels, manners and customs, and romances, which must tend to awaken their imagination and give them some of the meaning of self-devotion and heroism, in short, to unbrutalise them.[7]

This is the proper way, he insists, to acquire a knowledge of history and geography — except for children of the labouring classes, who may have to be taught them in school (presumably because they lack the books at home): 'And what an utter failure a system of education must be, if it has not given the pupil a sufficient taste for reading to seek for himself these most attractive and easily intelligible of all kinds of knowledge.'[8] (He adds the comment that such history and geography as can be taught in schools is no more than an exercise of memory — which no doubt reflects contemporary teaching methods but is wholly unacceptable today.)

But should children be allowed to read whatever comes into their hands, irrespective of its content and their own age or maturity? Mill does not discuss at any length this problem of censoring children's reading; he had given it some thought, however, and on the whole was against:

If careful selections are to be made for them, it becomes a most embarrassing question at what age are they to begin to be allowed to know any of the realities of life? and in many respects such knowledge is likely to be more mischievous if it comes startlingly upon them when they are of an age to understand it than if it is taken for granted in what they read when it has no particular interest for their childish minds.[9]

This, for one who had no children of his own, shows considerable psychological insight, and many would agree with him. Certainly, much of what younger children read in books and magazines on sexual matters (which is probably what Mill had in mind) passes over their heads. There is perhaps a stronger case for purging their reading of violence and its accompanying attitudes; for these they only too readily imitate. The commercialisation of reading matter — far greater now than in Mill's time and backed by psychological and market research as well as social forces — has made our problem more acute; it would therefore be difficult today, if not at any time, to justify allowing children unrestricted access to reading of all kinds. No doubt Mill had in mind the voracious and unhindered reading of his own childhood; but, like Rousseau's 'well-regulated liberty', it was unhindered only within a selected range of books.

Reading is for more than information, however; it should be for enjoyment too, leading to an established habit and love of reading and consequent intellectual improvement: 'The proper use of reading is to be subservient to thinking. It is by those who read to think that knowledge is advanced, prejudices dispelled, and the physical and moral condition of mankind improved.'[10] Unfortunately the general diffusion of the taste for reading has not yet had this desirable result — which is a principal reason, he thinks, for 'the degeneracy of our literature'. This was written in 1827-8, but the same view of reading and intellectual cultivation appears also in later writings. It occurs in the letter to Charles Friend quoted in the previous paragraph; and before that in 'The Claims of Labour', where he welcomes the cheap libraries in which even the poorest can find material both interesting and instructive. And the same article points approvingly to the Scottish peasant who for two centuries has been 'a reflecting, an observing, and therefore naturally a self-governing, a moral and a successful human being — because he has been a reading and a discussing one' — a blessing he owes chiefly to the parish schools.[11] Reading contributes also to improvement of character. It does so not only by the inspiration of heroic example (noted above) but also by cultivating feeling and imagination, by refining sensibility and broadening sympathy. Poetry is especially important here, though not so much in childhood, when, he thinks, it is 'least relished and least understood'; (there are compensations in children's intense passion for stories, 'almost any kind of story, merely as a story'). For poetry is 'impassioned truth'; it presents 'thoughts or images to the mind for the purpose of acting upon the emotions'. Herein lies its peculiar strength, in a union of intellect and emotion which empowers the will.[12] It may be objected that what Mill has in mind here hardly belongs to *elementary* education, but the educational meaning of 'elementary', it must be recalled, was more general in his day; in him it refers to the elements of a good education, such as, he hoped, would eventually be open to all.

For the remaining member of the three Rs, arithmetic, Mill also had a high regard; and that he had thought about the teaching of it seems clear from the review of Horace Grant's *Arithmetic* referred to above. Obviously, he was aware of its simple utility value in everyday life, but he required more than this. He insisted that arithmetic must be taught at the level of understanding, of reasoning, not of mere ciphering. Thus he criticises current methods, as a result of which 'hardly any child, and not many grown persons . . . have any idea of numbers but as marks on a slate, or of the rules of arithmetic but as a set of mechanical operations more like tricks of legerdemain than anything else'.[13] In his review of the Cousin Report (p.150 above) he cites an account of its teaching which relied purely on memory and left the children 'in absolute ignorance . . . concerning *number*', making them only 'blind instrument[s] of rules blindly learned by rote'. He cites too the abuse of wooden geometrical figures as visual aids:

> instead of making them the means of intellectual exercises, in which the children would be led every day to make new discoveries and to think for themselves, those figures are now pulled out, chiefly in the presence of visitors, and then the whole school bawls out together, 'This is a pentagon − this is a hexagon − this is an octagon' and so on.

In some schools, it seems, the tables were set to music or put to rhyme, demeaning in the process both pupil and subject.[14] The teaching should treat the child as having reason and should present arithmetic as an exercise of reason; in this way it would comply with the nature of both. For arithmetic leads to mathematics, and this Mill believed to be among the most valuable of intellectual studies. He explains why in a chapter of *Sir William Hamilton's Philosophy* and again, briefly, in the *Inaugural*.[15] Hamilton had discounted the value of mathematics as an intellectual discipline, thus revealing (according to Mill) 'fatal *lacunae* in the circle of his knowledge'. For although mathematics is not a complete intellectual education, it has important contributions to make to that education − standards of proof, habits of precision and attention (the latter of which Hamilton does allow), step-by-step division and testing of a train of reasoning, insight into coherent truth (which mathematics both exemplifies in itself and points to in the science of nature). Again, it may be objected that this belongs to a later stage of education than the elementary; but a building rises from its foundations, and appropriate teaching of arithmetic in childhood can at least facilitate mathematical under-standing in later years.

Geography and history, as already noted, would also have a place in Mill's elementary curriculum. Their intrinsic interest, he believed, should be sufficient to attract any child who had acquired the habit of reading and for whom the appropriate books were provided; children from poorer homes would need to be taught them. Interest apart, both have evident utility value, familiarising a child with his native culture and with himself as situated in time and place. Historical studies have inspirational value too, providing the stimulus of heroic example and high achievement; they give 'a certain largeness of conception to the student', revealing to him as nothing else can 'the infinite varieties of human nature' and correcting whatever is 'cramped and one-sided in his own standard of it'.[16] This too we have noted above, and in the next chapter we shall see how, at more advanced levels, he believed they should bring the student to a philosophy of history, to a conception of events unfolding themselves in a sequence of cause and consequence, a cosmic drama in which he has a responsible part to play. (Mill especially recommends the use of original sources, by means of which 'we are in actual contact with the contemporary minds' and with 'real history' — a practice long taken for granted in universities and widespread now in schools even among younger pupils.)[17]

Foreign languages would have no place in Mill's basic curriculum; for the poorest children there was little justification for them and no time any way. Even for pupils at what is now known as the secondary stage (such as in the endowed and public schools) he thought modern languages best learnt 'by intercourse with those who use them in daily life'.[18] A few months in the country itself were far more effective than years of lessons with books and masters, and he hoped that international colleges would eventually make this opportunity widely available. The value of acquiring a modern language he did not doubt: 'No one can in our age be esteemed a well-instructed person who is not familiar with at least the French language . . . and there is great use in cultivating a familiarity with German' (Mill learnt them both; see above, p.144). Thorough knowledge of any foreign language, modern or ancient, offers immense benefits, so he believed: it discourages the glib use of words without due care for meaning; it enables us to penetrate, to an extent otherwise impossible, into the thoughts and feelings of the native speakers; it thus, by comparison, illuminates our deficiencies — a first essential step to reform; without it 'we remain to the hour of our death with our intellects only half expanded'. Most valuable of all in these respects 'are the languages and literature of the ancients' — which means, of course, Latin and Greek. These had been the core of his own education, and even at the time of the *Inaugural Address* still formed the greater part of the normal secondary curriculum; this was a situation he wished to remain, and his defence of it (together with his castigation of current teaching methods) deserves a more detailed consideration.

We read in the *Autobiography* that Mill began learning Greek at three, Latin at eight. By the age of fourteen he had acquired a mastery of both languages rarely bettered by the modern university student at the end of his course; no less remarkable were the range and variety of his reading, which also far exceeded the achievement of most of today's undergraduates. The impact of his classical education was deep and permanent; throughout his life he remained a devotee, though not uncritically, of classical culture; it had become part of him; he was, as Alexander Bain describes him, 'a Greece-intoxicated man'.[19] Three things in particular it left with him: a conception of Athens as exhibiting the essential spirit of democracy and civilised culture; an unfailing regard for Plato as a master of intellectual method and a great moral teacher; and a belief in the educative force of the truly great, whether in man or in his achievements. These alone might seem sufficient justification for retaining classics at the centre of the secondary curriculum. In addition there was the literature of Greece and Rome, 'a rich store of experience of human nature and conduct' whose value was undiminished by the passage of time; moreover, it was a literature of unsurpassed stylistic excellence, which, though we cannot hope to rival it, serves as a model for our aspiration — 'early familiarity with the perfect makes our most imperfect production far less bad than it otherwise would be.' There were further benefits, issuing especially from the study of the languages: first, a training in attention to meaning and the precise use of words; second, 'on account of their regular and complicated structure', an intellectual discipline such as no modern language can provide.[20]

To secure these benefits efficient teaching was necessary, such as he had received from his father — and not just *efficient*, but appropriate in method and purpose. Teaching of this quality could not, save rarely (he mentions Arnold of Rugby), be found in English schools; Scotland, he claims, was better off in pedagogy and textbooks.[21] He complains of 'the wretched methods of teaching' which leave boys with no more than a smattering ('if even that') of the ancient languages, and of the 'shameful inefficiency of the schools . . . which pretend to teach these two languages and do not'.[22] The principal faults he alleges are these: the imposing of grammatical forms and rules on children before they have sufficient grasp of the language to make sense of them; the waste of time on composition, especially verse, which could be better spent in acquiring fluency in the language; the lack of this very fluency, without which language remains an obstacle to understanding instead of its instrument; finally, and especially at university level, an estimate of the constituent parts of classical instruction which (in Mill's view) precisely reverses their importance in educational value — first, the niceties of language, then a few poets, then ('at a great distance') some of the historians, next ('at a still greater interval') the orators, and, 'last of all and just above nothing, the philosophers'.[23] Among the remedies he proposes are, first, substituting practice in the forms and vocabulary of the languages for the traditional grammatical drilling ('the same principle on which a mere child learns with such ease and rapidity any modern language'). This recommendation (by no means new in Mill's time) anticipates the trend of modern practice in teaching Latin and Greek. Second, he suggests a shift in purpose from grammar and composition to fluency in reading: teaching should aim at enabling pupils 'to read the great works of ancient literature with ease' — again, an anticipation of the present day.[24]

Education must be incomplete, Mill believed, without a knowledge of the sciences; not that everyone should study all of them, but 'some should study all, and all some'.[25] Even at the elementary level of mere information the value of scientific instruction is obvious:

> We are born into a world which we have not made, a world whose phenomena take place according to fixed laws, of which we do not bring any knowledge into the world with us. In such a world we

are appointed to live, and in it all our work is to be done. Our whole working power depends on knowing the laws of the world — in other words, the properties of the things which we have to work with and to work among and to work upon.[26]

To us, whose daily lives are permeated and upheld by science and technology, this is a familiar and cogent argument — not simply for 'working power' but for very safety's sake; it may seem surprising that Mill found it no less cogent in his own comparatively unsophisticated age. Furthermore, we depend for this scientific knowledge mainly on the authority of others; unless, therefore,

an elementary knowledge of scientific truths is diffused among the public, they never know what is certain and what is not, or who are entitled to speak with authority and who are not; and they either have no faith at all in the testimony of science or are the ready dupes of charlatans and impostors

—again a claim which anticipates remarkably the even greater dangers of our own time. Science is important for its interest too; and here Mill is defending it on grounds more strictly pedagogical: 'Who would not wish to know why a pump raises water, why a lever moves heavy weights, why it is hot at the tropics and cold at the poles, why the moon is sometimes dark and sometimes bright, what is the cause of the tides?' Whatever be our specialised skills and training, if, through lack of such interest and the knowledge it brings, the universe remains 'a sealed book', then we have no right to call ourselves educated.

These are the most obvious benefits of scientific instruction, loss of which in youth can be made good without much difficulty in later life. More important (and less accessible once formal education is finished) is its value as 'a training and disciplining process, to fit the intellect for the proper work of a human being'. This 'proper work' is the discovery of truth, to which, in its many and varied aspects, there are two principal routes, observation and reasoning; in both of these the sciences provide, as can no other studies, an indispensable training. The former is the particular province of the experimental sciences (he mentions chemistry and experimental physics); these display at the highest level the skills which in the ordinary affairs of life most of us can only grope towards — preparation of experiment, assembling and testing of data, calculation of results, judgement of evidence and a 'wholesome scepticism' about conclusions. Indeed, 'hardly anyone who has not been a student of the physical sciences sets out with any just idea of what the process of interpreting experience really is'; a more general acquaintance with their skills would curb the facile addiction to 'popular notions and generalisations' and would contribute to a more effective conduct of politics and the economy. Reasoning is manifested in all the sciences, inductive mainly in the observational, deductive in the mathematical (astronomy, physics and mathematics itself, which Mill generally includes among the sciences). It is by reasoning that we are able 'from a few fundamental truths, to explain and predict the phenomena of material objects; and what is still more remarkable, the fundamental truths were themselves found out by reasoning', being statistically inferred from the data.[27] Moreover, the habits of analysis and abstraction involved in reasoning contribute also to integrity and independence of character; without them 'the mind is the slave of its own accidental associations, the dupe of every superficial appearance'.[28] In addition to this intellectual disciplining scientific instruction at its highest levels leads on to a grasp of the philosophy of science. By this Mill means not so much the actual truths which the sciences ascertain, as 'the processes by which the mind attains them, the marks by which it recognises them, and the co-ordinating and methodising of them with a view to the greatest clearness of conception and the fullest and readiest availability for use: in one word, the logic of the science'.[29] The concept includes also for him the place of the sciences in human culture, the picture of the universe they present to us, and the need (noted above) for a 'corrective and antagonistic principle' in poetry and the arts.[30]

On the practical pedagogy of science Mill has little to say. He tells us in the *Autobiography* of his own intense childhood interest in experimental science, but in a theoretical sense only, 'not trying experiments — a kind of discipline which I have often regretted not having had — nor even seeing, but merely reading about them'.[31] The implications of this comment for science teaching in schools are plain enough. In a letter to Comte he complains of the attitude to science and science education in England (Scotland is specifically excluded from this criticism): 'le véritable esprit scientifique est très rare chez nous,' he writes, attributing the defect either to the over-practical English character or to an excessive preoccupation with factual detail. Again: 'Il y a parmi les anglais en général une indifférence profonde envers l'éducation scientifique'; they regard science as a matter only for intellectuals or industrialists and in consequence allow excessive importance to literary studies. In a review of Harriet Martineau's 'Summary of Political Economy' he suggests that the function of the science teacher (where his teaching is for knowing rather than for practical application) is to select such scientific truths and present them in such order 'as will best exhibit the connectedness of the whole, and the completeness with which it solves all the questions which a contemplation of the subject matter suggests to the speculative inquirer'.[33] (To this one must add, from what Mill says elsewhere, the need to stimulate interest by attractive presentation of relevant information and to cultivate mental skills.)

Mill's curriculum would also include religious, moral and aesthetic components, partly as 'antagonistic' to the scientific and logical, but chiefly for their own essential contribution to what he conceived to be a good education. He believed that religion should be taught, but as fact (as he himself was taught it) not dogma, as a human pheno-and further inquiry.[34] To this knowledge everyone had a rightful freedom of the individual mind' and the possibility of questioning and further enquiry.[34] To this knowledge everyone had a rightful claim as a basis for personal decision on whether and what to believe. Within the Western tradition the Christian religion, 'the highest the world has yet known', could justifiably be taught (but always non-dogmatically), both as a part of that tradition and, no less, for its contribution to moral education: 'to exclude religious instruction is . . . to exclude moral instruction, or to garble it and deprive it of all systematic consistency.'[35] (Many will disagree with Mill here; indeed, so close an association between religion and morals is scarcely consistent with the independence of utilitarianism as a self-contained ethical position; but he is thinking particularly of morality as commonly conceived and practised among the English educated classes.) However, he was far from satisfied with the manner of its teaching, which was impaired partly by 'the literal and dogmatic character and sectarian spirit of English religion' and partly by poor methods.[36] He complains of authoritarian teaching by rote and memory, without understanding, so that religion, 'instead of a spirit pervading the mind, becomes a crust encircling it';[37] 'mere words', 'ideas unclear and confused' are complaints he quotes in his review of the Cousin Report (see above, p.150). He has no better opinion of the public schools, of Eton at least, which he cannot regard 'as a favourable specimen of what a school can do in the way of moral and religious training', judging 'by the kind of article turned out annually from Eton into the higher walks of life in this country'.[38] The most effective religious teaching, he claims, is that of home and childhood; social and public education can assist by 'a general pervading tone of reverence and duty' and by the information it can give — both 'extremely valuable'.[39] As for parents, he thinks they should

> point out to their children when the children begin to question them, or to make observations of their own, the various opinions on such subjects, and what the parents themselves think the most powerful reasons for and against. Then, if the parents show a strong feeling of the importance of truth, and also of the difficulty of attaining it, it seems to me that young people's minds will be sufficiently prepared to regard popular opinion or the opinions of those about them with respectful tolerance, and may be safely left to form definite conclusions in the course of mature life.[40]

No less important than the religious component is the aesthetic, 'the education of the feelings and the cultivation of the beautiful'.[41] This conclusion was impressed on Mill unforgettably by his nervous crisis and was in any case a natural inference from his own keen aesthetic sensitivity. It was not one, however, which he thought would appeal readily to the average Englishman, who found it incomprehensible that art could rank in equality of esteem with philosophy, science and other pursuits (a contrast, this, with the French and Germans, and a cause of the failure of understanding between England and the rest of Europe); the deficiency was due, he suggests, to Puritanism and the commercial spirit.[42] He makes a powerful plea for aesthetic education in the *Inaugural Address* as part of his conception of a liberal education; this is considered below (pp. 222ff.). What he says there is mainly in defence of its benefits — refinement of sensibility, elevation of sentiment and character, a sense of perfection in beauty which motivates towards moral goodness; he has little to say of the means of implementing it. From his comments in the *Autobiography* on the impact on himself of Ford Abbey, the Pyrenees and his country walks with his father, and from what he writes in the *Inaugural*, one must presume that he would require the educational environment to manifest beauty in its various aspects, natural and architectural as well as artistic (and how shocked he must have been by the school buildings of his time!). The study and, where possible, the *practice* of literature and the arts would also have an essential role; and all the school's activities he would wish to be permeated by the desire for perfection in execution, an intolerance of 'the smallest fault in ourselves or in anything we do'.[43] Literature, as the most accessible of the arts within the formal education of his time, would be especially important; and, remembering, no doubt, the influence of Wordsworth's poems in rescuing him from the depression of his nervous crisis, he was particularly sensitive to the claims of poetry (on literature see also above, pp. 185-7, and below, pp. 200-1). 'Where the sense of beauty is wanting or but faint,' he writes in his review of the writings of Junius Redivivus, 'the understanding must be contracted';[44] and not only the understanding but the whole personality. For aesthetic awareness contributes indispensably to 'the completeness of the human being', to the balanced growth of the individual towards his fulfilment;[45] there can be no genuine education without it.

Mill's concern for moral education is expressed repeatedly in his writings throughout his life. In the early 'Speech on Perfectibility' he emphasises its importance, especially in early years, and complains of its neglect — the latter due not so much to failure of intention as to sheer ignorance of appropriate methods. Interestingly, he points here to the need for a supportive social environment which, by the values it embodies, confirms the purposes of the moral educator.[46] Precisely the same message comes, towards the end of his life, from the *Inaugural*: moral education belongs peculiarly to the home 'in training the feelings and the daily habits', and this education is 'completed and modified, sometimes for the better, often for the worse, by society and the opinions and feelings with which we are there surrounded'.[47] Although this early training is 'in the main beyond the sphere and inaccessible to the control of public education', it does not follow that schooling has no contribution to make to moral education; indeed, Mill clearly believes that it has, but it must be the right kind of moral education — right in content and method. In a letter to W. J. Fox on his draft of a bill for compulsory secular education in England and Wales he suggests omitting the provision of moral instruction on the grounds that in practice it would mean, as already did existing religious education,

cramming the children *directly* with all the common *professions* about what is right and wrong and about the worth of different objects in life, and filling them indirectly with the spirit of all the notions on such matters which vulgar-minded people are in the habit of acting on without consciously professing. . . .

Much of this it is impossible to prevent, but the less of it the better. However, 'if it were possible to provide for giving *real* moral instruction it would be worth more than all else that schools can do.'[48]

That moral education is possible at all, he explains in *Sir William Hamilton*, depends on the fact that human beings can be trained to desire the right and reject the wrong; and it consists in 'subjecting them to the discipline which has most tendency to bring them into this state'. He continues:

> The object of moral education is to educate the will: but the will can only be educated through the desires and aversions; by eradicating or weakening such of them as are likeliest to lead to evil; exalting to the highest pitch the desire of right conduct and the aversion to wrong. . . The other requisites are, a clear intellectual standard of right and wrong, that moral desire and aversion may act in the proper places, and such general mental habits as shall prevent moral considerations from being forgotten or overlooked, in cases to which they are rightly applicable.[49]

Thus, the fundamental mechanism of moral education is association, operating through desire and aversion to establish habits which are built into character.

This conclusion is confirmed and amplified in other writings. We have already seen in his analysis of 'nature' that Mill acknowledges the need for 'artificial discipline' to shape man's given potential into something worthier than it could otherwise be. So too in his notes to his father's *Analysis* he argues that moral sentiments are not innate but are induced by associations of pleasure and pain and develop eventually into disinterested virtues.[50] The process is assisted, he suggests (also in the *Analysis*), by 'the natural force of sympathy'; and in 'Nature' too he asserts the naturalness of sympathy, adding that 'on that important fact rests the possibility of any cultivation of goodness and nobleness, and the hope of their ultimate entire ascendancy.'[51] 'Moral feeling,' he writes in a letter of 1859, is 'a natural outgrowth from the social nature of man', for 'a state of society is so eminently natural to human beings that anything which is an obviously indispensable condition of social life easily comes to act upon their minds almost like a physical necessity.'[52] Society, therefore, and the company of others are essential to moral development and can be used deliberately to promote it. (Thus in *Principles of Political Economy* he commends co-operation as 'a course of education in [the] moral and active qualities' which would result in a moral revolution and the transformation of human life, converting daily occupation into 'a school of social sympathies'; he is thinking here of industry and the conflict of capital and labour, but he would undoubtedly extend the principle to schools.)[53]

Psychological association is not the only requisite of moral education, as Mill points out in the passage quoted from *Sir William Hamilton*. Values too are necessary ('a clear intellectual standard of right and wrong'); the educator must know with what to link the child's desires and aversions, otherwise association is an empty mechanism lacking content and direction. Values come from the educator's own choice, be he parent or teacher; they come from the child's immediate environment of family and school, and they come ('sometimes for the better, often for the worse')[54] from the wider encircling social environment. Some (consideration, tolerance, honesty, justice, etc.) are by common consensus basic to democracy and may justifiably be imposed on children, but always, Mill would insist, and especially after childhood, by example and rational persuasion rather than by dogmatic inculcation. In any case, 'though direct moral teaching does much, indirect does more'; he would rely, therefore, more on the 'pervading tone' of home, school or university, reinforced where appropriate by the associative use of praise and blame, reward and punishment, rather than on moral instruction as such.[55] But the latter also has its place — again as Mill suggests in the passage quoted — especially in equipping children with the 'general mental habits' ('moral skills', we would call them now) which they need for opportune and effective moral decision.

There are two areas of the curriculum, highly regarded today, on which Mill has little or nothing to say, namely, physical education (including health) and the practical crafts. (In this he contrasts with John Locke, who includes in his *Thoughts concerning Education* detailed recommendations for bodily fitness, advice on physical recreation and a strong plea for acquiring manual skills — gardening and woodwork being especially 'fit and healthy recreations for a man of study or business'.)[56] Not that he disapproved of them or thought them unimportant: blessed with a sound constitution himself, as a result of temperance and much walking he grew up 'healthy and hardy, though not muscular'; walking, he tells us, satisfied his 'animal need of physical activity'.[57] Health he therefore took for granted, until he was smitten with tuberculosis, possibly in 1836 and quite certainly in 1853; and against this disease there was little advice to be given at that time. However, he does include physiology in his recipe for a liberal education, recognising not only its interest and intellectual value (as a science) but also its obvious practical uses. He also approved of 'military drill', explaining in a letter to Edwin Chadwick that his approval was not wholly for its military value — indeed, he would be 'a little frightened' if it were likely, as Chadwick had suggested, to 'make the majority of boys wish to be soldiers'.[58]

Manual skills he had no opportunity for acquiring: his education was more fitted 'for training me to *know* than to *do*', and in consequence he 'remained long, and in a less degree . . . always remained, inexpert in anything requiring manual dexterity'. He continues, in a tone of evident regret:

> My mind, as well as my hands, did its work very lamely when it was applied, or ought to have been applied, to the practical details which, as they are the chief interest of life to the majority of men, are also the things in which whatever mental capacity they have chiefly shows itself.[59]

(His father, he tells us, was the exact opposite.) However, in a letter of 1868 to Charles Friend (quoted earlier) he writes as follows:

> There is one other point in which a mother may, I believe, be of immense use to her children, which is apt to be too much overlooked in my opinion in modern education . . . and this is, teaching children (more especially if they are not going to be rich) to respect, to enjoy, and habitually to practise manual and domestic labour. The love of this, and the sense of moral dignity in doing it, are, next to the love of truth, the very most valuable possessions with which to begin life, whether we consider happiness or the power of getting on.[60]

For this he mentions approvingly Maria Edgeworth's *Popular Tales* (which he had himself read as a boy), Thomas Day's *Sandford and Merton*, and Harriet Martineau's *Household Education*. Evidently he was not insensitive to the importance, educationally and in themselves, of the skills which he lacked himself.

Mill made no attempt to formulate a systematic curricular theory; nevertheless, the underlying principles of such a theory are discernible in the preceding account of his views on method and content. At the heart of the curriculum are those 'primary elements and means of knowledge'[61] which, though differing from one kind or level of culture to another, are the need and the right of human beings everywhere. They include the information and the skills requisite for safe and effective living, among which literacy and numeracy, for us as in Mill's time, are of fundamental importance. To this central core he would add 'the most miscellaneous information', 'instruction of all kinds connected with the great interests of man and society'[62] — not as mere information to be registered computer-wise in the memory, but as an expansion of experience leading the pupil to increasing knowledge and command of himself (and this not simply as a self, but as a self *in history* and *in society*), and to the widest possible exercise of his abilities. In all this the emphasis is on learning rather than teaching, on the pupil's own interest, his activity in discovering, ordering and relating his knowledge, on openness, inquiry and the rejection of dogma; and this learner-centredness has its own inescapable implications for the selection and presentation of curricular content. Furthermore, despite his father's insistence on the utility of his studies, he warns against the acceptance of this as a criterion of the worth of knowledge: 'We know how easily the uselessness of almost every branch of knowledge may be proved, to the complete satisfaction of those who do not possess it.'[63] To approve only of empirical fact harnessed to vocation, production or sensory gratification is among those 'sinister interests' which prostitute knowledge in the market-place and is a principal danger of all forms of government, not least democracy. Specialisation, too, he rejects (at least until general or liberal education is completed); any study, if practised to the exclusion of others, narrows, perverts and prejudices the mind, stunting sympathy and public spirit. The curriculum must therefore be wide-ranging, balanced, incorporating as many as possible of the various forms of knowledge and experience.[64] Underlying all this is Mill's deep concern for the moral growth of the individual, for the development of his character as a whole person, acknowledging the claim of established values, yet critical of conformity and sensitive to 'the worth of different modes of life'.[65]

A superficial acquaintance with Mill's writings might suggest an over-intellectualised conception of education, emphasising excessively its cognitive aspects — an impression strengthened by the conspicuous imbalance of his own education, by his substantial scholarly achievement in the *Logic, Political Economy* and other writings, and by the common image of him as 'a cold, mechanical thinker . . . swathed in mournful black, hard-visaged and ice-veined'.[66] It is true that he writes of the intellect as 'the first of all human possessions, that which in its own nature is fitted to rule' (and calls on the state to recognise its value by subsidising scientific research);[67] that repeatedly he requires of education that it train the 'mental faculties', develop 'mental power' and exercise the skills requisite for intellectual exploration; that he extols the importance of logic, mathematics and languages, especially the classical, as intellectual disciplines promoting the capacity for thought; and that physical education and practical crafts have virtually no place in his educational thinking. But Mill was no narrow intellectual, either in himself or in his educational recommendations. As for himself, one need only recall his botanising, his constant travels abroad, his love of music and art, his sensitivity to beauty and his profound revulsion against the emotional anaesthesia induced by the inveterate habit of analysis. In education, despite the deficiencies mentioned and the extravagance of his claims for the classics, his proposals display (to the unprejudiced reader) a balance of view which was unusual in the mid-nineteenth century and which, it may fairly be claimed, constitutes a notable advance in English educational thinking.

Especially significant for our immediate purpose is his insistence on the due role of feeling and imagination, both as a necessary counterpoise to intellect and as themselves contributing to enlargement of knowledge and experience. It is conspicuous in his early essays on poetry and in his literary reviews of this same period of his life, when Wordsworth's poems had revealed to him 'thought coloured by feeling, under the excitement of beauty'.[68] Poetry is 'impassioned truth' which it sees 'through the medium of the imagination set in action by the feelings' and the faithful expression of which requires a 'matured and perfected intellect'.[69] In his review of Tennyson's *Poems* he distinguishes the innate sensitivity of the poet's 'nervous organisation', which is merely 'the capacity for poetry', from his acquired command of thought and expression, which is 'the work of cultivated reason'; it is the two together that produce great poetry.[70] He makes the same point in his review of Junius Redivivus, whom he commends for his union of intellect with sensitivity to beauty. The two are interdependent, for 'it is true of this as of all the other sensibilities, that without intellect they run wild; but without them, intellect is stunted'; he looks forward, therefore, to the day 'when the education of both will proceed hand in hand'.[71] It is the same with imagination: this too plays an essential role in human experience both as 'conceptive' (interpretative) and as creative. It assists self-observation; it enables us 'to conceive the absent as if it were present'; it is 'the power by which one human being enters into the mind and circumstances of another'; with sensation it is the medium which conveys to us from poet or artist the inspiration of beauty and moral greatness; it is a vital ingredient of originative genius.[72] He attacks J. A. Roebuck for his rejection of it: 'He saw little good in any cultivation of the feelings, and none at all in cultivating them through the imagination, which he thought was only cultivating illusions'; and he explains Bentham's deficiencies by a lack of it, which blinded him to vast areas of truth and left him 'a boy to the last' with much of human nature still dormant in him.[73] He regrets that 'the principles which ought to govern the cultivation and the regulation of the imagination' have never yet been seriously considered by philosophers.[74] One thing is clear to him, however, that imagination must be subjected to the discipline of reason, without which it may degenerate into fantasy and pervert judgement. No great work of imagination, he argues in 'Professor Sedgwick's Discourse', ever was or can be produced without great powers of reason; whatever the country, 'the age of her greatest eminence in poetry and the fine arts has been that of her greatest statesmen, generals, orators, historians, navigators — in one word, thinkers, in every department of active life.' (but not philosophers, he adds, for philosophy is 'the tardiest product of Reason itself').[75]

Thus, while Mill insists on the authority of reason (embodied in intellect) as the regulating, ordering, disciplining agent in human activity and on the highest standards of intellectual performance, he is true to his principle of 'antagonism' and to the reality of human nature in demanding due recognition of the illuminating, impassioning, energising function of imagination and emotion. He is indeed concerned with the whole person, with the fullest possible growth of his 'mental, moral, and aesthetic stature', which like a tree 'requires to grow and develop itself on all sides';[76] his proposals for the curriculum reflect this concern. In this he was ahead of his own time (as already suggested) and anticipates our own; for 'full development' is now an inevitable component of any respectable declaration of educational purpose. Inevitable, but not necessarily understood; and

Mill can help us here by his clear awareness of and adherence to its theoretical and practical implications. For there is a tendency among ourselves, in our anxiety to satisfy the demands of 'wholeness' and at the same time the educational claims of the common man (expressed, for example, in comprehensive education, mixed-ability classes and the provision of leisure pursuits), to undervalue intellect and its contribution to individual and social well-being. Consequently there is a danger of imbalance in our educational practice, to the detriment of intellectual and academic achievement; but without trained and disciplined intelligence, manifesting itself in clarity, accuracy and precision of thought and a resolute devotion to truth, no nation can survive. Perhaps it is no more than a danger, but it is one that Mill can help us avert by a concept of 'wholeness' which preserves in due balance the different aspects of human nature and their claims on the curriculum.

PHILOSOPHICAL ISSUES

Curriculum theory

Curricular principles — what to teach, why, in what sequence and proportion — have been a focus of attention for educationists since schools began. Once again, Plato initiates the discussion in his *Republic*, and it has continued through the history of European education. More recently attention has been directed to the philosophical bases of curricular choice and structure and to philosophical problems of justification; debate has been sharpened by demands for a 'core curriculum' of essential knowledge and skills (Mill's 'primary elements and means of knowledge') as a foundation for more specialised studies. Philosophical discussion of the curriculum can be found in: Phenix, P. H., *Realms of Meaning* (McGraw Hill, 1964); Peters, R. S., ed., *The Philosophy of Education*; White, J. P., *Towards a Compulsory Curriculum* (Routledge and Kegan Paul, 1973); Hirst, P. H., *Knowledge and the Curriculum*; Barrow, R., *Commonsense and the Curriculum* (Allen and Unwin, 1976); Warnock, M., *Schools of Thought* (Faber, 1977); Brent, A., *Philosophical Foundations for the Curriculum*. Chapters and articles on the curriculum are included in many of the books previously cited; and there are numerous articles in the journals, e.g., *J. Phil. Ed.*, vol. 5, no. 2, 1971 (Pring, R.); vol. 6, no. 1, 1972 (Sockett, H., Skilbeck, M.); vol. 12, 1978 (Carson, S., Carr, D.); and *Ed. Ph. and Th.*, vol. 6, no. 2, 1974 (Claydon, L. F.).

Herbert Spencer's *Education* (1861) and John Dewey's *The Child and the Curriculum* (1902) remain important and stimulating contributions to curricular discussion.

CHAPTER 5

Liberal Education

The concept of liberal education occupies a prominent place in Mill's educational thought — not to the extent of total dominance, but sufficiently to give a recognisable character and tone to most of what he wrote on and around education. The words themselves are not frequent in his writings; altogether there are probably fewer than twenty instances, and it is only in the *Inaugural Address* that they occur with any regularity. Nor did he attempt to impose on them a neat definition such as can be found, for instance, in Thomas and Matthew Arnold — preparation for 'the calling of a citizen and a man', the training which carries us to 'a knowledge of ourselves and the world'[1] — and in F. W. Farrar's *Essays on a Liberal Education.* He accepted the concept from the current vocabulary of educational thought and practice, assuming that, broadly, its meaning was understood, and impressed upon it emphases of content and structure which were peculiar to himself. His clearest and most direct account of it is in the *Inaugural Address*, which is certainly one of the most eloquent — if not the most penetrating — of apologias for liberal education; this is augmented and confirmed by numerous earlier writings.

Something of Mill's intention is revealed by his actual use of 'liberal education', 'liberal' and kindred terms. In the *Inaugural Address* he refers to the University of St Andrews as 'a seat of liberal education', praises the Scottish universities for providing 'the whole of a liberal education from the foundations upwards' and declares his purpose to be a review of the components of this education and of the claims of each to a place in it.[2] Classics, he argues at length, is an essential part of 'liberal education' because of its 'high rank among enlightening and liberalising pursuits' (which is not quite the tautology it may seem); in the early essay 'On Genius' he had suggested that classics was 'insensibly falling into disrepute as a branch of liberal education' and being replaced by 'the ready current coin of modern languages' and rote learning of scientific information.[3] In another early essay he refers to Professor Sedgwick of Cambridge as 'a commentator on the studies which form part of a liberal education' and as himself 'one of the most liberal members of the university'.[4] The obvious antidote to increasing specialisation, he writes in *Comte and Positivism*, is 'a large and liberal general education' (using 'large' here, surely, in something of its original Latin sense of 'copious', 'bountiful' — Tacitus' *largus animo*, 'generous-minded').[5] Elsewhere he commends Benjamin Jowett, the famous Master of Balliol, for his 'liberal tone of thought' and the poet Coleridge for contributing to 'liberality in matters of opinion'.[6] He refers too (in recommending a system of plural voting for the better-educated) to the 'liberal professions', though he does not specify what these are.[7] Further, Mill reveals a tendency to equate 'liberal' with 'good' and with 'general': 'Can anything deserve the name of a good education which does not include literature and science too?' — this in the *Inaugural*, where certainly no distinction is expressed or intended between 'liberal' and 'good'; and he rebukes Professor Sedgwick for ignoring the strong reasons for 'assigning to classical studies a high place in general education' and for failing to do justice to the physical sciences 'as branches of general education'.[8] In *On Liberty* he describes as 'liberal and large-minded' one whose interests are more than parochial; he writes of 'mental freedom' and 'mental slavery', of 'mental expansion and elevation', of 'the free development of individuality', and he condemns 'the education of restraint' — thus filling out the significance of 'liberal' from the related vocabulary of freedom and restraint.[9]

It is clear from this brief survey that Mill uses 'liberal education' with point and purpose to signify a well-established concept whose validity is unquestioned and which is meaningful both to himself and his readers. It is a term of commendation carrying the traditional seal of approval first impressed upon it by the Greeks, and is therefore readily identified with 'good education'. It refers in particular (but not, Mill would claim, exclusively) to university courses in which classics plays a prominent part, and it implies not only a higher level of studies but also a certain breadth, expansiveness and generality which transcend the immediacy of specialised or vocational purposes. Also detectable in the term as Mill employs it is the suggestion (as one would expect) of liberation, of resistance to restraint, of intellectual competence and openness which bring both release from conformity and the opportunity for individual growth. All this we shall find confirmed, together with much additional content, in the detailed exploration which follows.

Mill seems to envisage three kinds (which are also in a sense levels or stages) of education — elementary, liberal and vocational (the last including, for our present purpose, the academic specialisation of the scholar). 'There are certain primary elements and means of knowledge which it is in the highest degree desirable that all human beings born into the community should acquire during childhood'; and from this premise he proceeds to argue the need for legislation to impose on parents the obligation to provide them.[10] This elementary education is all that the mass of the population, 'the children of the labouring class', can at present hope to receive (many, of course, were not even receiving this much in the 1840s when Mill penned the words above); its aim should be 'to cultivate common sense, to qualify them for forming a sound practical judgement of the circumstances by which they are surrounded'. Any intellectual studies that go beyond this 'indispensable groundwork' are 'chiefly ornamental'.[11] Vocational studies there must also be for those who need them:

> It is very right that there should be public facilities for the study of professions. It is well that there should be Schools of Law and of Medicine, and it would be well if there were schools of engineering and the industrial arts. The countries which have such institutions are greatly the better for them; and there is something to be said for having them in the same localities and under the same general superintendence as the establishments devoted to education properly so called. But these things are no part of what every generation owes to the next, as that on which its civilisation and worth will principally depend.

Those who need professional training are comparatively few, he continues, 'and even those few do not require them until after their education, in the ordinary sense, has been completed'. Universities are not places of professional education; they 'are not intended to teach the knowledge required to fit men for some special mode of gaining their livelihood. Their object is not to make skilful lawyers or physicians or engineers, but capable and cultivated human beings.'[12]

Distinct from both elementary and vocational studies is liberal education, an advanced but not unduly specialised course, which builds on the former and is the proper foundation for the latter. It is distinct also from highly specialised academic studies; again, Mill admits the need for these. A system of education must 'kindle the aspirations and aid the efforts of those who are destined to stand forth as thinkers above the multitude'; 'the cultivation of speculative knowledge' is a service to the community, and he therefore recommends public financial assistance for 'the maintenance of what has been called a learned class'.[13] For those who are not professional scholars, however (and even for those who are), specialisation has its dangers:

> Experience proves that there is no one study or pursuit which, practised to the exclusion of all others, does not narrow and pervert the mind, breeding in it a class of prejudices special to that pursuit, besides a general prejudice, common to all narrow specialities, against large views, from an incapacity to take in and appreciate the grounds of them.[14]

This restriction of vision, he writes in *Comte and Positivism*, is 'one of the great and growing evils of the time, and the one which most retards moral and intellectual regeneration'.[15]

Some may perhaps find in these pronouncements a suggestion of the ancient disdain for the tradesman, the labourer and even the highly skilled professional, who have no leisure to cultivate their essential humanity. But this would be unfair to Mill: he quite genuinely believed in the value of specialised intellectual inquiry (for the few who were capable of it) and in the power of knowledge to promote human improvement. For such professions as law, medicine and engineering he had a respect quite independent of their obvious practical value — rightly conceived they could be genuinely educative; nor did he wish to impose on society a Platonic stratification of classes into gold, silver and bronze. It was his ideal that all men and women should develop their talents to the full and have the leisure to do so; but the condition of English society convinced him that the realisation of such hopes was far distant, that in present circumstances a necessary first step, however small, was to secure mass elementary education. Given intelligent economic management and the will for justice and improvement, further advance would come in due course, but meanwhile liberal education could be available only to those 'who are not obliged by their circumstances to discontinue their scholastic studies at a very early age'.[16] Even for the masses he envisaged something larger than literacy, numeracy and training in a trade: they were to be improved not as workmen merely, but 'as rational beings . . . capable of foresight, accessible to reasons and motives addressed to their understanding'.[17] Liberal education was not intended as a privileged alternative to elementary and vocational studies, but as a normal development from the former and a necessary preparation for the latter.

It was noted earlier that Mill tends to equate 'liberal education' with 'general education'; certainly he switches readily from the one term to the other, thus indicating that 'generality' is for him a major constituent of 'liberal'. But 'generality' is itself a complex notion whose meaning is not immediately obvious. Much of what Mill included in it is suggested in two passages, one of which follows his exclusion of professional training from university studies (p. 205 above), and the other introduces his attack on the Cambridge course in 'Professor Sedgwick's Discourse'. In the former he argues that any value which professional training has depends not so much on itself as on the 'sort of minds' the students bring to it, 'what kind of intelligence and of conscience the general system of education has developed in them'. He continues:

> Men are men before they are lawyers or physicians or merchants or manufacturers; and if you make them capable and sensible men, they will make themselves capable and sensible lawyers or physicians. What professional men should carry away with them from a university is not professional knowledge, but that which should direct the use of their professional knowledge and bring the light of general culture to illuminate the technicalities of a special pursuit. Men may be competent lawyers without general education, but it depends on general education to make them philosophic lawyers — who demand, and are capable of apprehending, principles instead of merely cramming their memory with details. And so of all other useful pursuits, mechanical included. Education makes a man a more intelligent shoemaker, if that be his occupation, but not by teaching him how to make shoes; it does so by the mental exercise it gives and the habits it impresses.[18]

In the latter passage Mill contrasts the 'English mind' with the Continental, noting in the former the absence of 'enlarged and commanding views', the inability to consider any problem in the light of 'principles more extensive than itself'. There is no 'eagerness for large and comprehensive inquiry', no interest in 'the investigation of truth *as* truth', in the 'prosecution of thought for the sake of thought', in 'the great problem of man's nature and life'; no 'curiosity respecting the nature and principles of human society, the history or the philosophy of civilisation'.[19]

There are numerous points here which will be considered in their turn; but first it is clear that Mill had in mind a generality which consists in range of knowledge — 'the light of general culture', 'enlarged and commanding views'; this is implied also by what he says of vocational training and confirmed by the course of studies which he outlines in the *Inaugural Address.* These studies include classics, of course, as a major component, but also the natural sciences, mathematics and logic, psychology and physiology, historical studies, international law, moral philosophy and religion, and finally the various aesthetic arts — a formidable programme indeed if Mill intends to impose it on every student in its entirety (he does not definitely say this). What he has in mind, however, is not a detailed familiarity with each subject (nor, he is careful to explain, a mere smattering of superficialities) but a thorough knowledge of 'its leading truths' and principles of procedure.[20] Moreover, he is strongly critical of the 'strangely limited estimate of what it is possible for human beings to learn', an estimate resting on 'a tacit assumption that they are already as efficiently taught as they can ever be'; and he judged the possibilities of achievement by what he himself accomplished in an education which began with Greek at the age of three and gave him 'an advantage of a quarter of a century over my contemporaries'.[21] Some studies he specifically excludes — history and geography at the purely factual level ('Whoever really learnt history and geography except by private reading?')[22] and modern languages, which (again judging from his own experience) he believed could be readily picked up by spending a few months in the country itself. But what, it may be asked, are his criteria for *inclusion*? The answer to this should become clear in the pages that follow, but to anticipate briefly, a particular study must contribute to the acquisition of intellectual skills, to a coherent view of the range of knowledge, to moral insight and an awareness of human problems; it must assist in opening up 'the accumulated treasure of the thoughts of mankind',[23] and it must provide standards to assess achievement, one's own and others', in one or more of the three principal areas of human experience — intellectual, moral, aesthetic. There is no inconsistency, Mill points out, between such wide-ranging studies and a detailed knowledge of some limited area; indeed, there are positive advantages: 'It is this combination which gives an enlightened public: a body of cultivated intellects, each taught by its attainments in its own province what real knowledge is, and knowing enough of other subjects to be able to discern who are those that know them better.'[24]

Liberal education is 'general' in another and equally important sense: it is an education which leads to an understanding both of the broader truths which lie within particular areas of knowledge — physical science, say, or history — and of those which pervade the whole structure of knowledge. Within any one science there is a wealth of detail which only the expert can hope (or needs) to acquire; but the general student can at least grasp its outlines, recognise its specific problems and the features of purpose and method which distinguish it from other sciences. In psychology, for instance, while he cannot be expected to master the intricacies of specialised argument for and against associationism or about the nature of 'mental faculties', 'it is a part of liberal education to know that such controversies exist and, in a general way, what has been said on both sides of them.'[25] He can also acquire some conception of science as a whole: his education will include 'a philosophic study of the methods of the sciences, the modes in which the human intellect proceeds from the known to the unknown'. 'We must,' Mill continues, 'be taught to generalise our conception of the resources which the human mind possesses for the exploration of nature; to understand how man discovers the real facts of the world and by what tests he can judge whether he has really found them.' So too in historical studies: the great mass of factual data is the province of the professional academic, but the general student can discern its broad outlines and can be assisted in inferring

> what are the main differences between human beings and between the institutions of society at one time or place and at another, in picturing to himself human life and the human conception of life as they were at the different stages of human development, in distinguishing between what is the same in all ages and what is progressive, and forming some incipient conception of the causes and laws of progress.

This 'generality' of liberal education applies not only within different areas of study but over knowledge as a whole. It provides a panoramic view of knowledge, a distant and inclusive perspective, which is barred, inevitably, to a restricted expertise. Thus the student learns to methodise his knowledge: to look at every separate part of it in its relation to the other parts and to the whole; combining the partial glimpses which he has obtained of the field of human knowledge at different points into a general map, if I may so speak, of the entire region; observing how all knowledge is connected, how we ascend to one branch by means of another, how the higher modifies the lower and the lower helps us to understand the higher, how every existing reality is a compound of many properties, of which each science or distinct mode of study reveals but a small part, but the whole of which must be included to enable us to know it truly as a fact in Nature and not as a mere abstraction.[26]

He learns that there is indeed a structure in knowledge which transcends and illuminates its separate parts, a coherence to which different disciplines, different modes of experience essentially contribute and within which diverse items leap into unexpected relatedness. Hence to isolate, whether it be facts, theories or academic disciplines, is in a sense to distort, to falsify; more than this, it is an impoverishment of experience, a diminution of life's enrichment. He learns of different approaches to truth — observation, experiment, reasoning, moral and aesthetic insight — and of the epistemological and metaphysical problems associated with them; he learns of the assumptions, the often unacknowledged premises, which support the search for truth — the uniformity of nature, the reality of moral obligation, personal identity, the existence of an ideal perfection. From all this comes the recognition of the value of investigating 'truth *as* truth', of engaging in 'thought for the sake of thought'.[27] Thus, generality, far from being synonymous with superficiality, becomes itself a kind of depth; the wider perspective (like aerial photography) throws up features which are hidden from the specialist's close-up preoccupation with detail. 'To have a general knowledge of a subject,' Mill agrees, 'is to know only its leading truths'; but, he adds, it is 'to know these not superficially but thoroughly, so as to have a true conception of the subject in its great features'. Here, as always, Mill pitches his expectations high, and one suspects that this 'crown and consummation of a liberal education' is a prize beyond the reach of most — but not the less worth striving for in the hope of at least partial realisation.[28]

Mill further required of liberal education that it should effect in the student certain intellectual skills and disciplines, certain attitudes towards truth and knowledge. There is clear evidence of this in the preceding paragraphs on generality, and it is confirmed by numerous explicit statements both in the *Inaugural Address* and in earlier writings. In the essay 'On Genius' he contrasts contemporary education, whose emphasis is on crammed absorption of sterile information and which results, therefore, in defective mental training, with that of ancient Greece, where knowledge was first-hand, *discovered*, not taught: 'Education *then* . . . was a series of exercises to form the thinking faculty itself, that the mind, being active and vigorous, might go forth and know.' The student was not measured into a 'suit of ready-made truths', but helped 'to form to himself an intellect fitted to seek truth for itself and to find it'. The disputations of the philosophers were 'a kind of mental gymnastics, eminently conducive to acuteness in detecting fallacies, consistency and circumspection in tracing a principle to its consequences, and a faculty of penetrating and searching analysis'. Thus, what a man knew was his own, 'and every new acquisition strengthened the powers, by the exercise of which it had been gained'. 'The end of education,' he asserts, 'is not to *teach*, but to fit the mind for learning from its own consciousness and observation.' There are some studies, he explains, whose obvious results are few, but whose justification is that they 'train the faculties', 'form the mind' and promote 'a vigorous intellect'; logic, metaphysics and the classical languages are those he names. 'As the memory is trained by remembering,' he confidently affirms, 'so is the reasoning power by reasoning, the imaginative by imagining, the analytic by analysing, the inventive by finding out. Let the education of the mind consist in calling out and exercising these faculties; never trouble yourself about giving knowledge — train the *mind*.'[29] He makes similar claims in other writings of this early period; in 'Civilisation', for instance, he asserts the principle that education should 'call forth the greatest possible quantity of intellectual *power* and . . . inspire the intensest *love of truth*'; and he states as if it were an established fact that 'habits of discipline once acquired qualify human beings to accomplish all other things for which discipline is needed.'[30]

Again, similar views occur in Mill's description of his own education in the early chapters of the *Autobiography*. He particularly commends his early and rigorous training in logic; nothing, he writes, 'in modern education tends so much, when properly used, to form exact thinkers, who attach a precise meaning to words and propositions and are not imposed on by vague, loose or ambiguous terms'. He owed a like debt to the Platonic dialogues and to the exercise imposed by his father of making abstracts of the books he studied. He praises too the habit, encouraged from the earliest years of his instruction, of being the author of his own knowledge: his father strove, he tells us, 'even in an exaggerated degree to call forth the activity of my faculties by making me find out everything for myself'.[31] In the *Inaugural* the notion of mental training is an essential part of his case for liberal education: it is a liberal (general) education, he argues in the passage already quoted, that raises a lawyer above the level of professional competence, makes him a *philosophic* lawyer 'capable of apprehending principles'; so too, 'by the mental exercise it gives and the habits it impresses', it makes a shoemaker into an *intelligent* shoemaker. Translation from Latin and Greek induces care and precision in the use of language: by habitual use words and phrases become a mere coinage of intercourse, glibly accepted, slotted unthinkingly into mental pigeon-holes; the close attention to meaning demanded by accurate translation provides a valuable corrective.[32] Scientific instruction is 'a training and disciplining process to fit the intellect for the proper work of a human being'; it cultivates the skills of factual inquiry, discrimination in assessing evidence, caution in accepting conclusions.[33] Mathematics habituates the mind to demand clear premises and precise definition of terms; logic 'compels us to throw our meaning into distinct propositions and our reasonings into distinct steps', it is 'the great disperser of hazy and confused thinking', clearing up 'the fogs which hide from us our own ignorance'.[34] All these separate components of a liberal education contributed, so Mill believed, to the ideal of a disciplined mind, skilled to apply itself with rigour and economy to the pursuit of truth.

This notion of a general mental training, of broad intellectual skills that can be taught (or learnt) in one field of study and transferred to others, is little accepted at the present time. It is no longer fashionable (though not uncommon in popular educational discourse) to speak of 'mental faculties' — memory, imagination, observation, judgement, accuracy and so on — which can be trained for general application to any sphere of use. Psychological research and a more subtle analysis of these 'faculties' have given us a picture of the mind which is far more complex and at the same time more specific in its skills than is assumed in Mill's notion of mental training. To some extent, no doubt, Mill was misled by the implications of association psychology, whose conception of the mind was closer to physical and mechanical models and perhaps lent itself more readily to the idea of transferable training. It does not follow, however, that he was wholly wrong: though accuracy, for instance, is specific to Latin or mathematics or history rather than a generalised skill, it is possible to cultivate an *ideal* of accuracy which, whatever the subject of study, can protect against slipshod, unevidenced, unchecked conclusions; an *ideal* of truth which resists both self-deception and the blandishments of external persuasion; an *ideal* of initiative in inquiry as preferable to dressing up in borrowed information. It seems, therefore, not unreasonable to suppose that the kind of education which Mill conceives as liberal, by forming in the student appropriate ideals and attitudes, would lead him to a more discerning, honest, rationally controlled yet creative intellectual activity.

So far this discussion of liberal education has been confined to 'cognitive perspective' — the range of knowledge and the intellectual skills and habits of mind that Mill thought desirable. But liberal education, he believed, is more than cognitive; it is directed also towards personal growth, the *liberation* of potential, the development of the student as an individual and as a member of society. Personal growth is part of Mill's concept of individuality; it is a central theme of chapter iii of *On Liberty*, where he insists on 'the free development of individuality' and on man's humanity as something worth cultivating in its own right: 'Among the works of man which human life is rightly employed in perfecting and beautifying, the first in importance surely is man himself.'[35] It occurs in the *Inaugural*, here in close association with liberal education: 'Men are men before they are lawyers or physicians or merchants or manufacturers' and education is aimed at 'the perfection of our nature', at producing 'capable and cultivated human beings'.[36] Individuality is not enough, however: man is social; he owes obligations to society; he is a citizen; liberal education must therefore prepare him for this role. It must 'present all knowledge as chiefly a means to worthiness of life, given for the double purpose of making each of us practically useful to his fellow-creatures and of elevating the character of the species itself'. Liberally educated, a man will contribute to the formation of public opinion, protest against wrong, acquaint himself with public business and exercise a critical judgement on its transactions:

> Let not anyone pacify his conscience by the delusion that he can do no harm if he takes no part and forms no opinion. Bad men need nothing more to compass their ends than that good men should

look on and do nothing. He is not a good man who, without a protest, allows wrong to be committed in his name and with the means which he helps to supply, because he will not trouble himself to use his mind on the subject. It depends on the habit of attending to and looking into public transactions and on the degree of information and solid judgement respecting them that exists in the community, whether the conduct of the nation as a nation, both within itself and towards others, shall be selfish, corrupt and tyrannical or rational and enlightened, just and noble.[37]

In all this Mill is reasserting (with the added force of his own conviction, of course) the ancient ideal — Greek, Roman and Renaissance — of the involved and responsible citizen, the man (and, for Mill, the woman too) whose developed powers are used to enhance not only his own quality of life, but that of his fellow beings. Liberal education is thus both liberation and discipline, a freeing of capacity in growth and self-realisation, and at the same time a purposive direction of that capacity towards the obligations of citizenship and of humanity.

Mill accepted as axiomatic that to be human is to be moral, to be involved in situations and relationships which require decision as to what *ought* to be done. 'It is a fact in human nature,' he writes in 'Professor Sedgwick's Discourse', 'that we have moral judgements and moral feelings.'[38] All education should therefore include a moral element: 'It is a very imperfect education which trains the intelligence only and not the will. No one can dispense with an education directed expressly to the moral as well as the intellectual part of his being.'[39] The foundations of moral education, Mill recognises, are laid in the home 'in training the feelings and the daily habits': 'It is the home, the family, which gives us the moral or religious education we really receive' — though this, he adds, 'is completed and modified, sometimes for the better, often for the worse, by society and the opinions and feelings with which we are there surrounded'. What, then, is the peculiar task of liberal education? It is, first, to provide moral knowledge — knowledge of the principal systems of morality, ancient and modern, and of the different ethical premises which have been proposed as justifying moral decision: utility, natural justice, 'principles of practical reason' and so on. The instruction should be expository rather than dogmatic; the teacher's task is not 'to impose his own judgement, but to inform and discipline that of his pupil'. This does not prevent him from presenting reasoned argument for his own preference, if he has one; nor does it suppose 'an essentially sceptical eclecticism'; it does, however, entail an honest attempt to present the strengths and weaknesses of each system, each ethical premise with a view to eliciting 'the rules of conduct most advantageous to mankind'. A second task is to cultivate in students the skills required for moral judgement — such skills, for instance, as the capacity to seek out relevant facts and to assess them impartially, reference to moral premises and the ability to reason from them, an awareness (not unlike the scientist's) of the fallibility of one's conclusions. Mill says little on this aspect of moral education, but its necessity, as well as its possibility, can be inferred from his remarks on mental training.

Liberal education should also, thirdly, confront the student with standards of excellence to stimulate and assess his own endeavours, to promote elevation of character by the 'habitual vision of greatness'.[40] Mill has in mind here not only moral standards, but also intellectual and aesthetic; for these latter two are valuable both in themselves, as intimations of perfection in truth and beauty, and also in contributing significantly to moral improvement: 'There is . . . a natural affinity,' he writes, 'between goodness and the cultivation of the Beautiful', and 'to know the truth is already a great way towards disposing us to act upon it.'[41] It is part of the value of the classical writers that 'they show us . . . what excellence is and make us desire it'; of historical studies that they present a record 'of all great things which have been achieved by mankind . . . [of] the great principles by which the progress of man and the condition of society are governed'. Mathematics and experimental science provide 'the most perfect and successful models' of intellectual activity; art engenders a 'sense of perfection' which makes us 'demand from every creation of man the very utmost that it ought to give and render[s] us intolerant of the smallest fault in ourselves or in anything we do'.[42] Apart from its positive contribution to moral growth, this constant stimulus of the ideal serves also to counteract the bias towards mediocrity which Mill saw as a principal danger in democracy: 'To have a high standard of excellence often makes the whole difference of rendering our work good when it would otherwise have been mediocre.'[43] It was this fear that prompted his demand for a franchise weighted in favour of the better-educated; it also confirmed a predisposition (born, one suspects, of his early study of Plato's *Republic*) towards a kind of cultural elitism, a moral, intellectual and aesthetic leadership of 'the more cultivated few over the many'.[44]

High standards are themselves an incentive to moral endeavour, but they need also the inspiration of altruism which springs from a deep love of virtue and the habit of good will towards others. A negative conscience of restraint is not enough — to refrain from harm, to avoid illegality, while devoting one's energies to the pursuit of wealth or ambition:

> If we wish men to practise virtue, it is worth while trying to make them love virtue and feel it an object in itself and not a tax paid for leave to pursue other objects. It is worth training them to feel not only actual wrong or actual meanness, but the absence of noble aims and endeavours as not merely blamable but also degrading; to have a feeling of the miserable smallness of mere self in the face of this great universe, of the collective mass of our fellow creatures, in the face of past history and of the indefinite future — the poorness and insignificance of human life if it is to be all spent in making things comfortable for ourselves and our kin and raising them a step or two on the social ladder. Thus feeling, we learn to respect ourselves only so far as we feel capable of nobler objects.[45]

The roots of altruism, as of all moral training, are in the home, but liberal education has a part to play in reinforcing and extending the lessons learnt there. It does so by the inspiration of excellence derived from different studies, by the example of teachers and by 'the pervading tone of the place':

> Whatever it teaches it should teach as penetrated by a sense of duty; it should present all knowledge as chiefly a means to worthiness of life, given for the double purpose of making each of us practically useful to his fellow-creatures and of elevating the character of the species itself, exalting and dignifying our nature. There is nothing which spreads more contagiously from teacher to pupil than elevation of sentiment; often and often have students caught from the living influence of a professor a contempt for mean and selfish objects and a noble ambition to leave the world better than they found it. . . .

Even religion may have some influence; for despite his personal rejection of Christian theology, Mill admits that altruism can be sustained not only by envisaging 'an idealised posterity' in some Utopia yet to come, but also by 'the contemplation . . . of ideal perfection embodied in a Divine Being'.

It is in these recommendations for moral education that the present-day reader may be least disposed to agree with Mill. Is there not, he may ask, an excess of moral ardour here, an exaggerated paternalism which is inconsistent both with Mill's concern for freedom and with our own concept of the democratic open society? It is clearly impossible to argue out here a defence of Mill and of moral education, but some points can usefully be made. He is right to insist that man is a moral being, that moral training is an essential part of education and that its foundations are laid at home in childhood; these propositions are surely beyond dispute. Nor is it unreasonable to require that this basic moral training should be continued at school, where it can be amplified, possibly corrected and raised to the level of informed rational decision; to do this entails precisely what Mill suggests — providing moral knowledge, moral skills, standards of excellence and an environment which encourages altruism — and his views are confirmed by the findings of current moral education projects. A good education (or liberal or general, as one chooses) cannot exclude this moral component. Our present predicament is certainly no less urgent than in the England of Mill's time: greater freedom, greater permissiveness, greater opportunity for choice, all of them accentuated by the seductive pressures of commercialism, point to a need for guidance in responsible moral decision. What is questionable is whether the large modern comprehensive school, representing in staff and children a vast range of moral attitudes and motives, can ever provide (as smaller selective schools — and not only grammar schools — have been able to do) that 'pervading tone' which Mill rightly deemed necessary to support the direct moral instruction. Also questionable is the extension of his conception of moral education to the university. Students now are adults when they enter university; they expect to manage their own lives, choose their own moral principles, make their own moral decisions with a freedom and independence which resists any hint of moral conditioning. Moral direction is unwelcome unless specifically asked for; professors are not expected to radiate a noble altruism; and the complexity of a modern university is even less congenial to Mill's 'pervading tone' than the comprehensive school. Yet one expects a university to exemplify excellence, not only in scholarship and administration but also in the integrity, impartiality, dedication and human concern of its staff; to this extent at least one can agree with Mill in regarding it as an instrument of moral education. One can also respect his solicitude, exaggerated though it may now seem, that liberal education should include a strong moral element. Moreover, one must in fairness acknowledge his anxiety to avoid dogmatism, indoctrination and a prejudiced partiality of fact; of one thing he has no doubt: 'A university ought to be a place of free speculation.'[46] A conspicuous element in the concept of liberal education throughout much of its history has been the notion of balance. It has been conceived as an education which fosters a broad range of potential, allowing no one aspect of human nature to predominate, excluding none of the principal modes of experience; thus, it has aimed to cultivate body *and* mind, the man *and* the citizen, to give due weight to the sciences *and* the arts; it has opposed specialisation and vocational training as inimical to a balanced, proportioned development. The notion certainly appears in Mill, though not throughout his presentation of liberal education; for he says virtually nothing on the promotion of health and physique or on the cultivation of practical skills (though in the *Autobiography* he regrets the absence of the latter in himself). It is most obvious in the curriculum of studies proposed in the *Inaugural* (p.208 above), which not only opens to the student's gaze a panoramic sweep of knowledge but is particularly notable for its inclusion in equal partnership of a diversity of subjects — languages, sciences, mathematics, history, the arts — and for its special emphasis on the last.

Languages for Mill in this context meant Latin and Greek; modern languages could be acquired readily enough, he thought, in a few months' residence abroad. In the early part of the nineteenth century the role of classics as the core of any education beyond the elementary level was little questioned; James Mill took it for granted, so too did John, while deploring the inefficiency of the teaching. By 1867, the date of the *Inaugural Address*, the situation had changed; though much of his audience would be sympathetic, Mill could no longer assume a general assent to the educational value of classics. He therefore defends it at some length and with obvious feeling; his arguments were summarised above. Scientific instruction he also defends, not only in deference to the increasing demand for its recognition as a normal subject of the curriculum, but also from his own conviction (as the author of an eminent exposition of scientific method in his *Logic*) of its inherent value; it is, he writes, 'an indispensable necessity . . . recommended by every consideration which pleads for any high order of intellectual education at all'.[47] Science is valuable, of course, for the information it provides: civilised life and culture would be impossible without a steady advance in knowledge of natural laws and the properties of 'the things which we have to work with and to work among and to work upon'. It is not enough, however, that this should be available to the expert; an elementary knowledge of science must be diffused among the public, partly for its sheer interest — 'It is surely no small part of education to put us in intelligent possession of the most important and most universally interesting facts of the universe' — partly too to protect against the charlatan and the impostor. In conjunction with mathematics, its indispensable instrument, science is also valuable for its intellectual discipline: it induces the habit of seeking out the truth, exercises the skills of observation, experiment and reasoning, encourages discriminating selection of evidence and guards against hasty and ill-considered judgement. At the very least a familiarity with the methods of science 'does the useful service of inspiring a wholesome scepticism about the conclusions which the mere surface of experience suggests'; and this can be of immense benefit in daily life as well as in more specialised activities such as politics, industry and commerce. The value of mathematics for Mill was not merely, or even chiefly, its instrumentality as a tool of science. Its claim for a place in liberal education lay rather in its vindication of the power of reasoning — its implicit support for the claim 'that there actually is a road to truth by means of reasoning' — and in the training it provides in correct logical procedures along that road; it lay too in the notion, initially derived from mathematics and momentous in its intellectual significance, that there is 'a connected body of truth', including not only 'abstract number and extension, but the external facts of the universe'.

The importance of historical studies lies not so much in the acquisition of factual information — though this is necessary, of course, and should be accomplished, Mill believes, by the student's private reading — as in the generalisations derived from it. In this area liberal education should assist the student

> in collecting from history what are the main differences between human beings and between the institutions of society at one time or place and at another; in picturing to himself human life and the human conception of life as they were at the different stages of human development; in distinguishing between what is the same in all ages and what is progressive, and forming some incipient conception of the causes and laws of progress.

It should help him to view the great process of history

not as a mere narrative, but as a chain of causes and effects still unwinding itself before his eyes and full of momentous consequences to himself and his descendants; the unfolding of a great epic or dramatic action, to terminate in the happiness or misery, the elevation or degradation, of the human race; an unremitting conflict between good and evil powers, of which every act done by any of us, insignificant as we are, forms one of the incidents; a conflict in which even the smallest of us cannot escape from taking part, in which whoever does not help the right side is helping the wrong, and for our share in which, whether it be greater or smaller, and let its actual consequences be visible or in the main invisible, no one of us can escape the responsibility.[48]

Thus, history introduces the student to different conceptions of life and culture; it enables comparison and contrast of peoples and institutions; it provides stimulus to the imagination and the moral sense; it reveals something of the complex interchange of cause and effect over vast stretches of space and time. All this, one can agree, is of immense educational value in broadening and 'liberalising' thought and attitude. But Mill asks more than this: in the second of these passages he sees history as the unfolding of a cosmic drama, a struggle between good and evil in which each of us has an inescapable responsibility to side with the forces of happiness and elevation; he is imposing an interpretation on history and prescribing a moral duty for the student. Now this is the expression of a noble ideal and wholly in keeping with Mill's constant aspiration towards human improvement; but what he seems to be recommending here is not history merely but a kind of historicism, as Professor Popper describes it in *The Poverty of Historicism*, and it is questionable whether this is consistent with the neutral view of historical processes which he proposes elsewhere (e.g. in *Logic* VI, x, 3) or, more pertinently, with his own concept of a liberal education as non-dogmatic and non-prescriptive. In moral education, he tells us, it is no part of the teacher's task 'to impose his own judgement'; religious teaching 'should not be in the spirit of dogmatism, but in that of inquiry'; and 'whatever you do,' he tells his university audience at St Andrews, 'keep at all risks your minds open; do not barter away your freedom of thought.'[49]

That Mill's liberal curriculum should include a balance of linguistic, scientific and historical studies is hardly surprising: the place of classics was ensured by its still virtually unchallenged role in contemporary education as well as by his own profound admiration for the best in classical culture; the author of *A System of Logic* was unlikely to underestimate the educational value of the sciences; historical reading was among his earliest and most persistent delights, and there appears repeatedly in his writings a view of history as a texture of cause and effect, persons and processes, which offers interest, intellectual stimulus and moral insight. What *is* surprising, perhaps, to those who are only superficially acquainted with Mill, is the inclusion of religion in his programme of liberal studies and his passionate plea for aesthetic experience as an essential part of liberal education.

It is common knowledge that J. S. Mill, like his father, was agnostic in matters of religion: he was 'brought up from the first without any religious belief' and was thus 'one of the very few examples in this country of one who has not thrown off religious belief, but never had it'.[50] Yet he was not insensitive to the nature and importance of religion: 'The essence of religion is the strong and earnest direction of the emotions and desires towards an ideal object, recognised as of the highest excellence, and as rightfully paramount over all selfish objects of desire.' Its value 'as a source of personal satisfaction and of elevated feelings is not to be disputed'. He found cause for awe and wonder in the mystery of human existence in its setting of infinite space and time; he was impressed by the nobility of Jesus and the worth of the Christian ethic; and though he was unable to reconcile the existence of a perfect Creator with the manifest imperfection of 'so clumsily made and capriciously governed a creation as this planet and the life of its inhabitants', he accepted that the conception of such a Being was a possible source of altruistic inspiration.[51] The most effective religious (as also moral) education, he believed, is that of home and childhood; the function of institutional instruction, whether at school or university, is to provide factual information about religion — its history, its diversity, its psychology — and to encourage open discussion and honest commitment. The overriding consideration is truth — truth of fact and of conscience; and although Mill would no doubt grant, albeit reluctantly, a parent's right to imbue his children with his own beliefs, he rejected 'dogmatic inculcation from authority' from any place in the teacher's role: 'the teaching should not be in the spirit of dogmatism, but in that of inquiry. The pupil should not be addressed as if his religion had been chosen for him, but as one who will have to choose it for himself.'[52]

It might be suggested that Mill's (admittedly somewhat guarded)

defence of religious studies in the *Inaugural Address* was a mark of
respect for his audience, which included members of the Theological
Faculty and students preparing for the ministry (the latter, Alexander
Bain records, received with 'vociferous applause' the statement on
'free speculation').[53] This may be partly true, though it in no way
impairs the sincerity of what he says. However, no such reason can
be assumed for his apologia for the arts, which was prompted by no
motive save his own intense belief in their educational value. The
intellectual and the moral, about which he has spoken his mind in the
earlier part of the *Address*, 'are the two main ingredients of human
culture, but they do not exhaust the whole of it'. There is, he explains,

a third division which, if subordinate and owing allegiance to the
two others, is barely inferior to them and not less needful to the
completeness of a human being; I mean the aesthetic branch, the
culture which comes through poetry and art and may be described
as the education of the feelings and the cultivation of the beautiful.[54]

Behind the austere conventional image of Mill — 'the solemn bald
head, the black clothes, the grave expression, the measured phrases,
the total lack of humour'[55] — there lie a sensitivity to beauty, both in
nature and the various forms of art, and a feeling for the romantic
unsuspected by those who know him only in his major works. There
are glimpses of them in his childhood years: the grounds of Ford
Abbey, 'umbrageous and full of the sound of falling waters', which
provided for him 'a sort of poetic cultivation'; the mountain grandeur
of the Pyrenees; his delight in history and the heroic; the fascination
of Pope's *Iliad*; his early pleasure in music.[56] But James Mill had little
use for emotion; passionate feeling he deemed a form of moral
aberration.[57] For Bentham music and poetry were on a level with
pushpin, and the arts generally were merely a diversion for the idle
who might otherwise amuse themselves only 'in the hazardous and
bloody game of war'.[58] From the dreariness of emotional atrophy
imposed on him by his father's character and utilitarian orthodoxy
John eventually escaped as if into a world of spring sunshine and
flowers; starved and stifled by his education his capacity for aesthetic
and emotional response broke out rebelliously in the period of his
nervous crisis and thereafter established itself securely in his mature
personality. Henceforth, he tells us, 'the cultivation of the feelings
became one of the cardinal points in my ethical and philosophical
creed. . . I now began to find meaning in the things which I had read

or heard about the importance of poetry and art as instruments of human culture.'[59]

In the years that followed, up to 1843, he thought much and deeply about aesthetic experience and the arts, especially poetry. He read, and later met and conversed with, Wordsworth, Coleridge and Southey;[60] he delighted in Shelley and other romantic poets;[61] he wrote a number of reviews and critical articles, mainly on poetry but also on music and drama, and expounded in his two essays 'What is Poetry?' and 'The Two Kinds of Poetry' a developed theory of poetry and the arts.[62] In these and other writings he considers the nature of imagination ('the power by which one human being enters into the mind and circumstances of another', the artist's instrument of identification with his subject); of art ('the expression or embodying in words or forms of the highest and most refined parts of nature', 'a language for the most earnest feelings of the most susceptible minds', 'the endeavour after perfection in execution'); of style (the expression of meaning 'exactly and without any appearance of effort . . . as a man of sense and education, filled with his subject and quite indifferent to display, might be supposed to express it spontaneously').[63] Emotion, he is now convinced, is not only valuable in itself but has an essential role in the application of knowledge to morality.[64] Thus, it is hardly surprising to find him asserting in a letter to Carlyle that the artist is superior even to the logician and metaphysician in his intuitive perception and 'impressive' communication of truth:

> I conceive that most of the highest truths are, to persons endowed by nature in certain ways which I think I could state, intuitive; that is, they need neither explanation nor proof but, if not known before, are assented to as soon as stated. Now it appears to me that the poet or artist is conversant with *such* truths and that his office in respect to truth is to declare *them* and to make them *impressive*.[65]

The logician and metaphysician have a function in explaining the truths of the artist's insight to those who are incapable of understanding them intuitively; but 'the artist's is the highest part, for by him alone is real *knowledge* of such truths conveyed' and it is by him alone that truth becomes 'a living principle of action'.

This intense interest in poetry and aesthetic theory was not, as has been suggested, a transient phase in his experience, to be eclipsed by his absorption in logic, political economy and practical social problems; nor was it simply a campaign to convert his fellow utilitarians to a more balanced view of human nature.[66] The evidence suggests that Mill possessed an innate aesthetic sensitivity which was suppressed by his education, burgeoned after his emotional crisis and, at a lower level of intensity, remained an active and fruitful element in his personality; that once the void of his education had been filled, the emotional and aesthetic were established in him at a deep level of satisfaction and acceptance which no longer needed justification either to himself or to others. It is true that he ceased writing reviews and articles on poetry and that his energies shifted towards the composition and revision of his books, his administrative responsibilities at India House (until 1858) and his increasing involvement in social and political issues. Yet it is clear from references in Bain's biography,[67] from contemporary letters and journals, from his own correspondence and from his notes to James Mill's *Analysis* that his interest in literature and the arts persisted. Writing to Clara and George Mill in 1849 his mother mentions that 'we played at cards till 12 o'clock last night while he [John] played upon the piano without music some of his own compositions.'[68] Years later, in a note to the *Analysis*, he comments on the sensuous delight of music — single notes, harmony and melody — and its enrichment by associated ideas and feelings; in another note he defends the associationist account of beauty and cites Ruskin's *Modern Painters* in support of his argument.[69] In 1855 he writes enthusiastically to Harriet of his visits to museums and galleries in Rome and Florence — 'I find the pleasure which pictures and statues give me increases with every experience'; from Athens he writes with equal fervour of its temples and sculptures whose 'extreme beauty' surpassed his expectations. Nor did he lose his susceptibility to natural beauty: after climbing Pentelicus, on the outskirts of Athens, he comments: 'I never saw any combination of scenery so perfectly beautiful and so magnificent . . . the more than earthly beauty of this country quite takes away from me all care or feeling about historical associations'; in an earlier letter during the same tour he had written from Italy: 'Nothing can be more beautiful than this place. You can . . . imagine how I enjoy the beauty when I am *not* looking at it — now in this bedroom by candlelight I am in a complete nervous state from the sensation of beauty I am living among.'[70] Finally, it is inconceivable that Mill's undeviating integrity and intellectual honesty would have allowed him to write of the arts as he did in the closing pages of the *Inaugural Address* had his words not wholly matched what he, then in his sixties, still thought and felt.

Aesthetic experience was not only a lasting source of pleasure for Mill, an integral part of his personal life; he saw it also as an essential element in any mature and balanced person and vitally important for morality and democracy. 'Every human action,' he writes in his criticism of Bentham, 'has three aspects: its *moral* aspect, or that of *right* and *wrong*; its *aesthetic* aspect, or that of its *beauty*; its *sympathetic* aspect, or that of its *loveableness*.'[71] This is true of human action because it is true also of human nature; and although Mill's list is arguably incomplete, it establishes the aesthetic alongside the moral and social as an essential component of our humanity. Without it (as he knew from his bitter period of nervous depression) a man's growth is thwarted, his potential unfulfilled; for fullness of personal development aesthetic experience is indispensable. It is also, as he knew equally well, an abundant source of deeply satisfying enjoyment.

While necessary for personal completeness, it contributes also to the moral and social facets of our nature. There is space here only for a brief statement of Mill's position; for fuller discussion reference should be made to the articles noted.[72] Aesthetic experience purifies and elevates character by purging emotion of its more selfish elements, by the inspiration of perfection in beauty of form, colour, sound or language, and by its representation of loftiness in human character and achievement. The noblest end of poetry, he writes in his review of Tennyson's poems, is 'that of acting upon the desires and characters of mankind through their emotions to raise them towards the perfection of their nature'[73] — a purpose which Mill would certainly have extended to any other of the arts. 'Not what a boy or girl can repeat by rote,' he writes elsewhere, 'but what they have learnt to love and admire is what forms their character.'[74] Such elevation is itself a form of moral improvement; but the impact of aesthetic experience goes beyond this. It promotes imaginative sympathy, an identification of oneself with the lives, thoughts and feelings of others, and thereby thrusts one out of the sterile closed circuit of mere rules and precepts into a genuine and active concern for the well-being of one's fellow men. Further, it can provide a motivation for right action which moral knowledge and moral rules do not in themselves possess. The gap between knowing the good and doing it was a problem for Mill as it has been for all ethical thinkers; its solution, he thought, lay at least partly in the association of moral knowledge with the energising emotion derived from the arts — not by using them crudely as instruments of rhetorical indoctrination, but simply by the persuasion of their own aesthetic integrity; only thus can it become 'a living principle of action' (p.223 above). The relevance of the arts to democracy is now obvious: by elevating the individual, extending his sympathies and giving motivation to his moral beliefs, it both improves the quality of society ('the worth of a state . . . is the worth of the individuals composing it'),[75] thereby protecting it from the mediocrity which Mill considered a danger inherent in democratic institutions, and at the same time raises the level of mutual understanding and concern which are indispensable to the realisation of the democratic ideal.

Mill's view of aesthetic experience and the arts has been considered at length, partly to correct the false view — a shadow cast on him by James Mill and the cold utilitarianism of Bentham — that he was insensitive to beauty and the finer feelings, partly to emphasise his firm conviction of their essential place in any programme of liberal education. The passage of the *Inaugural Address* in which he makes his plea for the arts is eloquent and moving in itself, and aptly summarises much of his thought about them; it should be read as a whole — and, of course, as part of the total *Address*. Its final sentences, however, leave the reader in no doubt of the nobility of Mill's conception of the arts and of the earnestness with which he pleads their inclusion in a balanced education:

> No other human productions come so near to perfection as works of pure Art. In all other things we are, and may reasonably be, satisfied if the degree of excellence is as great as the object immediately in view seems to us to be worth; but in Art the perfection is itself the object. If I were to define Art, I should be inclined to call it the endeavour after perfection in execution. If we meet with even a piece of mechanical work which bears the marks of being done in this spirit — which is done as if the workman loved it and tried to make it as good as possible, though something less good would have answered the purpose for which it was ostensibly made — we say that he has worked like an artist. Art, when really cultivated and not merely practised empirically, maintains what it first gave the conception of, an ideal Beauty to be eternally aimed at, though surpassing what can be actually attained; and by this idea it trains us never to be completely satisfied with imperfection in what we ourselves do and are, to

idealise as much as possible every work we do and most of all our own characters and lives.[76]

In conclusion it may be asked whether the concept of liberal education retains any significance for the present time. Could the phrase be omitted now without semantic loss from our educational vocabulary and its place taken by terms which, if no more precise, are at least more appropriate to the social and pedagogic climate of comprehensive schools and mixed ability? Was Mill defending an ideal which, though meaningful to himself and his contemporaries, was doomed by social and educational change to ultimate irrelevance? These are large and complex questions which cannot be examined here in the depth they deserve, but the following comments may provide some guidance in seeking the answers.

Over the centuries there has accumulated within the concept a reservoir of ideas and values which have been available for the selective construction of different patterns of educational purpose. This reservoir includes: the distinction between slave and free, and, closely associated with this, vocational detachment, leisure for self-cultivation and a certain aura of privilege; liberation — release from restriction, whether positive in the deliberate limitation of experience for social, political or religious ends, or negative in the absence of opportunity; personal fulfilment in the realisation both of essential human characteristics (social, moral, aesthetic, etc.) and of individual capacities and aptitudes; excellence, particularly moral excellence, and high standards; intrinsic value, the notion that certain experiences are valuable or enjoyable just in themselves — beauty, for instance, in nature or art; citizenship and the acceptance of responsibility within and for the community; balance, harmony and proportion, both generally in personal growth and more specifically in curriculum content — a due attention to the range of knowledge, to different modes of knowing and experiencing, the avoidance of narrowness or excessive specialisation; particular curricular patterns — the Seven Liberal Arts of the Renaissance or, at the present time, Professor Hirst's 'forms of knowledge';[77] particular curricular emphases — 'music' (in the ancient sense), grammar and logic, eloquence, classical languages and literature; and finally liberality of *method* and the exclusion, as inconsistent with a proper education, of certain practices such as rote learning of information and indoctrination.

Of these items some have lost all significance for twentieth-century

Western societies and can be firmly discarded; such are the notion of privilege, the slave/free distinction (implicit in the Latin *liber, liberalis*) and vocational detachment. This last, built into the concept from classical times and assumed over the centuries to be an essential component, is clearly incompatible, in Mill's time as in ours, with the educational needs of an industrial society. Today vocational orientation is commonly accepted as educationally legitimate and is embodied both in the organisation of schools and in curricular practice. Other items are of greatly diminished importance: already by the time of the *Inaugural* it was evident that classics, which Mill so enthusiastically extolled, could not continue as the staple of the curriculum. Even with the best of teaching the ordinary schoolboy, as T. H. Huxley remarked, 'finds Parnassus uncommonly steep' and rarely gets to the top;[78] today Latin and Greek have but a tenuous hold in a diminishing number of schools.

The concept has been further eroded by the association of 'liberal' with social class — a relic in part of the ancient division between slave and free; thus, a liberal education is supposedly one that is imbued with 'middle-class values' (regularly a pejorative phrase), rejects 'working-class culture' and perpetuates undesirable social distinctions. For those who take this view the concept is not merely obsolete but socially and educationally obstructive. In addition, there has been a semantic weakening, brought about partly by the inclusion of new meanings, partly by the substitution of other terms — 'good', 'general', 'balanced', 'all-round' — to describe educational purpose. By making science an essential component, Mill, Huxley and others of the nineteenth century were adding a new dimension of meaning which rendered the traditional usage inadequate. More recently Professor Whitehead has rejected as fallacious the antithesis between technical and liberal education: 'There can be no adequate technical education which is not liberal, and no liberal education which is not technical.'[79] Here again, the merging of 'liberal' and 'technical', however amply justified in educational practice, diminishes the effectiveness of the concept by blunting its semantic edge.

There are several items, however, which have assumed far greater prominence and are now widely regarded as central to educational purpose and practice, criteria to judge not merely whether an education is good but whether it can be deemed education at all. Such are the notions of growth and release of potential, of full development, of man as man, possessed of an essential humanity to be appropriately fostered into maturity. Less crucial but nevertheless of acknowledged importance are generality, balance and the pursuit of excellence; citizenship too, preparation for life in a community of free but mutually dependent individuals, is a widely affirmed ideal; and education for leisure, not to the exclusion of vocational purpose but in recognition that life is more than livelihood, has an established place in educational programmes.

Should 'liberal education' be retained, then, to signify these current emphases and any new patterns of educational purpose which may be formed from the accumulated reservoir of components? There are arguments for and against. On the one hand it may be said that a concept of such Protean diversity, whose content is the product of historical accretion in widely different social environments and whose meaning can be selectively imposed according to individual prefer- ence, is more likely to impede than promote clarity of thought and communication. It is, furthermore, an emotionally charged term, to which there is attached a flavour compounded of elitist ideals, the public school tradition and middle-class privilege, a flavour which is distasteful in the present social and educational climate. Even the literary and humane bias of the traditional concept, though it points to objectives in themselves desirable, can obscure the necessary contribution to education of science and technology (despite the claims of Mill, Huxley, Whitehead and many others); likewise, its emphasis on intellect and reason, even when this includes the sciences, can distract attention from the needs of children whose gifts are practical and artistic. In reply it can be countered that emphasis on literary and humane studies is of greater importance in the present era of technology and computers than ever it has been in the past; that excellence and high standards are indispensable in any society and especially in one threatened by a pervasive mediocrity; that intellectual rigour is likewise of enhanced value in a culture where mass communication and the proliferation of stimulus-response techniques are eroding the need and the capacity to think. Further, besides its obsolete and now only dimly audible echoes of slavery, dominance and privilege, 'liberal education' has obvious etymological, conceptual and even emotive links with freedom; it thus directs attention to, and may help to revitalise, an essential element in our social and educational ideals.

These arguments are less about *usage*, which is the question at issue, than about content, method and aims. What needs to be asked is whether thought and discussion will gain or lose in clarity, precision and intelligibility by the continued use of 'liberal' to describe education. Historical significance it certainly has: Aristotle knew what he meant by it; so did the writers and educators of the Renaissance and of the nineteenth century; in such contexts the word can scarcely be avoided. But what of today? To the present writer the balance of argument seems against it. Historical associations can easily mislead by diverting attention from present realities; emotive suggestion, especially when, as in this instance, it conveys ambivalently both disfavour and approval, is a notorious impediment to clear thought and rational discussion. Add to this the complexity of the concept, its diversity of content and the lack of agreement as to what sort or quality of education it signifies, and one must incline to the conclusion that for the time being at least educators would be well advised to exclude it from their vocabulary.

PHILOSOPHICAL ISSUES
Liberal education

Liberal education is another topic which has been discussed down the centuries — ever since Aristotle gave his account of it in *Politics* VIII; the different meanings attached to the words make an interesting study in the relation between education and its cultural context. New impetus has been given to debate on the meaning and content of liberal education by Professor Hirst's paper 'Liberal Education and the Nature of Knowledge', referred to on p. 227 above (see also chapters 4 and 6 of his *Knowledge and the Curriculum*. His views have been criticised in a number of papers and partially modified as a result; see *J. Phil. Ed.,* vol. 6, no. 2, 1972 (Hindess, E.); vol. 7, no. 2, 1973 (Hirst, P. H.); *Ed. Ph. and Th.*, vol. 2, no. 1, 1970 (Gribble, J.); vol. 3, no. 1, 1971 (Hirst, P. H.); no. 2 (Phillips, D. C.); vol. 6, no. 1, 1974 (Watt, A. J.); vol. 7, no. 2, 1975 (Simpson, K., Simons, M.); there is also chapter 3 of Brent, A., *Philosophical Foundations for the Curriculum.* Professor Peters has two papers on liberal education in his *Education and the Education of Teachers* (Routledge and Kegan Paul, 1977).

For nineteenth-century interpretations of liberal education more or less contemporary with Mill, see Farrar, F. W., ed., *Essays on Liberal Education* (1867); Newman's *The Idea of a University* (1852) embodies another statement of liberal education which affords an interesting comparison with Mill's.

Notes

The following abbreviations are used in the notes to the text:

Autob.   *Autobiography*, ed. Laski, H.J. (World's Classics, Oxford University Press, 1924, etc.).

CW   Collected Works (University of Toronto Press and Routledge and Kegan Paul).

D & D   *Dissertations and Discussions,* vols. I-III (2nd edn, 1867), vol. IV (1875).

EERS   *Essays on Ethics, Religion and Society* (Collected Works X).

EES   *Essays on Economics and Society* i and ii (Collected Works IV and V).

EL   *Earlier Letters, 1812-1848* i and ii (Collected Works XII and XIII).

EPC   *Essays on Philosophy and the Classics* (Collected Works XI).

EPS   *Essays on Politics and Society* i and ii (Collected Works XVIII and XIX).

Hamilton   *An Examination of Sir William Hamilton's Philosophy* (6th edn, 1889).

Inaugural   *Inaugural Address at the University of St Andrews,* in *John Stuart Mill on Education*, ed. Garforth, F.W. (Teachers College Press, 1971).

Lib   *On Liberty,* ed. Fawcett, M.G., (World's Classics, Oxford University Press, 1912, etc.; in one volume with *Representative Government* and *The Subjection of Women*).

LL   *Later Letters, 1849-1873* i-iv (Collected Works XIV-XVII).

Logic   *A System of Logic: Ratiocinative and Inductive* i and ii (Collected Works VII and VIII).

PPE	*Principles of Political Economy* i and ii (Collected Works II and III).
Repr. Gov.	*Considerations on Representative Government,* ed. Fawcett, M.G. (World's Classics, Oxford University Press, 1912, etc.; in one volume with *On Liberty,* etc.).
S. of W.	*The Subjection of Women,* ed. Fawcett, M.G. (World's Classics, Oxford University Press, 1912, etc.; in one volume with *On Liberty,* etc.).
Schn. *ELS*	*Mill's Essays on Literature and Society,* ed. Schneewind, J.B. (Collier Books, 1965).
Schn. *EW*	*Mill's Ethical Writings,* ed. Schneewind, J.B. (Collier Books, 1965).
Warnock	*Utilitarianism, On Liberty,* etc., ed. Warnock, M. (Collins, 1962).

Wherever possible quotations are taken from and references made to the volumes of the Collected Works; some important works have not yet appeared in this series, notably the *Autobiography,* the *Inaugural Address, Sir William Hamilton's Philosophy* and *The Subjection of Women;* the editions used for these are indicated above. Since the Collected Works may not be easily available to all readers, I have added, for some of Mill's writings, references to more accessible editions.

PART I: Personal and Historical

1   *Autob.,* p. 7.
2   *ib.,* pp. 7-8.
3   *ib.,* p. 6.
4   *ib.,* p. 16.
5   *ib.,* p. 19.
6   *ib.,* p. 18.
7   *ib.,* p. 20.
8   *ib.,* p. 25.
9   Packe, M. St. J., *The Life of John Stuart Mill,* pp. 56-9.
10   *Autob.,* p. 92.
11   *ib.,* ch. 5.
12   *ib.,* p. 31.
13   *ib.,* p. 26.
14   *ib.,* p. 213.
15   Packe, M. St. J., *op. cit.,* p. 450.
16   *Hansard,* vol. 191, col. 1048, 21 April 1868.
17   For these see: *Autob.,* pp. 226-30, and 'The Contest in America', *Fraser's Magazine* 65 (February 1862); 'The Negro Question', *Fraser's Magazine*

41 (January 1850), and, for Jamaica and Governor Eyre, *Autob.*, pp. 251-4, and Packe, M. St. J., *op. cit.,* pp. 466-72.
18 Packe, M. St. J., *op. cit.,* pp. 501-3.
19 'The Tom-foolery at Oxford', *Monthly Repository* 8 (1834), p. 525; 'Debate on the Universities Admission Bill', *ib.*, p. 592.
20 'Sedgwick's Discourse', *EERS*, pp. 33-4. For another attack on the universities, see his essay 'Civilisation' (1836).
21 Burston, W.H., ed., *James Mill on Education,* p. 71.
22 Quoted in Lawson, J. and Silver, H., *A Social History of Education in England,* p. 241.
23 An Infant School Society was founded in London in 1824 under the direction of Samuel Wilderspin, who travelled the country lecturing and helping to establish schools; a Glasgow Infant School Society was founded in 1827, and the Home and Colonial Infant Society in 1836, with the express purpose of promoting Pestalozzi's ideas.
24 *Hansard,* vol. 20. col. 166, 30 July 1833.
25 'The Claims of Labour', *EES* i, p. 378.
26 Quoted in Lawson, J. and Silver, H., *op. cit.,* p. 275.
27 This is the commonly accepted view; for another, more favourable, see Hurt, J.S., *Education in Evolution: Church, State, Society and Popular Education 1800-1870* (Hart-Davis, 1971) and Sylvester, D.W., *Robert Lowe and Education* (Cambridge University Press, 1974).
28 Quoted in Lawson, J. and Silver, H., *op. cit.,* p. 305.
29 'Civilisation', *EPS* i, p. 143n. (Schn. *ELS*, p. 178n.).
30 *Hansard*, vol. 182, col. 1263, 13 April 1866.
31 *ib.*, vol. 187, cols 826-7, 20 May 1867.
32 *ib.*, vol. 189, col. 374, 29 July 1867.
33 *ib.*, vol. 192, cols 1928-9, 23 June 1868.
34 *Parliamentary Papers* 1854-5, vol. XX, pp. 92-8.
35 *Parliamentary Papers* 1867-8, vol. XXVIII, Part II, vol. ii, pp. 61ff. (quotations on pp. 65, 66).
36 *The Times,* 26 March 1870.
37 See the bibliography, Mill's Writings (ii), 1831/3, Despatches to India.
38 *EL* i, p. 233.
39 *PPE* ii, p. 950.
40 'Thoughts on Parliamentary Reform', *EPS* ii, p. 327.
41 'Centralisation', *EPS* ii, p. 591.
42 'Lord Brougham's Defence of the Church Establishment', *Monthly Repository* 8 (1834), p. 443.
43 *EPS* i, p. 303 (*Lib.*, p. 130); *PPE* ii, p. 950.
44 *EPS* i, p. 302 (*Lib.*, p. 130).
45 Quoted in Himmelfarb, G., ed., *J. S. Mill On Liberty* (Penguin Books, 1974), p. 45.
46 *EPS* i, p. 263 (*Lib.*, p. 73).
47 *ib.*, p. 269 (*Lib.*, p. 82).
48 'National Education', *Monthly Repository* 8 (1834), p. 357.

PART II: Scientific Foundations

1 *Experientialism*

1 'Professor Sedgwick's Discourse', *EERS,* p. 49.
2 *Essay concerning Human Understanding* II, i, 2.
3 *EL* ii, p. 412.

4   *Autob.*, pp. 190-1.
5   *Hamilton*, p. 627.
6   'Coleridge', *EERS*, pp. 128-9.
7   *Logic* ii, p. 930; *ib.*, p. 792; *Hamilton*, p. 627.
8   *Autob.*, p. 233.
9   Anschutz, R.P., *The Philosophy of J. S. Mill*, p. 121.
10   *Autob.*, p. xv.
11   'Nature', *EERS*, pp. 379-80.
12   *Logic* ii, p. 949.
13   'Of the Definition of Political Economy', *EES* i, p. 312. In making the 'is/ought' distinction, Mill no doubt had in mind the celebrated passage in Hume's *Treatise* III, i, 1; the distinction has become a well-worn topic of twentieth-century ethical discussion, for which see above, p.79.
14   *Logic* ii, p. 844; he qualifies this misleadingly by requiring that the facts 'follow one another according to constant laws, although those laws may not have been discovered, nor even be discoverable by our existing resources'. He thus seems to stipulate a metaphysical definition of fact which is inconsistent with a strict experientialism; there may well be 'rogue' or random facts which resist inclusion within any system of explanation; to suppose otherwise is to assume a uniformity in nature of which there is no proof (which is what he apparently did — see the following paragraphs).
15   *Hamilton*, p. 622.
16   'Nature', *EERS*, p. 374.
17   *Logic* ii, pp. 845-6.
18   For instance, Anschutz, R.P., *The Philosophy of J. S. Mill;* Ryan, A., *The Philosophy of John Stuart Mill.*
19   *Logic* i, p. 309.
20   *Hamilton*, p. 477.
21   *Logic* i, pp. 304, 430.
22   *Logic* i, pp. 307-9; on pp. 574-5 he does qualify his position by saying that causal uniformity must be taken as holding only in those parts of the universe where it has been found to hold. See also *Comte and Positivism, EERS*, p. 293.
23   *Hamilton*, p. 248; Locke, *Essay* IV, iii, 29; Hume, *Enquiries* IV, i, 26. See also *Logic* i, p. 471: explanation 'is but substituting one mystery for another, and does nothing to render the general course of nature other than mysterious; we can no more assign a *why* for the more extensive laws than for the partial ones'.

2   *Science and Human Nature*

1   *EL* i, p. 36.
2   *Autob.*, p. 112.
3   *The Improvement of Mankind*, p. 67.
4   *Logic* ii, pp. 943ff. ('the Art of Life', p. 949).
5   *Autob.*, pp. 133ff.
6   *Logic* ii, p. 835. Mill's 'moral sciences' are roughly equivalent to our 'social sciences', including psychology, sociology, political science and economics — the 'human sciences' as distinct from the 'natural sciences'.
7   *ib*, p. 834.
8   *ib.*
9   e.g. *Lib.*, ch. 3; *EL* i, pp. 207-8.
10   *Hamilton*, p. 2; *Inaugural*, pp. 200ff. (Cf. *LL* iv, p. 1586: 'Psychology,

ethics, and politics, in the widest sense of the terms, are the really important studies now, both for one's own instruction and for exercising a useful influence over others.')

11 *Logic* ii, pp. 844, 833. On the difficulties of experimental inquiry, see pp. 865-6.

12 *ib.* i, p. 379.

13 *ib.*, pp. 835, 836-7. See *Autob.*, pp. 143-4; it is clear from this passage that Mill's interest in the problem of freedom and necessity was not only philosophical but also deeply personal; the same concern is apparent in a letter which he wrote to de Tocqueville a few months after the publication of the *Logic* (*EL* ii, p. 612).

14 *Logic* ii, pp. 836, 841, 839, 838, 839.

15 *Hamilton*, p. 576.

16 *Logic* ii, p. 837.

17 *ib.*, p. 838.

18 The quotations that follow are in *Logic* ii, pp. 840, 839, 840, 839, 840, 841.

19 *ib.*, p. 841.

20 *Hamilton*, p. 578.

21 *Repr. Gov.*, ch. 2.

22 *Logic* ii, p. 937.

23 *Hamilton*, p. 576.

24 Professor A. J. Ayer discusses these issues in his essay 'Man as a Subject for Science' (delivered as the sixth Auguste Comte Memorial Lecture at the London School of Economics, 1964; published in Laslett, P. and Runciman, W.G., eds, *Philosophy, Politics and Society*, 3rd series); he concludes:

> The strength of the determinists lies in the fact that there seems to be no reason why the reign of law should break down at this point [i.e. human behaviour], though this is an argument which seemed more convincing in the age of classical physics than it does today. The strength of the indeterminists lies in the fact that the specific theories which alone could vindicate or indeed give any substance to their opponents' case have not yet been more than sketched, though this not to say that they never will be. Until such theories are properly elaborated and tested, I think that there is little more about this topic that can be usefully said. (p. 24)

25 *Logic* ii, p. 846; the quotations that follow are on pp. 847-8.

26 *ib.*, p. 849.

27 *ib.*, pp. 851, 852; on observation and experiment, see *Logic* ii, pp. 865ff. and *Hamilton*, p. 178; Locke's 'ideas' (mentioned below) referred to virtually any mental content — sensations and feelings as well as thoughts.

28 *Logic* ii, p. 851.

29 *Hamilton*, p. 380.

30 James Mill, *Analysis of the Phenomena of the Human Mind*, vol. 2, pp. 174-5 (J.S.M.'s note).

31 On this see 'Nature', *EERS*, pp. 418-19: 'Human existence is girt round with mystery: the narrow region of our experience is a small island in the midst of a boundless sea, which at once awes our feelings and stimulates our imagination by its vastness and its obscurity' (and the remainder of the paragraph).

3   *Association Psychology*

 1   *LL* i, p. 239.
 2   'Bain's Psychology' *EPC*, pp. 344-5 (*D & D* III, p. 103).
 3   *ib.*, p. 341 (*D & D* III, p. 97).
 4   *de Memoria* II, 45lb ff.
 5   *Essay* II, xxxiii, 2.
 6   *Treatise* I,4
 7   *Logic* ii, p. 851.
 8   *Autob.*, pp. 191, 233.
 9   *Hamilton*, p. 401.
 10 *Logic* ii, p. 852.
 11 *ib.*, p. 854; on 'mental chemistry', see his note in James Mill's *Analysis*, vol. 2, pp. 233ff.
 12 *ib.*
 13 *Analysis*, vol. 1, pp. 403-4.
 14 *ib.*, p. 412.
 15 *ib.*, p. 423.
 16 *Logic* ii, pp. 856, 859.
 17 *ib.*
 18 *Hamilton*, pp. 188-9.
 19 *ib.*, p. 225 (cf. pp. 231-2).
 20 *ib.*, p. 227.
 21 *ib.*, p. 231; the quotations that follow are on p. 232.
 22 *ib.*, p. 238.
 23 *ib.*, p. 241.
 24 *ib.*, p. 248.
 25 *ib.*, pp. 186, 184; and on introspection, see also pp. 177-9.
 26 'Bain's Psychology', *EPC*, pp. 354ff. (*D & D* III, pp. 119ff.).
 27 *Hamilton*, pp. 342, 345.
 28 *ib.*, p. 355.
 29 *ib.*, p. 241.

4   *Ethology*

 1   *EPS* i, p. 310 (*Lib.*, p. 141).
 2   *Logic* ii, p. 863.
 3   *ib.*, p. 864.
 4   *ib.*, pp. 864-5. Mill's argument is not as clear as it might be, for it is not immediately obvious that 'universal laws' in the passage quoted are not in fact the basic causal laws of psychology; later, however, he says plainly (p. 869) that the laws of the formation of character are 'derivative laws, resulting from the general laws of mind'. He cites lying as an instance of how general laws of mind may combine with specific patterns of circumstances to produce effects which may be generalised into laws of behaviour (p. 862).
 5   Bain, A., *John Stuart Mill*, pp. 78-9; see also *LL* ii, p. 645: 'a subject I have long wished to take up, at least in the form of Essays, but have never felt myself sufficiently prepared'.
 6   *Logic* ii, p. 873; the following quotations are on the same page.
 7   *ib.*, pp. 873-4.
 8   *ib.*, p. 874.
 9   *ib.*, p. 869.

10 *ib.*, pp. 861, 864, 862; on the status of 'empirical laws', 'derivative laws' and 'causal laws', see Anschutz, R.P., *op. cit.,* p. 93, and Ryan, A., *The Philosophy of John Stuart Mill,* pp. 68ff. and 182-3.
11 *ib.*, p. 870.
12 *ib.*, pp. 870, 869; cf. p. 872. 'ethology, the deductive science, is a system of corollaries from psychology, the experimental science.'
13 *ib.*, p. 873.
14 *ib.*
15 Ward, J., 'John Stuart Mill's Science of Ethology', p. 450; *Logic* ii, p. 873.
16 Bain, A., *John Stuart Mill,* p. 79.
17 *Logic* ii, p. 943. Packe has an interesting comment on ethology in his *Life of John Stuart Mill,* p. 271:

> The Science of Ethology is still unwritten. It is a sobering reflection that until it is, until it can be fully understood how people and races come to be as they are as a result of their circumstances, no great improvement can be hoped for in the field of human relations; and all our tremendous advances in material science must serve more to the constriction than to the enlargement of the human spirit.

He refers also to a warning of its possible dangers in Hayek, F.A., *The Counter Revolution of Science.*

5 *The Practical Arts*

1 In a note to his text Mill distinguishes his present use of 'art' in its 'older and, I hope, not yet obsolete sense', i.e. as a systematic body of purposive skills (Greek T∈χνη), from the aesthetic meanings.
2 *Logic* ii, pp. 943, 874.
3 *ib.*, p. 949.
4 *ib.*, pp. 944-5.
5 *ib.*, p. 946.
6 *ib.*
7 *ib.*, pp. 947-8.
8 *ib.*, p. 948.
9 Quotations thus far, *ib.*, pp. 950, 949.
10 *ib.*, p. 951 (also the following quotation); cf. the opening paragraphs of Aristotle's *Ethics*, Book I; the term *philosophia prima* is Aristotle's, but not quite in his sense; for him it was 'the science of being', more akin to metaphysics.
11 *ib.*, p. 952.
12 *Republic* 420b, 519e (ed. Lee, 2nd edn, pp. 185-6, 323-4); see Barrow, R., *Plato, Utilitarianism and Education,* ch. 1.
13 *Logic* ii, p. 950.
14 *ib.*, p. 946.
15 *ib.*, p. 895; 'barbarism' presumably because it is (for a classicist) a somewhat abhorrent combination of Latin and Greek roots. This is the wording of the 8th edition; earlier he had written: 'which I shall henceforth, with M. Comte, designate by the more compact term sociology.'
16 *ib.*, pp. 875, 878.
17 *ib.*, pp. 877, 879.
18 *ib.*, p. 895.
19 *ib.*, p. 911.
20 *ib.*, p. 926.
21 *ib.*, p. 936.

22   *ib.*, pp. 929-30.
23   *Autob.*, p. 19.
24   *Times Educational Supplement*, 10 March 1972.
25   Juvenal, *Satires* II, vi, 347-8; Mill is perhaps echoing this quotation in his diary entry of 22 January 1854: 'and who will educate the educators?' (Schn. *ELS*, p. 350).

PART III: The Educative Process

1   *Introductory*

1   *Inaugural*, pp. 153-4.
2   'Tocqueville on Democracy in America' (1840), *EPS* i, pp. 168-9 (*D & D* II, pp. 24-5, Schn. *EW*, pp. 121-2).
3   *Autob.*, p. 293; *EPS* i, pp. 264-5 (*Lib.*, pp. 75-6); *EPS* ii, pp. 393ff., 467-9, 478-9 (*Repr. Gov.*, pp. 172ff., 274-7, 289-90).
4   *Autob.*, pp. 46-8; *PPE* ii, p. 756.
5   *LL* i, p. 22; 'Utility of Religion', *EERS*, p. 409.
6   *Utilitarianism, EERS*, p. 235 (Schn. *EW*, p. 309; Warnock, p. 289).
7   *ib.*, *EERS*, pp. 217-18 (Schn. *EW*, p. 291; Warnock, p. 268).
8   *Comte and Positivism, EERS*, p. 339.
9   *PPE* ii, p. 940; *EPS* i, p. 268 (*Lib.*, p. 81).
10 *EPS* i, pp. 261, 270 (*Lib.*, pp. 70-1, 83).
11 *EPS* ii, p. 389 (*Repr. Gov.*, p. 166); *S. of W.*, pp. 442ff., 477ff., 507ff. and *passim*.
12 *EERS*, p. 397.
13 *EPS* i, p. 261 (*Lib.*, p. 70).
14 *S. of W.*, pp. 542-3.
15 *PPE*, p. 208; the two following quotations are on pp. 208-9.
16 *Utilitarianism, EERS*, p. 236 (Schn. *EW*, p. 311; Warnock, p. 290).
17 'Bentham', *EERS*, p. 109 (Schn. *ELS*, p. 279).
18 'Utility of Religion', *EERS*, p. 404.
19 'Civilisation', *EPS* i, p. 144 (*D & D* I, p. 201; Schn. *ELS*, p. 179).
20 *EPS* i, p. 243 (*Lib.*, p. 43).
21 *Inaugural*, pp. 177, 184ff.
22 *LL* iii, p. 1346.
23 *EPS* i, p. 243 (*Lib.*, p. 44).
24 'On Genius', Schn. *ELS*, pp. 96-8.
25 'Civilisation', *EPS* i, pp. 129, 133 (*D & D* I, pp. 177, 183; Schn. *ELS*, pp. 161, 165).
26 See above, pp.46-7.
27 *Autob.*, pp. 232-3.
28 *Thoughts concerning Education*, p. 95 (para. 67).
29 *The English Utilitarians*, vol. 3, p. 273; quoted in Roellinger, F.X., 'Mill on Education', p. 247, from Ward, W., *Men and Matters* (Longmans, 1914).
30 'Utility of Religion', *EERS*, p. 409. In fairness, one should bear in mind Mill's consistent view of education as wider than schooling; and it is true that *total* control of environment can achieve far more than the few daily hours of compulsory attendance (and is correspondingly more dangerous!). James Mill took the same extended view of education. In letters to Comte John twice writes of Helvetius' exaggerations (*EL* ii, pp. 526, 605).
31 *Essay* II, i, 2.
32 *John Stuart Mill*, pp. 146, 147.
33 *Autob.*, p. 26: 'If I had been by nature extremely quick of apprehension. . . .'

34 'Bain's Psychology', *EPC*, p. 354 (*D & D* III, pp. 119, 120); and see James Mill's *Analysis*, vol. 2, pp. 354ff.

35 *ib.*, p. 355 (*D & D* III, p. 122).

36 *Analysis*, vol 2, pp. 372ff. (quotations on pp. 373, 375).

37 *ib.*, pp. 279, 262. See also *Autob.*, pp. 15, 16, where James Mill strove to make John 'as far as possible understand and feel the utility of' his studies — aware, no doubt, of the effect of this on attention. It is interesting to note what Bentham says about it in *Chrestomathia:*

> *Experience, observation, experiment;* in these three words may be seen the sources of all our knowledge. Of these, *experience* is without effect, any farther than as it has had *observation* for its accompaniment; and, in the very idea of *experiment*, that of observation is included. Upon *observation* therefore it is — upon *observation*, that is upon *attention* applied to the subject with effect — that everything depends. (Notes to Chrestomathic Tables, Table I, no 33)

38 'Bain's Psychology', *EPC*, p. 349 (*D & D* III, p. 110).

39 'Grote's Aristotle', *EPC*, p. 510 (*D & D* IV, p. 228).

40 'Sedgwick's Discourse', *EERS*, p. 56. He complains in a letter to Comte of the neglect of educational theory (to which 'les exagérations d'Helvetius' have at least given some impetus), *EL*, ii, p. 526.

41 *EPS* i, p. 263 (*Lib.*, p. 73).

42 *Autob.*, pp. 116-17.

43 McCloskey, H.J., *John Stuart Mill*, p. 97: '. . . Mill was seriously exposed to the danger of becoming (what he for a brief time became) a moral totalitarian'; see also Cowling, M., *Mill and Liberalism*, and, for an opposing view, Rees, J.C., 'Was Mill for Liberty?'

44 *Inaugural*, p. 163; *Thoughts concerning Education*, p. 197 (para. 165).

45 'Education', in Burston, W.H., ed., *James Mill on Education*, p. 98 and n. 16, p. 196.

46 For the experimental schools and influences of the period, see Stewart, W.A.C., *Progressives and Radicals in English Education.* For Robert Owen, see *EL* i, p. 47; *LL* iv, p. 1948; *Hamilton*, pp. 586ff. For Charles Dickens, see *EL* i, p. 343; *LL* i, p. 190, iv p. 1740. On Mill and the 'Gradgrindery' of Dickens the following articles are of interest: Fielding, K.J., 'Mill and Gradgrind'; Alexander, E., 'Disinterested Virtue: Dickens and Mill in Agreement'; Baker, W.J., 'Gradgrindery and the Education of J. S. Mill'.

47 *Autob.*, pp. 31, 24, 26-7.

48 'On Genius', Schn. *ELS*, p. 101.

2 *Environmentalism*

1 'Education', in Burston, W.H., *op. cit.,* pp. 58, 52.

2 *ib.*, pp. 99, 70.

3 *Autob.*, p. 115.

4 *ib.*, p. 116.

5 *ib.* See also *The Early Draft*, pp. 178ff.

6 *ib.*, pp. 47ff.

7 'Education', in Burston, W.H., *op. cit.*, p. 69.

8 *ib.*, p. 71.

9 *Thoughts concerning Education*, pp. 25-6 (para. 1); the quotations that follow are on pp. 92 (para. 66), 59 (para. 102), 92 (para. 66), 95 (para. 67).

10 *S. of W.,* pp. 494ff. (quotations on pp. 499, 496, 502, 507).

11 *ib.*, p. 501.

12 'Tennyson's Poems', Schn. *ELS*, p. 140.
13 *Autob.*, pp. 25-6.
14 *Logic* ii, p. 859.
15 'Nature', *EERS*, pp. 392, 393. On instinct, see also his letter to Comte, *EL* ii, p. 526: 'Mais c'est encore pour moi un grand problème s'il existe peu ou beaucoup de ces instincts primitifs'; and Rothblatt, S., *The Revolution of the Dons*, p. 111, where he refers to Mill's 'curious debate' with Samuel Bailey on Berkeley's theory of vision and suggests that Mill 'came dangerously close to erecting his own theory of innate ideas'. Mill's article, here referred to, is in *EPC* and *D & D* II (originally, *Westminster Review,* October 1842).
16 *S. of W.*, p. 494; 'Tennyson's Poems', Schn. *ELS*, p. 141; *Logic* ii, p. 859.
17 'The Negro Question', p. 29; cf. also on the Irish (pp. 124-5); also his review of de Tocqueville, where he warns against supposing that the advanced state of European civilisation is due 'to any superiority of nature, and not rather to combinations of circumstances which have existed nowhere else, and may not exist for ever among ourselves' *EPS* i, p. 197 (*D & D* II, p. 72; Schn. *EW*, p. 155).
18 'Utility of Religion', *EERS*, pp. 408-10.
19 'Lord Brougham's Defence of the Church Establishment', *Monthly Repository* 8 (1834), p. 442.
20 *Autob.*, pp. 232-3.
21 *EL* ii, p. 526.
22 In the following summary of Mill's analysis (pp. 116-23) page references to 'Nature' (all CW) are inserted in the text.
23 For Mill's 'proof' of utility, see ch. 4 of *Utilitarianism*, especially the third paragraph; there has been much discussion of this — see, for instance, Mary Warnock's introduction to her edition, pp. 25ff., Hudson's *Modern Moral Philosophy,* Cowan's *Pleasure and Pain*, and the essays in Schneewind, J.B., ed., *Mill: a Collection of Critical Essays.*
24 On reason and instinct, see *S. of W.*, p. 430: 'It is one of the characteristic prejudices of the reaction of the nineteenth century against the eighteenth to accord to the unreasoning elements in human nature the infallibility which the eighteenth century is supposed to have ascribed to the reasoning elements. For the apotheosis of Reason we have substituted that of Instinct. . . .'
25 *Emile*, pp. 5, 14.
26 Cf. Peters, R.S., *Ethics and Education*, p. 55: the educator's 'plea for self-realisation is a plea for the principle of options within a range of activities and modes of conduct that are thought to be desirable'.
27 *ib.*, p. 25.
28 'On the Present State of Literature', *Adelphi* 1 (1923-4), p. 683.
29 *Logic* ii, pp. 863-4.
30 *S. of W.*, p. 452.
31 *ib.*, p. 453.
32 *PPE* i, p. 319.
33 'Utility of Religion', *EERS*, pp. 409-10.
34 'Civilisation', *EPS* i, pp. 129ff. (*D & D* I, pp. 176ff.; Schn. *ELS*, pp. 161ff).
35 *Autob.*, p. 26.
36 'Civilisation', *EPS* i, p. 136 (*D & D* I, p. 188; Schn. *ELS*, p. 169).
37 'Perfectibility', in *Autob.*, p. 294.
38 *EL* i, pp. 31-32.
39 *PPE* i, pp. 371-2.

40 *S. of W.*, pp. 469, 479.
41 *Morning Chronicle*, 13 March 1850, p. 5 (Mill states that 'very little of this was mine' — MacMinn, etc., *op. cit.*, p. 73).
42 *PPE* i, p. 103, ii, p. 943.
43 *EPS* i, pp. 267, 270 (*Lib.*, pp. 80, 84).
44 *PPE* i, pp. 208, 209.
45 'Grote's History', *EPC*, pp. 315ff. (*D & D* II, pp. 520ff.).
46 *PPE* ii, p. 594.
47 'Civilisation', *EPS* i, p. 133 (*D & D* I, p. 183; Schn. *ELS*, p. 165); *PPE* ii, pp. 794ff. (cf. i, p. 205). Mill makes a number of comments on competition, not all of them in agreement: he allows that it is not necessarily evil (*PPE* ii, pp. 986-7), and that in the present state of industry and commerce it is well nigh indispensable (*ib.*, pp. 794ff.); on the other hand, it is not the moral ideal (*Comte and Positivism, EERS*, pp. 340-1), nor are the moral arguments against it to be disdained ('Newman's Political Economy', *EES* ii, p. 444).
48 *PPE* ii, p. 861; 'Civilisation', *EPS* i, pp. 133-5 (*D & D* I, pp. 184-6; Schn. *ELS* pp. 166-8).
49 *Logic* ii, p. 838.
50 'Tocqueville on Democracy in America', *EPS* i, pp. 197-8 (*D & D* II, p. 73; Schn. *EW*, p. 155).
51 *Curriculum and Examinations in Secondary Schools* (H.M.S.O., 1943), p. 2.
52 'Tocqueville on Democracy in America', *EPS* i, p. 199 (*D & D* II, pp. 75-6; Schn. *EW*, p. 157).
53 *S. of W.*, pp. 502-3.
54 *Morning Chronicle,* 3 December 1846.
55 *PPE* i, pp. 318-19, 326-7.
56 *EPS* ii, pp. 467-8 (*Repr. Gov.*, p. 274).
57 *ib.*, quotations on pp. 390, 392, 393, 392, 396, 404 and *Repr. Gov.*, pp. 167, 170, 171, 170, 176, 186.
58 On democracy and mediocrity, see, for example, *EPS* i, pp. 268-9 (*Lib.* pp. 81-2); ii, p. 508 (*Repr. Gov.*, p. 329); 'Tocqueville on Democracy in America', *EPS* i, pp. 194ff. (*D & D* II, pp. 67ff.; Schn. *EW*, pp. 151ff).
59 *Autob.*, pp. 144-5.
60 'Carlyle's French Revolution', Schn. *ELS*, pp. 201-2.
61 'Tocqueville on Democracy in America', *EPS* i, p. 169 (*D & D* II, pp. 25-6; Schn. *EW*, p. 122).
62 'Bentham', *EERS*, p. 105 (Schn. *ELS*, p. 275).
63 *PPE* ii, p. 886.
64 *EPS* ii, p. 387 (*Repr. Gov.*, p. 162).
65 *LL* i, pp. 268ff.; e.g., Corfu, pp. 413-14: 'The sparkle of the sea waves in the sunlight at this place can be compared to nothing but raining stars into the water'; the sculptures in the Theseum at Athens, p. 426: 'I was not at all prepared for their extreme beauty.'
66 'The Claims of Labour', *EES* i, p. 384.
67 *PPE* ii, p. 756.
68 'Land Tenure Reform', *D & D* IV, p. 257. See also *LL* iii, pp. 1140-1:

> I have all my life been strongly impressed with the importance of preserving as much as possible of such free space [i.e. commons] for healthful exercise, and for the enjoyment of natural beauty as the growth of population and cultivation has still left to us. The desire to engross the whole surface of the earth in the mere production of the greatest possible

quantity of food and the materials of manufacture, I consider to be founded on a mischievously narrow conception of the requirements of human nature.

(Mill is writing from Avignon approving the formation of the Commons Preservation Society).

69 'State of Politics in 1836', *London and Westminster Review* 3 and 25 (April, 1836), pp. 277-8.
70 *LL* iii, pp. 1136-7.
71 See bibliography.
72 *Autob.*, pp. 6, 47, 125: 'What made Wordsworth's poems a medicine for my state of mind was that they expressed, not mere outward beauty, but states of feeling, and of thought coloured by feeling, under the excitement of beauty' (and were therefore, one may add, more powerfully educative than simple aesthetic pleasure).
73 For the continuing nature/nurture controversy, see Professor Eysenck's two books, *Race, Intelligence and Education* and *The Inequality of Man,* and his review of Wilson, E.O., *Sociobiology: The New Synthesis* (Harvard University Press, 1975), in *The Times,* 29 December 1975; also Jencks, C. and others, *Inequality: A Reassessment of the Effect of Family and Schooling in America* (Allen Lane, 1973).
74 Reeves, M., *Growing up in a Modern Society,* pp. 12-13.
75 *Emile*, pp. 56, 84.
76 *EPS* i, p. 232 (*Lib.* p. 28).
77 *Republic* 492c-493a (2nd edn, pp. 287-8).
78 *Inaugural*, p. 154.

3 *Method*

1 'Education', in Burston, W.H., ed., *op. cit.,* p. 92.
2 *Analysis*, vol. 2, p. 262.
3 'Civilisation', *EPS* i, p. 124 (*D & D* I, p. 168; Schn. *ELS,* p. 154).
4 *Logic* ii, p. 842-3.
5 *PPE* i, p. 124.
6 'Sedgwick's Discourse', *EERS,* p. 40.
7 *Inaugural*, p. 167, and *Autob.* pp. 48, 101. The Hamiltonian method, mentioned by Mill in the *Autobiography*, used interlinear translations (at first in French readers) in order to allow more rapid reading; grammar was to be acquired inductively from the reading (see Gilbert, M., 'The Origins of the Reform Movement in Modern Language Teaching').
8 'The Spirit of the Age', Schn. *ELS,* p. 66.
9 *EPS* i, p. 250 (*Lib.,* p. 54).
10 'On the Definition of Political Economy', *EES* i, p. 333.
11 *Autob.*, pp. 71-2.
12 'On Genius', Schn. *ELS,* pp. 89, 90.
13 'Civilisation', *EPS* i, p. 141 (*D & D* I, p. 196; Schn. *ELS,* p. 175).
14 The *Globe,* 23 October 1835
15 *Autob.*, pp. 26-7 (cf. p. 24).
16 *ib.*, pp. 20, 14.
17 'On Genius', Schn. *ELS,* p. 97.
18 *PPE* i, p. 281.
19 'Civilisation', *EPS* i, p. 124 (*D & D* I, p. 168; Schn. *ELS,* p. 154).
20 *EPS* i, p. 262 (*Lib.,* pp. 72-3).
21 *op. cit.*

22 'On Genius', *op. cit.*; the quotations that follow are on pp. 99, 100, 96, 97-8, 101.
23 *Autob.*, p. 26.
24 *EPS* i, pp. 243ff. (*Lib.*, pp. 45ff).
25 'Mrs. Austin's Translation of M. Cousin's Report on the State of Public Instruction in Prussia', *Monthly Repository* 8 (1834), p. 506 (Mill is quoting Sir William Molesworth).
26 *ib.* p. 504.
27 *ib.*, pp. 507-8.
28 *ib.*, p. 510.
29 'The Claims of Labour', *EES* i, p. 378.
30 'Civilisation', *EPS* i, p. 144 (*D & D* I, p. 201, Schn. *ELS*, p. 179); 'On Genius', Schn. *ELS*, p. 98; *Comte and Positivism, EERS*, p. 352.
31 'On Genius', Schn. *ELS*, p. 99; 'The Spirit of the Age', Schn. *ELS*, p. 33; *Autob.*, p. 24; Paper relating to the Re-organisation of the Civil Service (1854/5) p. 98, *EPS* i, p. 211.
32 *Inaugural*, pp. 215, 177.
33 'Grote's Plato', *EPC*, p. 404 (*D & D* III, p. 319).
34 'On Genius', Schn. *ELS*, p. 99; *Inaugural,* p. 215.
35 *PPE* i, p. 280 (difficulties).
36 *Inaugural*, pp. 191-2.
37 'Grote's Plato', *EPC*, p. 411 (*D & D* III, p. 331).
38 'On Genius', Schn. *ELS*, p. 100; 'The Spirit of the Age', *ib.*, pp. 39-40.
39 *Inaugural*, p. 156; 'Civilisation', *EPS* i, p. 146 (*D & D* I, p. 204; Schn. *ELS*, p. 181); 'On Genius', Schn. *ELS*, p. 101.
40 *Autob.*, pp. 16-19, 23-4, 57, 98-9.
41 The *Globe*, 23 October 1835.
42 On the 'Orbilian tradition' (Orbilius was Horace's schoolmaster), see Castle, E.B., *Ancient Education and Today.*
43 Chs 1, 2. On 'Gradgrindery', see the articles cited in Part II, Introductory, n. 46.
44 *EPS* ii, pp. 47 5-6 (*Repr. Gov.*, pp. 284, 286); *EPS* i, pp. 303-4 (*Lib.*, pp. 130-2).
45 'Endowments', *EES* ii, p. 624.
46 *op. cit.*
47 'Bain's Psychology', *EPC*, p. 350 (*D & D* III, p. 113).
48 Bain, A., *op. cit.*, ch. 6, p. 173.
49 *Autob.*, p. 137.
50 'On Genius', Schn. *ELS*, pp. 90, 92.
51 *PPE* ii, p. 949.
52 'National Education', *Monthly Repository* 8 (1834), p. 357; *LL* iii, p. 1304.
53 *Inaugural*, p. 215.
54 'Lord Brougham's Defence of the Church Establishment', *Monthly Repository* 8 (1834), p. 444.
55 *LL* iii, pp. 1246, 1304. On teachers and teaching, see also *EPS* ii, p. 545 (*Repr. Gov.*, pp. 379-80); 'Civilisation' *EPS* i, p. 144 (*D & D* I pp. 201-3; Schn. *ELS*, pp. 179-80); *Autob.* pp. 12ff.
56 *LL* iii, p. 1304; 'Endownments', *EES* ii, p. 627.
57 *Autob.*, p. 27.
58 *EPS* i, p. 250 (*Lib.*, p. 53).
59 *EPS* ii, p. 545 (*Repr. Gov.*, p. 379).
60 *Inaugural*, p. 214.

61 'Lord Brougham's Defence of the Church Establishment', *op. cit.*, p. 443.
62 *ib.*, p. 444.
63 'National Education', *op. cit.*, p. 357.
64 *LL* iii, p. 1093.
65 *Inaugural*, p. 164; *Autob.* p. 25.
66 *LL* iv, pp. 1549-50; cf. *Comte and Positivism, EERS*, p. 303, where he criticises Comte for exaggerating the amount of knowledge that can be taught 'by good methods of teaching'.
67 *Autob.* p. 8. See also Burston, W.H., 'The Utilitarians and the Monitorial System of Teaching'.
68 'Mrs. Austin's Translation', *op. cit.*, p. 509.
69 'Endowments', *EES* ii, pp. 622ff.
70 'Claims of Labour', *EES* i, p. 377.
71 'National Education', *op. cit.*, p. 358.
72 *Inaugural*, p. 163.
73 In Schn. *ELS*, p. 350.
74 'Coleridge', *EERS*, p. 133 (Schn. *ELS*, p. 308).
75 *Comte and Positivism, EERS*, p. 339.
76 *Autob.*, p. 44.
77 *ib.* pp. 44-5.
78 *EPS* i, pp. 226, 294 (*Lib.*, pp. 18, 118).
79 *EPS* i, p. 224 (*Lib.*, p. 15).
80 *Inaugural*, p. 154.
81 'Bentham', *EERS*, p. 106 (Schn. *ELS*, p. 276).
82 *ib.*, *EERS*, pp. 108, 109 (Schn. *ELS*, pp. 278, 279).
83 'The Spirit of the Age', Schn. *ELS*, p. 44.
84 'Sedgwick's Discourse', *EERS*, p. 33.
85 *EPS* i, 246 (*Lib.*, p. 48).
86 *Logic* ii, p. 951.
87 *Inaugural*, p. 226.
88 *Utilitarianism, EERS*, pp. 246, 248-9 (Schn. *EW*, pp. 321-2, 324-5; Warnock, pp. 303-4, 306-7).
89 *ib.*, *EERS* pp. 250-1 (Schn. *EW*, pp. 327-8; Warnock, pp. 309-10).
90 *Analysis*, vol. 2, pp. 324-6.
91 *LL* ii, p. 650.
92 *Hamilton*, pp. 586ff; quotations on pp. 586, 594 ('the rule of right').
93 *ib.*, p. 597.
94 *Utilitarianism, EERS*, pp. 253, 256 (Schn. *EW*, pp. 330, 334; Warnock, pp. 313, 317); *Analysis*, vol. 2, pp. 324-6; *EPS* i, p. 280 (*Lib.*, p. 98). See also his letter to Florence Nightingale, *LL* ii, p. 712, where he seems to suggest that retaliation is a natural consequence of being wronged, and indignation against wrongdoing a legitimate reaction.
95 'On Punishment', *Monthly Repository* 8 (1834), p. 734.
96 *LL* ii, p. 712.
97 *Utilitarianism, EERS*, pp. 248, 250-1, (Schn. *EW* pp. 325, 327-8; Warnock, pp. 306-7, 309-10); *Hamilton*, pp. 592-6; 'On Punishment', *op. cit.*, p. 736.
98 *EPS* i, pp. 223-4 (*Lib.*, p. 15).
99 *Hansard*, vol. 191, cols 1052, 1048 (21 April 1868).
100 'Exception to the Objections to Nominal Punishments', *Examiner*, 16 September 1838; 'On Punishment', *op. cit.*, p. 735.
101 'On Punishment', *op. cit.*, p. 736.
102 *Hamilton*, pp. 593-4 n. (including the two following quotations).
103 *LL* iii, p. 1116.

104 *Sunday Times*, 2 June 1850.
105 *Autob.*, pp. 67-8, 101ff. (quotation on p. 104).
106 'Grote's Aristotle', *EPC*, pp. 509-10 (*D & D* IV, p. 228); for Locke's 'principling', see Garforth, F.W., ed., *Conduct of the Understanding*, p. 116.
107 'The Spirit of the Age', Schn. *ELS*, p. 35.
108 *EPS* i, p. 231 (*Lib.*, p. 27).
109 *Autob.*, p. 18; 'Grote's Plato', *EPC*, pp. 382ff. (*D & D* III, pp. 284ff.).
110 'Sedgwick's Discourse', *EERS*, pp. 38-9 ('antagonist principle'); for the second phrase, 'antagonism of influence', I have not been able to trace the reference, but it is certainly Mill's; 'Coleridge', *EERS*, p. 122 (Schn. *ELS*, p. 295) ('antagonist modes of thought').
111 'Sedgwick's Discourse', *EERS*, p. 39.
112 'The Two Kinds of Poetry', Schn. *ELS*, p. 126.
113 *EPS* i, p. 309 (*Lib.*, p. 139).
114 *Autob.*, pp. 7, 95, 39; 'Grote's Plato', *EPC*, p. 415 (*D & D* III, p. 338); 'Grote's History', *EPC*, p. 334 (*D & D* II, p. 550); *Autob.*, pp. 56, 86.
115 'Letters for Palmyra', *London and Westminster Review* 28 (January 1838). p.469 (these passages also in 'A Prophecy', *D & D* I, pp. 284-5).
116 'Writings of Junius Redivivus', *Monthly Repository* 7 (1833), p. 263.
117 *EPC*, p. 150, and Borchard, R., ed., *Four Dialogues of Plato*, p. 170.
118 'Civilisation', *EPS* i, p. 145 (*D & D* I, pp. 202-3; Schn. *ELS*, pp. 180-1); *Inaugural*, pp. 171ff.
119 *Inaugural*, p. 212.
120 'National Education', *op. cit.*, p. 357.
121 'Civilisation', *EPS* i, p. 144 (*D & D* I, pp. 202-3; Schn. *ELS*, p. 180); cf. *Inaugural*, p. 215.

4 *Content*

1 *British Parliamentary Papers*, 1831-2. Irish University Press, *Colonies: East India*, vol. 6, p. 392.
2 *LL* iv, p. 1663; *Inaugural*, p. 155; 'The Claims of Labour', *EES* i, p. 378.
3 *PPE* ii, p. 948.
4 *British Parliamentary Papers*, *op. cit.*, p. 523; cf. *LL* i, p. 80, below.
5 'Mrs. Austin's Translation', *op. cit.*, p. 508.
6 'National Education', *op. cit.*, pp. 357-8.
7 *LL* i, p. 80.
8 *Inaugural*, p. 168.
9 *LL* iii, p. 1470.
10 'On the Present State of Literature', *op. cit.*, p. 685.
11 'The Claims of Labour', *EES* i, p. 378. For detailed advice on reading, see Mill's letter to Florence May, *LL* iii, pp. 1472ff.
12 'What is Poetry?', schn. *ELS*, pp. 105, 104, 108, 104. The following two articles are of particular interest for Mill's views on poetry: Price, A., 'J. S. Mill and the Combination of Logic and Poetry in Education'; Robson, J.M., 'J. S. Mill's Theory of Poetry'.
13 *op. cit.*
14 'Mrs. Austin's Translation', *op. cit.*, pp. 507, 511, 512.
15 *Hamilton*, ch. 27 (quotation on p. 607); *Inaugural*, pp. 188-90. For Mill's views on the nature of arithmetic, see Britton, K., 'The Nature of Arithmetic: a Reconsideration of Mill's Views'.
16 'Civilisation', *EPS* i, p. 145 (*D & D* I, p. 203; Schn. *ELS*, pp. 180-1).

17 *Inaugural*, p. 173.
18 *ib.*, p. 167; the following quotations are on pp. 167, 170, 171.
19 Bain, A., *op. cit.*, p. 94.
20 *Inaugural*, pp. 176, 181, 174.
21 *ib.*, pp. 163, 162.
22 *ib.*, p. 161.
23 *ib.*, pp. 162-3, 182-3; 'The Protagoras', *EPC*, p. 39, and Borchard, R., ed.,
    Four Dialogues of Plato, p. 41.
24 *Inaugural*, pp. 163, 182.
25 'Civilisation', *EPS* i, p. 146 (*D & D* I, p. 204; Schn. *ELS*, p. 181).
26 *Inaugural*, p. 184; also the two following quotations; 'a sealed book',
    p. 185.
27 *ib.*, pp. 185, 192, 191, 189.
28 'Sedgwick's Discourse', *EERS*, p. 39.
29 *Comte and Positivism, EERS*, p. 291.
30 'Sedgwick's Discourse', *EERS*, pp. 38-9. On science and art see also
    pp. 218-19 and 222.
31 *Autob.*, p. 14.
32 *EL* ii, pp. 566, 667.
33 'Miss Martineau's Summary of Political Economy', *EES* i, p. 225.
34 'Lord Brougham's Defence of the Church Establishment', *op. cit.*, p. 443
    (cf. *Inaugural*, p. 215, and *LL* iii, pp. 1235-6). Mill goes on to make some
    general observations on the teacher's function which are worth quoting
    fully:

    An enlightened instructor limits his operations in this respect to apprizing
    the learners what are the opinions actually entertained; and by
    strengthening their intellects, storing their minds with ideas, and
    directing their attention to the sources of evidence, not only on every
    doubtful, but on every undisputed point, at once qualifies and stimulates
    them to find the truth for themselves. Let the teaching be in this spirit,
    and it scarcely matters what are the opinions of the teacher; and it is for
    their capacity to teach thus, and not for the opinions they hold, that
    teachers ought to be chosen. (p. 444)

35 *LL* iii, p. 1469; 'Lord Brougham's Defence of the Church Establishment',
    op. cit., 443.
36 'Lord Brougham's Defence of the Church Establishment', *ib.*
37 'On Genius', Schn. *ELS*, p. 99.
38 *LL* iii, p. 1305.
39 *Inaugural*, p. 214.
40 *LL* iii, p. 1469.
41 *Inaugural*, p. 219.
42 *ib.*, p. 221.
43 *ib.*, p. 226.
44 'Writings of Junius Redivivus', *op. cit.*, p. 269.
45 *Inaugural*, p. 219.
46 In *Autob.*, pp. 293-4.
47 *Inaugural*, p. 211; also the following quotation.
48 *LL* i, p. 39.
49 *Hamilton*, pp. 585-6.
50 *Analysis*, vol. 2, pp. 233-4, 308-9.
51 *ib.*, p. 309; 'Nature', *EERS*, p. 394.
52 *LL* ii, pp. 649-50.
53 *PPE* ii, pp. 792-3 (and cf. pp. 768-9).

54 *Inaugural*, p. 211.
55 *Autob.*, p. 40; *Inaugural*, p. 212.
56 *Thoughts concerning Education*, p. 225 (para. 204).
57 *Autob.*, p. 30; he also writes in his French diary of bathing every morning in the River Garonne (Bain, A., *op. cit.*, p. 16).
58 *LL* iii, p. 1224; on military drill, see Chadwick's paper submitted to the Education Commission in 1861, *Parliamentary Papers*, 1861-2, Irish University Press, *Education: General*, vol. 8, pp. 835ff.
59 *Autob.*, pp. 30-1.
60 *LL* iii, p. 1469.
61 *PPE* ii, p. 948.
62 *LL* i, p. 80; 'Lord Brougham's Defence of the Church Establishment', *op. cit.*, p. 443.
63 *EPS* ii, p. 446 (*Repr. Gov.*, p. 244).
64 *Inaugural*, p. 165; *Comte and Positivism, EERS*, pp. 312-13.
65 *EPS* i, p. 261 (*Lib.*, p. 70).
66 Robson, J.M., 'J. S. Mill's Theory of Poetry', p. 420.
67 'Honours to Science', *Monthly Repository* 8 (1834), p. 455.
68 *Autob.*, p. 125.
69 'What is Poetry?' Schn. *ELS*, pp. 108, 107, 118.
70 'Tennyson's Poems', Schn. *ELS*, pp. 140-1.
71 'Writings of Junius Redivivus', *op. cit.*, pp. 269-70.
72 'On Genius', Schn. *ELS*, pp. 92, 93; 'Bentham', *EERS*, p. 92 (Schn. *ELS*, p.258); The Gorgias', *EPC*, p. 150, and Borchard, R., ed., *Four Dialogues of Plato*, p. 170.
73 *Autob.*, p. 128; 'Bentham', *EERS*, pp. 92-3 (Schn. *ELS*, pp. 259-60).
74 'Theism', *EERS*, p. 483.
75 'Sedgwick's Discourse', *EERS*, p. 42.
76 *EPS* i, pp. 270, 263 (*Lib.*, pp. 84, 73). On the balance of Mill's view, see the article by Price, note 12 above, especially the final paragraph: 'he was the first, in the nineteenth century at least, really to evaluate the main and diverse elements of training and to synthesise them into a living unity proper for the education of the whole man.'

5 *Liberal Education*

1 Bamford, T.W., *Thomas Arnold on Education*, p. 55; the second quotation is from Matthew Arnold's report on secondary education in France, Germany, Italy and Switzerland, included in the *Report of the Schools Inquiry Commission* (1868), vol. 6, p. 599.
2 *Inaugural*, pp. 153, 158.
3 *ib.*, p. 172; 'On Genius', Schn. *ELS*, p. 100.
4 'Sedgwick's Discourse', *EERS*, pp. 72, 36.
5 *Comte and Positivism, EERS*, p. 312; Tacitus, *Histories* II, 59.
6 *LL* ii, p. 819; 'Coleridge', *EERS*, p. 122 (Schn. *ELS*, p. 295).
7 *LL* ii, p. 543.
8 *Inaugural*, p. 160; 'Sedgwick's Discourse', *EERS*, pp. 42-3, 39.
9 *EPS* i, pp. 230, 243, 243, 310, 261, 299 (*Lib.*, pp. 25, 44, 43, 141, 70, 124).
10 *PPE* ii, p. 948.
11 *ib.* i, pp. 374-5.
12 *Inaugural*, p. 155.
13 *ib.*, pp. 202-3; *PPE* ii, p. 968.
14 *Inaugural*, p. 165.

15 *Comte and Positivism, EERS*, p. 312; on the same page he writes: 'A man's mind is as fatally narrowed, and his feelings towards the great ends of humanity as miserably stunted, by giving all his thoughts to the classification of a few insects or the resolution of a few equations, as to sharpening the points or putting on the heads of pins.'
16 *Inaugural*, p. 182.
17 *EES*, i, p. 378.
18 *Inaugural*, pp. 155-6.
19 'Sedgwick's Discourse', *EERS*, p. 34.
20 *Inaugural*, p. 165.
21 *ib.*, p. 164; *Autob.*, p. 26.
22 *Inaugural*, p. 168.
23 *ib.*, p. 212.
24 *ib.*, p. 166.
25 *ib.*, p. 202; the following quotations are on pp. 157, 205.
26 *ib.*, pp. 156-7.
27 'Sedgwick's Discourse', *EERS*, p. 34.
28 *Inaugural*, pp. 165, 157.
29 'On Genius', Schn. *ELS*, pp. 96, 97, 100 – 101.
30 'Civilisation', *EPS* i, pp. 144, 124 (*D & D* I, pp. 201, 168; Schn. *ELS*, pp. 179, 154). On philosophical disputation and dialectic, see also *Autob.*, pp. 18-19; *Inaugural*, pp. 176-7.
31 *Autob.*, pp. 16, 24.
32 *Inaugural*, pp. 169-70.
33 *ib.*, pp. 184ff. (quotation on p. 185).
34 *ib.*, pp. 188ff. (mathematics); pp. 193ff. (logic). (Quotations on pp. 195, 194).
35 *EPS* i, pp. 261, 263 (*Lib.*, pp. 70, 73).
36 *Inaugural*, pp. 156, 153, 155.
37 *ib.,* pp. 212, 210.
38 'Sedgwick's Discourse', *EERS*, p. 50.
39 *Inaugural*, p. 211; the following quotations are on pp. 211, 213, 214, 213.
40 Whitehead, A.N., *The Aims of Education,* p. 106.
41 *Inaugural*, pp. 226, 210.
42 *ib.*, p. 178; 'Civilisation', *EPS* i, p. 145 (*D & D* I, p. 203; Schn. *ELS*, pp. 180-1); *Inaugural*, p. 192; *ib.*, p. 226.
43 *ib.*, p. 181.
44 'Civilisation', *EPS* i, p. 134 (*D & D* I, p. 184; Schn. *ELS*, p. 166).
45 *Inaugural*, p. 223; the following quotations are on pp. 212, 223.
46 *ib.*, p. 216.
47 *Inaugural*, p. 184; the following quotations are on pp. 184, 185, 192, 188, 189.
48 *ib.*, pp. 205, 205-6.
49 *ib.*, pp. 214, 215, 217.
50 *Autob.*, pp. 32, 36.
51 'Utility of Religion', *EERS,* pp. 422, 420, 423.
52 *Inaugural*, pp. 214, 215.
53 Bain, A., *op. cit.,* p. 128.
54 *Inaugural*, p. 219.
55 Berlin, Sir Isaiah, *John Stuart Mill and the Ends of Life*, p. 11.
56 *Autob.*, pp. 47, 48, 6-7 and 10 (history and the heroic), 9 (Pope's *Iliad*), 122 (music).
57 *ib.*, p. 41.

58 For Bentham's comments on poetry, etc., see *Works*, ed. Bowring, J., vol. 2, pp. 253-4, and Mill's essay on Bentham, *EERS*, pp. 113-14 (Schn. *ELS*, pp. 285-6); see also Warren, A.H., *English Poetic Theory 1825-65*, pp. 66-7, and Sharpless, F.P., *The Literary Criticism of John Stuart Mill*, pp. 16ff. Sharpless argues, with justification, that these familiar quotations from Bentham, as they stand, give a misleading impression of his position — as Mill also suggests in the passage referred to.

59 *Autob.*, p. 122. The following passage is notable for its expression of Mill's appreciation of aesthetic experience and its educational role:

> Where the sense of beauty is wanting, or but faint, the understanding must be contracted: there is so much which a person, unfurnished with that sense, will never have observed, to which he will never have had his attention awakened: there is so much of the value of which to the human mind he will be an incompetent and will be apt to be a prejudiced judge: so many of the most important means of human culture which he will not know the use of, which he is almost sure to undervalue, and of which he is at least unable to avail himself in his own efforts, whether for his own good or for that of the world. It is true of this as of all the other sensibilities, that without intellect they run wild; but without them, intellect is stunted. A time will come, when the education of both will proceed hand in hand; let us rather say, when the aid of culture will be more particularly invoked to strengthen the part which is relatively deficient: or at lowest, to bestow the power of *appreciation*, when the quality to be appreciated is one which only nature can give.

('Writings of Junius Redivivus', *op cit.*, pp. 269-70)

60 On Mill's visit to Wordsworth, see the article by Anna J. Mill, 'John Stuart Mill's visit to Wordsworth, 1831', which uses Mill's unpublished journal of his tour of the Lakes in the summer of that year (he also met Southey during this tour). A letter to John Sterling, written in October of the same year, recalls the visit: 'I am convinced that the proper place to see him is in his own kingdom' (*EL* i, pp. 80-2).

61 J. M. Robson, in 'J. S. Mill's Theory of Poetry', p. 437, quotes from Bertrand and Patricia Russell's *Amberley Papers* a passage describing the effect on Mill of reading aloud Shelley's 'Ode to Liberty': 'He got quite excited and moved over it, rocking backwards and forwards and nearly choking with emotion; he said to himself: "It is almost too much for one" ' (this in 1870).

62 The most important of his reviews are those of Tennyson's early poems (1835) and of the writings of Alfred de Vigny (1838); he also reviewed Macaulay's *Lays of Ancient Rome* (1843) and numerous other works, in poetry, music and drama; see Hainds, J.R., 'J. S. Mill's *Examiner* Articles on Art'.

63 'Bentham', *EERS*, p. 92 (Schn. *ELS*, p. 258); *EL* i, p. 81; *Examiner*, 4 April 1832 (Hainds, J.R., *op. cit.*, p. 223); *Inaugural*, p. 226; 'Present State of Literature', *op. cit.*, p. 688.

64 See the passage quoted on p.179 above from 'The Gorgias', *EPC*, p. 150 (Borchard., R., ed., *Four Dialogues of Plato*, p. 170).

65 *EL* i, p.163 (also the following quotation).

66 See Warren, A.H., *op. cit.*, pp. 77-8, and Robson, J.M., 'J. S. Mill's Theory of Poetry', pp. 421, 437.

67 Bain, A., *op. cit.*, pp. 149ff.

68 Hayek, F.A., *John Stuart Mill and Harriet Taylor*, p. 133. There is further testimony to Mill's love of and competence in music in a book of memories, *Memoires of a Student*, written by his stepson, Algernon Taylor. After

mentioning that there were certain persons whose playing had a lasting effect on him, he continues:

> Among these perhaps the most remarkable and interesting was that of Mr. Mill, who used, now and then, to perform on the piano, but only when asked to do so by my mother; and then he would at once sit down to the instrument and play music entirely of his own composition, on the spur of the moment: music of a singular character, wanting, possibly, in the finish which more practice would have imparted, but rich in feeling, vigour and suggestiveness: the performer taking for his theme, may be, the weird grandeur of cloud and storm, the deep pathos of a dirge, the fierce onset of the battlefield, or the triumphant, joyous time of a processional march. (pp. 10-11)

69 *Analysis*, vol. 2, pp. 241-2, 246-7, 252ff.
70 *LL* i, pp. 295 (cf., 286, 312), 426, 428-9, 322.
71 'Bentham', *EERS*, p. 112 (Schn. *ELS*, p. 283).
72 Alexander, E., 'Mill's Theory of Culture: The Wedding of Literature and Democracy'; Robson, J.M., *art. cit.*; and Warren, A.H., *op. cit.*
73 'Tennyson's Poems', Schn. *ELS*, p. 141.
74 'Letters from Palmyra', *op. cit.*, p. 469 (*D & D* I, p. 285).
75 *EPS* i, p. 310 (*Lib.*, p. 141).
76 *Inaugural*, pp. 226-7.
77 Hirst, P.H., 'Liberal Education and the Nature of Knowledge'.
78 Huxley, T.H., *Science and Education*, p. 100 (see pp. 97-101 on classics in schools).
79 Whitehead, A.N., *The Aims of Education*, p. 74.

Bibliography

The following lists of Mill's writings include only works used or referred to in the text and notes. Mill compiled his own full list of his published writings; this has been edited by MacMinn, N., Hainds, J.R. and McCrimmon, J.M., *Bibliography of the Published Writings of John Stuart Mill* (Evanston: Northwestern University Press, 1945); it excludes the few works published posthumously.

Since the present book is confined to a limited area of Mill's thought, no attempt has been made to provide a full bibliography of secondary sources. The list includes those drawn on in the text and notes, others which have helped the writer in understanding Mill and his educational thought, and others again which supply useful biographical, historical or critical material. More extensive bibliographies can be found in van Holthoon's *The Road to Utopia*, Robson's *The Improvement of Mankind* and Ryan's *J. S. Mill* and *The Philosophy of John Stuart Mill*; a complete, cumulative list is provided in *The Mill News Letter*, nos. 1ff. (1965-   ).

For the life of Mill one should, of course, read the *Autobiography* (including Stillinger's *Early Draft*); there is also much biographical material in the six volumes of letters in the Collected Works. Bain's *John Stuart Mill* is a valuable contemporary source; also useful is another nineteenth-century book, Courtney's *The Life of John Stuart Mill*, and there are many fascinating personal glimpses of Mill in Caroline Fox's *Memories of Old Friends*. Of modern biographies the fullest is Packe's; there are also Borchard's and Cranston's (the latter a brief critical essay). Hayek's *John Stuart Mill and Harriet Taylor* and Pappé's *John Stuart Mill and the Harriet Taylor Myth* deal with a specific (and crucial) personal relationship; so too does Josephine Kamm's *John Stuart Mill in Love*. Mazlish's *James and John Stuart Mill* combines biography with psychology in what is claimed to be 'a contribution to psychohistory'.

252   Bibliography

The abbreviations used in the Bibliography are the same as those used in the Notes.

1 Mill's Writings (in chronological order of publication)

(i) Books

1843   A System of Logic: Ratiocinative and Inductive i and ii (CW VII and VIII), textual editor Robson, J.M., introduction by McRae, R.F., 1973.
1844   Essays on Some Unsettled Questions of Political Economy; in EES i (CW IV).
1848   Principles of Political Economy i and ii (CW II and III); textual editor Robson, J.M., introduction by Bladen, V.W., 1965.
1859   Dissertations and Discussions, an anthology of Mill's periodical writings, of which two volumes were published in 1859, a third in 1867 and a fourth in 1875.
1859   On Liberty; in EPS i (CW XVIII); ed. Fawcett, M. G., Oxford University Press, World's Classics, 1912, etc. (with Representative Government and The Subjection of Women); and ed. Himmelfarb, G., Penguin Books, 1974.
1861   Considerations on Representative Government; in EPS ii (CW XIX); ed. Fawcett, M. G., Oxford University Press, World's Classics, 1912, etc. (with On Liberty and The Subjection of Women).
1863   Utilitarianism (reprinted from Fraser's Magazine 64 (1861); in EERS (CW X); ed. Warnock, M., Fontana, 1962; and in Mill's Ethical Writings, ed. Schneewind, J. B., Collier Books (New York) 1965.
1865   Auguste Comte and Positivism (reprinted from the Westminster Review of the same year, vols 83, 84, N. S. 27, 28); in EERS (CW X).
1865   An Examination of Sir William Hamilton's Philosophy.
1867   Inaugural Address at the University of St. Andrews; in Garforth, F. W., ed., John Stuart Mill on Education, Teachers College Press, 1971; and in Schneewind, J. B., ed., Mill's Essays on Literature and Society, Collier Books (New York), 1965.
1869   The Subjection of Women; ed. Fawcett, M. G., Oxford University Press, World's Classics, 1912, etc. (with On Liberty and Representative Government).
1873   Autobiography (published posthumously); Laski's edition (Oxford University Press, World's Classics, 1924, etc.) is the text as published by Mill's stepdaughter, Helen Taylor, with certain passages excised; the full text is in the Columbia University Press editions of 1924 and 1944 (ed. Howson, R., preface by Coss, J.J.). The original draft, written probably between 1853 and 1856, has been published as The Early Draft of John Stuart Mill's Autobiography, ed. Stillinger, J., University of Illinois Press, 1961.
1874   Three Essays on Religion (published posthumously); in EERS (CW X). The three essays are 'Nature', 'Utility of Religion' and 'Theism'.

Collected writings have been published in the following volumes of the Collected Works:

Earlier Letters, 1812-1848 i and ii (CW XII and XIII), ed. Mineka, F.E., 1963.

Later Letters, 1849-1873 i-iv (CW XIV-XVII), ed. Mineka, F.E. and Lindley, D.W., 1972.
Essays on Economics and Society i and ii (CW IV and V), textual editor Robson, J.M., introduction by Lord Robbins, 1967.
Essays on Ethics, Religion and Society (CW X), textual introduction by Robson, J.M., introduction by Priestley, F.E.L., and Dryer, D.P., 1969.
Essays on Philosophy and the Classics (CW XI), textual editor Robson, J.M., introduction by Sparshott, F.E., 1978.
Essays on Politics and Society i and ii (CW XVIII and XIX), textual editor Robson, J.M., introduction by Brady, A., 1977.
Selected writings include:
Essays on Politics and Culture by John Stuart Mill, ed. Himmelfarb, G. (New York: Doubleday, 1962).
John Stuart Mill: A Selection of his Works, ed. Robson, J. M., (Toronto: Macmillan, 1966); this includes *On Liberty* and *Utilitarianism* in full.
Mill's Essays on Literature and Society, ed. Schneewind, J.B., (New York: Collier Books, 1965).
Mill's Ethical Writings, ed. Schneewind, J.B., (New York: Collier Books, 1965).
John Stuart Mill on Politics and Society, ed. Williams, G.L., (Glasgow: Fontana/Collins, 1976).

(ii) *Articles, essays, etc.*

1827-8   'On the Present State of Literature'; an unpublished speech; *Adelphi* 1, no. 2 (1923-4).
1828   'Speech on Perfectibility'; an unpublished speech, included in Laski, H.J., ed., *Autobiography*.
1831   'The Spirit of the Age', *Examiner*, January-May, 1831; Schneewind, J.B., ed., *Mill's Essays on Literature and Society*.
1831-2   Despatches to India, *British Parliamentary Papers*, Session 1831-2; Irish University Press edition, *Colonies: East India*, vol. 6, pp. 377ff.
1832   'Miss Flower's "Songs of the Seasons" ', *Examiner*, 8 April 1832; see Hainds, J.R., 'J. S. Mill's *Examiner* articles on Art', *Journal of the History of Ideas* 11 (1950).
    'On Genius', *Monthly Repository* 6 (October 1832); Schneewind, J.B., ed., *Mill's Essays on Literature and Society*; Borchard, R., *Four Dialogues of Plato*.
1833   'What is Poetry?', *Monthly Repository* 7 (January 1833); combined with 'The Two Kinds of Poetry' in *D & D* I, 'Thoughts on Poetry and its Varieties'; Schneewind, J.B., ed., *Mill's Essays on Literature and Society*.
    'Corporation and Church Property', *Jurist* 4 (February 1833); *D & D* I, 'The Right and Wrong of State Interference with Corporation and Church Property'.
    'Writings of Junius Redivivus' [W. B. Adams], *Monthly Repository* 7 (April 1833); another review, of one work only, in *Tait's Edinburgh Magazine* in June of the same year.
    'The Two Kinds of Poetry', *Monthly Repository* 7 (November 1833); combined with 'What is Poetry?' in *D & D* I; Schneewind, J.B., ed., *Mill's Essays on Literature and Society*.

1834   'National Education', in 'Notes on the Newspapers', *Monthly Repository*
        8 (17 April 1834).
        'Miss Martineau's Summary of Political Economy', *Monthly Repository*
        8 (May 1834); *EES* i (CW IV).
        'Lord Brougham's Defence of Church Establishment', in 'Notes on the
        Newspapers', *Monthly Repository* 8 (13 May 1834).
        'Honours to Science!' in 'Notes on the Newspapers', *Monthly Repository*
        8 (25 May 1834).
        'Mrs. Austin's Translation of M. Cousin's Report on the State of Public
        Instruction in Prussia', *Monthly Repository* 8 (July 1834); MacMinn,
        etc. have 'Miss' in their *Bibliography* (p. 40), but the article has 'Mrs'.
        'On Punishment', *Monthly Repository* 8 (October 1834).
1834-5 'Notes on Some of the More Popular Dialogues of Plato', *Monthly
        Repository* 8, 9 (February 1834-March 1835); *EPC* (CW XI). These
        'Notes' are a combination of comment, paraphrase and translation;
        Protagoras, Phaedrus, Gorgias, Apology are published in Borchard,
        R., ed., *Four Dialogues of Plato* (London: Watts, 1946).
1835   'Professor Sedgwick's Discourse — State of Philosophy in England',
        London Review 1 (April 1835); *D & D* I, 'Professor Sedgwick's
        Discourse on the Studies of the University of Cambridge'; *EERS*
        (CW X).
        'Tennyson's Poems', *London Review* 1 (July 1835); Schneewind, J.B.,
        ed., *Mill's Essays on Literature and Society*.
        'De Tocqueville on Democracy in America', *London Review* 1 (October
        1835); a later review appeared in the *Edinburgh Review* (October
        1840); *EPS* i (CW XVIII).
        Notice of Grant's *Arithmetic for Young Children* and *Exercises for the
        Improvement of the Senses*, the *Globe*, 23 October 1835.
1836   'Civilisation' *London and Westminster Review* 3 and 25 (April 1836);
        EPS i (CW XVIII); *D & D* I; Schneewind, J.B., ed., *Mill's Essays on
        Literature and Society*.
        'State of Politics in 1836', *London and Westminster Review* 3 and 25
        (April 1836).
        'On the Definition of Political Economy', Essay V in *Essays on Some
        Unsettled Questions of Political Economy* (1844); reprinted from
        London and Westminster Review 4 and 26 (October 1836); *EES* i
        (CW IV).
1837   'Carlyle's French Revolution', *London and Westminster Review* 5 and
        27 (July 1837); Schneewind, J.B., ed., *Mill's Essays on Literature and
        Society* (omits excerpts from Carlyle).
1838   'Letters from Palmyra', *London and Westminster Review* 6 and 28
        (January 1838); review of William Hare's *Letters of Lucius Manlius
        Piso, from Palmyra, to his Friend, Marcus Curtius, at Rome*, a historical
        novel; reprinted in part in *D & D* I, 'A Prophecy'.
        'Writings of Alfred de Vigny', *London and Westminster Review* 7 and
        29 (N.S. 31) (April 1838); *D & D* I; Schneewind, J.B., ed., *Mill's Essays
        on Literature and Society*.
        'Bentham', *London and Westminster Review* 7 and 29 (N.S. 31)
        (August 1838); *D & D* I; *EERS* (CW X); Schneewind, J.B., ed., *Mill's
        Essays on Literature and Society*.
        'Exception to the Objections to Nominal Punishments', *Examiner*,
        16 September 1838.
1840   'Coleridge', *London and Westminster Review* 33 (March 1840); *D & D*

I; *EERS* (CW X); Schneewind, J.B., ed., *Mill's Essays on Literature and Society.*

'M. de Tocqueville on Democracy in America', *Edinburgh Review* 72 (October 1840); *EPS* i (CW XVIII); *D & D* II; Schneewind, J.B., ed., *Mill's Ethical Writings.* An earlier review, of the first volume, appeared in the *London Review* 1 (October 1835).

1843   'Macaulay's Lays of Ancient Rome', *Westminster Review* 39 (February 1843).

1845   'The Claims of Labour', *Edinburgh Review* 81 (April 1845); *D & D* II; *EES* i (CW IV).

1846   Leading article, *Morning Chronicle*, 3 December 1846; on the beneficial effect on intelligence of ownership of land.

1850   'The Negro Question', *Fraser's Magazine* 41 (January 1850); a vehement reply to an article by Carlyle in the previous issue.
         Leading article, *Morning Chronicle*, 13 March 1850; inadequate punishment of crimes of violence, especially against women and children ('Very little of this was mine' — MacMinn, etc., *op. cit.*, p. 73).
         'Punishment of Children', *Sunday Times*, 2 June 1850 ('Very little of this article was mine' MacMinn, etc., *op. cit.*, p. 75).

1851   'Newman's Political Economy', *Westminster Review* 56 (October 1851); *EES* ii (CW V).

1852   'Dr. Whewell on Moral Philosophy', *Westminster Review* 58 (October 1852); *D & D* II; *EERS* (CW X); Schneewind, J.B., ed., *Mill's Ethical Writings.*

1853   'Grote's History of Greece', *Edinburgh Review* 98 (October 1853); a review of vols 9, 10, 11; *D & D* II; *EPC* (CW XI). An earlier review, of volumes 1 and 2, had appeared in the *Edinburgh Review* in October 1846; this is in *D & D* II, 'Early Grecian History and Legend'; *EPC* (CW XI). Various shorter notices had appeared in the *Spectator* in April 1846, June 1847, March 1849 and March 1850.

1854   Diary, 8 January to 13 April 1854; in Elliot, H.S.R., *The Letters of John Stuart Mill*, vol II pp. 357-86; excerpts in Schneewind, J.B., ed., *Mill's Essays on Literature and Society.*

1854-5 Paper relating to the reorganisation of the Civil Service (competitive examinations), *Parliamentary Papers* 1854-5, vol. XX, pp. 92-8; *EPS* i (CW XVIII).

1859   'Bain's Psychology', *Edinburgh Review* 110 (October 1859); *D & D* III; *EPC* (CW XI).

1864   Letter to the *Gardeners' Chronicle and Agricultural Gazette*, 26 January 1864; published in Mill's obituary in this journal, 17 May 1873; *Mill News Letter* 10, no. 1 (Winter 1975).

1866   'Grote's Plato', *Edinburgh Review* 123 (April 1866); *D & D* III; *EPC* (CW XI).

1868   Speech against the abolition of capital punishment, *Hansard*, 21 April 1868, cols 1047ff.

1869   'Endowments', *Fortnightly Review* 11 (1 April 1869); *D & D* IV; *EES* ii (CW V).
         Notes to James Mill's *Analysis of the Phenomena of the Human Mind* (new edn, 1869), edited by Bain, A., Findlater, A. and Grote, G., with additional notes by J. S. Mill.

1871   *Speech on Land Tenure Reform*, delivered 15 May 1871, and published by the Land Tenure Reform Association; *D & D* IV.

1873   'Grote's Aristotle', *Fortnightly Review* 19 (1 January 1873); *D & D*
        IV; *EPC* (CW XI)
1874   'Nature' (written 1850-8), in *Three Essays on Religion.*
        'Utility of Religion' (written 1850-8), in *Three Essays on Religion.*
        'Theism' (written 1868-70), in *Three Essays on Religion.*

2   *Secondary Sources*

ALEXANDER, E. *Matthew Arnold and John Stuart Mill* (London: Routledge and
    Kegan Paul, 1965).
    'Mill's Theory of Culture: The Wedding of Literature and Democracy',
    University of Toronto Quarterly 35 (1965-6).
    'Disinterested Virtue: Dickens and Mill in Agreement', the *Dickensian* 65
    (1969).
ANON 'Mr. Mill on Education', a review of the *Inaugural Address, Saturday
    Review* 23 (9 February 1867).
ANON Review of the *Autobiography, Edinburgh Review* 139 (January-April
    1874).
ANON Review of the *Autobiography, Quarterly Review* 136 (January-April
    1874).
ANSCHUTZ, R.P. *The Philosophy of J. S. Mill* (Oxford: Clarendon Press, 1953;
    repr. with appendix, 1963).
ARNOLD, M. Report on secondary education in France, Germany, Italy and
    Switzerland, *Report of the Schools Inquiry Commission* (1868), Irish University
    Press, vol. VI.
AUGUST, E. *John Stuart Mill: A Mind at Large* (London: Vision Press, 1976).
AYER, A.J. 'Man as a Subject for Science', in Laslett, P. and Runciman, W.G.,
    eds, *Philosophy, Politics and Society*, 3rd series (Oxford: Blackwell, 1967).

BAIN, A. *John Stuart Mill: A Criticism with Personal Recollections* (London:
    Longmans Green, 1882; repr. New York: Kelley, 1969).
    Education as a Science (London: Kegan Paul, Trench, 7th edn, 1889).
BAKER, W.J. 'Gradgrindery and the Education of J. S. Mill: A Clarification',
    Western Humanities Review 24 (Winter 1970).
BAMFORD, T.W., ed. *Thomas Arnold on Education* (London: Cambridge
    University Press, 1970).
BARROW, R. *Plato, Utilitarianism and Education* (London: Routledge and Kegan
    Paul, 1975).
BENTHAM, J. *Chrestomathia*, in *Works* vol. 8, ed. Bowring, J. (Edinburgh:
    William Tait, 1843).
BERLIN, SIR ISAIAH *John Stuart Mill and the Ends of Life* (Robert Waley Cohen
    Memorial Lecture, London: Council of Christians and Jews, 1959).
BOARD OF EDUCATION *Curriculum and Examinations in Secondary Schools*,
    Report of the Committee of the Secondary School Examinations Council
    (Norwood Report) (London: H.M.S.O., 1943).
BORCHARD, R. *John Stuart Mill: The Man* (London: Watts, 1957).
BOURNE, H.R. FOX, ed. *John Stuart Mill: Notices of his Life and Works together
    with two Papers written by him on the Land Question* (London: E. Dallow,
    1873; repr. from the *Examiner*, 17 May 1873).
BOYD, D. *Elites and their Education* (Windsor: National Foundation for
    Educational Research, 1973).
BRITTON, K. 'The Nature of Arithmetic: A Reconsideration of Mill's Views',

Proceedings of the Aristotelian Society 48 (1947-8).
'John Stuart Mill: The Ordeal of an Intellectual', *Cambridge Journal* 2, no. 2 (1948).
John Stuart Mill (Harmondsworth: Penguin Books, 1953).
'J. S. Mill and the Cambridge Union Society', *Cambridge Review* 76 (29 October 1955).
'J. S. Mill: A Debating Speech on Wordsworth, 1829', *Cambridge Review* 79 (8 March 1958).
BRITTON, K. and ROBSON, J.M. 'Mill's Debating Speeches', *Mill News Letter* 1, no. 1 (Fall 1965).
BROGAN, H. *Tocqueville* (London: Collins/Fontana, 1973).
BURNS, J.H. 'J. S. Mill and Democracy, 1829-61', in Schneewind, J.B., ed., *Mill: a Collection of Critical Essays* (London: Macmillan, 1969).
BURSTON, W.H. 'The Utilitarians and the Monitorial System of Teaching', *The Year Book of Education 1957* (London: Evans, 1957).
ed. *James Mill on Education* (London: Cambridge University Press, 1969).
James Mill on Philosophy and Education (London: Athlone Press, 1973).

CAPES, J.M. 'The Autobiography of John Stuart Mill', *Contemporary Review* 23 (December 1873-May 1874).
CARR, R. 'The Religious Thought of John Stuart Mill: A Study in Reluctant Scepticism', *Journal of the History of Ideas* 23 (1962).
CASTLE, E.B. *Ancient Education and Today* (Harmondsworth: Penguin Books, 1961).
CHADWICK, E. 'Communications on Half-Time Teaching and on Military Drills', with a letter explanatory of the former, in Papers submitted to the Education Commission, 1 July 1861, *Parliamentary Papers 1861-2,* Irish University Press edition, *Education: General,* vol. 8.
COMMISSION ON RELIGIOUS EDUCATION IN SCHOOLS *The Fourth R: The Durham Report on Religious Education* (London: National Society and S.P.C.K., 1970)
COURTNEY, W.L. *Life of John Stuart Mill* (London: Walter Scott, 1889).
COWAN, J.L. *Pleasure and Pain* (London: Macmillan, 1968).
COWLING, M. *Mill and Liberalism* (London: Cambridge University Press, 1963).
CRANSTON, M. *John Stuart Mill* (London: Longmans, Green, Writers and their Work no. 99, 1958).
CUMMING, I. *A Manufactured Man* (Auckland: University of Auckland, Bulletin no. 55, Educational Series no. 2, 1960).

DEWEY, J. *John Dewey: Selected Educational Writings*, ed. Garforth, F.W. (London: Heinemann, 1966).
DICKENS, C. *Hard Times* (London: 1854; Oxford University Press, World's Classics, 1924, etc.).
DUNCAN, G. *Marx and Mill* (London: Cambridge University Press, 1973).
DURHAM, J. 'The Influence of J. S. Mill's Mental Crisis on his Thoughts', *American Imago* 20 (1963).

ELLIOT, H.S.R., ed. *The Letters of John Stuart Mill*, 2 vols (London: Longmans, Green, 1910).
EYSENCK, H.J. *Race, Intelligence and Education* (London: Temple Smith, 1971).
The Inequality of Man (London: Temple Smith, 1973).

FARRAR, F.W., ed. *Essays on a Liberal Education* (London: Macmillan, 1867).

FEUER, L.S. 'John Stuart Mill as a Sociologist: The Unwritten Ethology', in Robson, J.M. and Laine, M., eds, *James and John Stuart Mill.*

FIELDING, K.J. 'Mill and Gradgrind', *Nineteenth Century Fiction* 11 (1956-7).

FOX, CAROLINE *Memories of Old Friends,* ed. Pym, H.N. (London: Smith, Elder, 1882).

FRIEDMAN, R.B. 'An Introduction to Mill's Theory of Authority', in Schneewind, J.B., ed., *Mill: a Collection of Critical Essays* (London: Macmillan, 1969).

GARFORTH, F.W. *The Scope of Philosophy* (London: Longmans, 1971).

GILBERT, M. 'The Origin of the Reform Movement in Modern Language Teaching', *Durham Research Review* 4 (September, 1953).

GOMPERZ, H. *Theodor Gomperz, 1832-1912* (Vienna: Gerold, 1936).

HAINDS, J.R. 'J. S. Mill's *Examiner* Articles on Art', *Journal of the History of Ideas* 11 (1950).

HALLIDAY, R. J. 'Some Recent Interpretations of John Stuart Mill', *Philosophy* 43 (January 1968).

John Stuart Mill (London: Allen and Unwin, 1976).

HAMBURGER, J. *Intellectuals in Politics* (New Haven: Yale University Press, 1965).

HARRIS, A.L. 'John Stuart Mill's Theory of Progress', *Ethics* 66 (April 1956).

'John Stuart Mill: Servant of the East India Company', *Canadian Journal of Economics and Political Science* 30 (1964).

HARRISON, F. 'John Stuart Mill', *Nineteenth Century* 40 (July-December, 1896).

HAYEK, F.A. *John Stuart Mill and Harriet Taylor* (London: Routledge and Kegan Paul, 1951).

The Counter Revolution of Science (Chicago: 1952; London: Collier-Macmillan, 1964).

HIMMELFARB, G. 'The Two Mills', *New Leader*, 10 May 1965.

'Mill on Liberty', *Inquiry* 10 (1967).

Victorian Minds (London: Weidenfeld and Nicolson, 1968), ch. 4, 'The Other John Stuart Mill'.

On Liberty and Liberalism: The Case of John Stuart Mill (New York: Knopf, 1974).

HIRST, P.H. 'Liberal Education and the Nature of Knowledge', in Archambault, R.D., *Philosophical Analysis and Education* (London: Routledge and Kegan Paul, 1965).

HOLTHOON, F.L., VAN *The Road to Utopia: A Study of John Stuart Mill's Social Thought* (Assen: van Gorcum, 1971).

HUDSON, W.D. *Modern Moral Philosophy* (London: Macmillan, 1970).

HUME, D. *A Treatise of Human Nature,* ed. Selby-Bigge, L.A. (London: Oxford University Press, 1888, etc.).

Enquiries concerning the Human Understanding and concerning the Principles of Morals, ed. Selby-Bigge, L.A. (London: Oxford University Press, 2nd edn, 1902).

HUXLEY, T.H. *Science and Education* (London: Macmillan, 1925; first publ. 1893).

'A Liberal Education and where to find it', *ib.,* ch. 4.

JACK, D.R.L. *John Stuart Mill: Philosophy and Education,* M.Ed. Thesis, University of Birmingham, 1972-3.

JANES, G.M. 'J. S. Mill's Education', *Quarterly Journal of the University of North Dakota* 21, no. 2 (1931).

KAMM, J. *John Stuart Mill in Love* (London: Gordon and Cremonesi, 1977).

LEVI, A.W. 'The "Mental Crisis" of John Stuart Mill', *Psychoanalytic Review* 32 (1945).

'The Idea of Socrates: The Philosophic Hero in the Nineteenth Century', *Journal of the History of Ideas* 17 (1956).

LOCKE, J. *An Essay concerning Human Understanding*, abridged and ed. Pringle-Pattison, A.S. (London: Oxford University Press, 1924, etc.).

Some Thoughts concerning Education, ed. Garforth, F.W. (London: Heinemann, 1964).

Of the Conduct of the Understanding, ed. Garforth, F.W. (New York: Teachers College Press, 1966).

McCLOSKEY, H.J. *John Stuart Mill: A Critical Study* (London: Macmillan, 1971).

'Mill's Liberalism', *Philosophical Quarterly* 13 (1963).

McREADY, H.W. The Defence of Individualism', *Queen's Quarterly* 52 (1945).

MAGID, H.M. 'Mill and the Problem of Freedom of Thought', *Social Research* 21 (1954).

MATTHEWS, C. 'Argument through Metaphor in John Stuart Mill's *On Liberty*', *Language and Style* 4 (1971).

MAZLISH, B. *James and John Stuart Mill: Father and Son in the Nineteenth Century* (London: Hutchinson, 1975).

MILL, ANNA J. 'John Stuart Mill's Visit to Wordsworth, 1831', *Modern Languages Review* 44 (1949).

John Mill's Boyhood Visit to France (Toronto: University of Toronto Press, 1960).

MILL, JAMES 'Education', article contributed to the 5th edition of the *Encyclopaedia Britannica* (written in 1818, according to Bain, A., *James Mill*, p. 247).

Analysis of the Phenomena of the Human Mind, 2 vols, notes by Bain, A., Findlater, A., Grote, G., edited with additional notes by John Stuart Mill (London: Longmans, Green, Reader and Dyer, new edition, 1869).

The History of British India, 3 vols (London: Baldwin, Cradock and Joy, 2nd edn, 1820).

Elements of Political Economy (London: Baldwin, Cradock and Joy, 2nd edn, 1824).

MILL NEWS LETTER Toronto: University of Toronto Press in association with Victoria College, 1965-.

MORLEY, J. 'The Death of Mr. Mill', *Fortnightly Review* 78 N.S. (1 June 1873).

NEFF, E. *Carlyle and Mill: An Introduction to Victorian Thought* (New York: Columbia University Press, 1926; Octagon Books, 1964, repr. 1974).

PACKE, M. ST. J. *The Life of John Stuart Mill* (London: Seckcr and Warburg, 1954).

PAPPE, H.O. *John Stuart Mill and the Harriet Taylor Myth* (London: Cambridge University Press, 1960).

'Mill and Tocqueville', *Journal of the History of Ideas* 25 (1964).

PETERS, R.S. *Education as Initiation* (London: London University Institute of Education, 1964).

Ethics and Education (London: Allen and Unwin, 1966).

'Survival or the Soul?', *Times Educational Supplement,* 10 March 1972.

PILLON, F. 'La Raison Profonde de la Crise Mentale de Stuart Mill', *La Critique Philosophique* 2 (1873).

PLAMENATZ, J. *The English Utilitarians* (Oxford: Blackwell, 2nd edn, 1958).
PLATO *Republic*, transl. and ed. Lee, H.D.P. (Harmondsworth: Penguin Books, 1955, 2nd edn. 1974).
POPPER, SIR KARL *The Open Society and its Enemies* (London: Routledge and Kegan Paul, 1945; 4th edn. 1962).
  The Poverty of Historicism (London: Routledge and Kegan Paul, paperb. edn. 1961).
PRICE, A. 'J. S. Mill and the Combination of Logic and Poetry in Education', *Researches and Studies* 24 (October 1962).
PRINGLE, G.O.S. 'Mill's Humanity', *Westminster Review* 150 (July-December 1898).

RANDALL, J.H. 'John Stuart Mill and the Working-Out of Empiricism', *Journal of the History of Ideas* 26 (1965).
REES, J.C. *Mill and his Early Critics* (Leicester: University College, Leicester, 1956).
  'A Phase in the Development of Mill's Ideas on Liberty', *Political Studies* 6 (1958).
  'A Re-reading of Mill on Liberty', *Political Studies* 8 (1960).
  'H. O. Pappé on Mill', *Political Studies* 10 (1962); a review of Pappé, *op. cit.*, 1960.
  'Was Mill for Liberty?' *Political Studies* 14 (1966); a review of Cowling, M., *op. cit.*
REEVES, M. *Growing up in a Modern Society* (London: University of London Press, 1946).
ROBSON, J.M. 'Harriet Taylor and John Stuart Mill: Artist and Scientist', *Queen's Quarterly* 73 (1966).
  The Improvement of Mankind (Toronto: University of Toronto Press; London: Routledge and Kegan Paul, 1968).
  'J. S. Mill's Theory of Poetry', *University of Toronto Quarterly* 29 (1960).
  'Rational Animals and Others', in Robson, J.M. and Laine, M., eds, *James and John Stuart Mill*.
ROBSON, J.M. and LAINE, M., eds *James and John Stuart Mill: Papers of the Centenary Conference* (Toronto and Buffalo: University of Toronto Press, 1976).
ROEBUCK, J. 'National Education', *Tait's Edinburgh Magazine* 2 (March 1833); see also his speeches in *Hansard*, vol. 20, 30 July 1833, and vol. 24, 3 June 1834.
ROELLINGER, F.X. 'Mill on Education', *Journal of General Education* 6, no. 3 (April 1952).
ROTHBLATT, S. *Revolution of the Dons* (London: Faber, 1968).
ROUSSEAU, J.J. *Emile*, transl. Foxley, B. (London: Dent, Everyman Library, 1911, repr. 1948).
RUSSELL, BERTRAND 'John Stuart Mill', *Proceedings of the British Academy* 41 (1955).
RUSSELL, BERTRAND and PATRICIA, eds *The Amberley Papers*, 2 vols (London: Hogarth, 1937).
RYAN, A. 'John Stuart Mill's Art of Living', *Listener* 74 (21 October 1965).
  The Philosophy of John Stuart Mill (London: Macmillan, 1970).
  J. S. Mill (London: Routledge and Kegan Paul, 1974).

SCHAPIRO, J.S. 'Utilitarianism and the Foundation of English Liberalism', *Journal of Social Psychology* 4 (1939).

'John Stuart Mill, Pioneer of Democratic Liberalism in England', *Journal of the History of Ideas* 4, no. 2 (April 1943).

SCHNEEWIND, J.B., ed. *Mill: A Collection of Critical Essays* (London: Macmillan, 1969).

SHARPLESS, F.P. *The Literary Criticism of John Stuart Mill* (The Hague: Mouton, 1967).

SKINNER, B.F. *Walden Two* (New York: Macmillan, paperb. edn. 1962). *Beyond Freedom and Dignity* (London: Jonathan Cape, 1972).

STEPHEN, L. 'Social Macadamisation', *Fraser's Magazine* 6 N.S. (July-December, 1872). *The English Utilitarians*, 3 vols (London: Duckworth, 1900).

STEWART, W.A.C. *Progressives and Radicals in English Education, 1750-1970* (London: Macmillan, 1972).

STOKES, E. *The English Utilitarians and India* (London: Oxford University Press, 1959).

SUMNER, L.W. 'More Light on the Later Mill', *Philosophical Review* 83 (October 1974).

TAYLOR, A. (son of Harriet Taylor) *Memories of a Student* (London: Simkin, Marshall, etc., 1895).

TAYLOR, H. *Autobiography*, 2 vols (London: Longmans, Green, 1885).

THILLY, F. 'The Individualism of John Stuart Mill', *Philosophical Review* 32 (January 1923).

THOMAS, W. 'John Stuart Mill and the Uses of Autobiography', *History* 56, no. 188 (October 1971).

THORNTON, W.T. 'John Stuart Mill at the India House', *Examiner*, 17 May 1873 (see above, Bourne, H.R. Fox, ed.).

THWING, C.F. 'Education according to John Stuart Mill', *School and Society* 3, no. 53 (January 1916).

WARD, J. 'J. S. Mill's Science of Ethology', *International Journal of Ethics* (later *Ethics*) 1 (July 1891).

WARD, J.W. 'Mill, Marx and Modern Individualism', *Virginia Quarterly Review* 35 (1959).

WARD, WILFRID *Men and Matters* (London: Longmans, 1914), quoted in Roellinger, F.X., *op. cit.*

WARREN, A.H. *English Poetic Theory*, 1825-65 (New York: Octagon Books, 1966).

WEINBERG, A. *Theodor Gomperz and John Stuart Mill* (Geneva: Librairie Droz, 1963).

WEST, E.G. 'The Role of Education in Nineteenth Century Doctrines of Political Economy', *British Journal of Educational Studies* 12 (1963-4). 'Liberty and Education: John Stuart Mill's Dilemma', *Philosophy* 40 (1965).

WEST, M. 'A Boy's Education', *Education* (Boston, Mass.) 19 (March 1899).

WHITEHEAD, A.N. *The Aims of Education* (London: Benn, 2nd edn, 1950, paperb. edn. 1962).

WOODS, T. *Poetry and Philosophy: A Study in the Thought of John Stuart Mill* (London: Hutchinson, 1961).

Index

Academies   10,12
Accuracy   152
Activity   144ff., 155, 157-8
Aesthetic experience   194-5,
    200-1, 215, 221, 222ff.
Altruism   71, 88, 91, 163, 178-9,
    215ff.
American Civil War   9
Anglicans   see Church of England
Anschutz, R.P.   32
'Antagonism'   102, 176-7, 192,
    193, 201
Aristotle   5, 47, 48, 50, 71, 91,
    148, 151, 230
Arithmetic   146, 150, 161-2,
    187-8 (see also Mathematics)
Arnold, Matthew   18, 203
Arnold, Thomas   19, 20, 158,
    190, 203
Art   33, 62, 67ff., 72, 79
    of life   33, 36, 70
Arts   167, 179, 192, 194-5, 201
    215, 218, 222ff.
Association psychology   4, 46ff.,
    59ff., 65-6, 93ff., 103, 107ff., 111,
    123-4, 137-8, 142-4, 155, 169,
    171, 173, 178, 196-7, 212-13, 224
Athens   129, 189, 224
Attention   52, 98-9
Authority   80, 92, 93, 101, 102,
    139, 140, 154, 157, 159, 165-7,
    181, 201, 221 (see also under
    Freedom)
Avignon   5,8,9,136
Ayer, A.J.   43 note 24

Bacon, Francis 29, 31, 63
Bacon, Roger 29
Bain, Alexander 3, 49, 57, 61, 65,
    97, 98, 99, 157, 189, 222, 224
Balance 199, 200, 201-2, 218, 227,
    228

Beauty   87, 134-7, 167, 194-5,
    200-1, 215, 222, 224, 225, 226
Behavioural engineering   75-7,
    80-1, 102
Belief   52-3
Bell, Andrew   13, 101
Bentham, Jeremy   xi, 3-4, 5, 6,
    11, 25, 30, 36, 76, 96, 99 note 37,
    104, 134, 153, 160, 178, 201,
    222, 225, 226
Bentham, Sir Samuel   5
Berkeley, George   30, 48, 50
Biber, G.E.   150, 184
Birth control   6
Blame   101, 108, 197
British and Foreign School Society
    13, 14, 16
Brougham, Henry, Lord   15, 184
Bureaucracy   23, 89, 127

Cambridge, University of   10-11,
    20
Campbell, Thomas   20
Carlyle, Thomas   114, 133, 223
Causality   48, 59-60, 62-3, 73-5,
    93, 94
Causation   33, 38ff., 48, 55, 73-5
Censorship   80, 96-7, 138-9, 141,
    180, 185-6
Chadwick, Edwin   198
Character   39-42, 43, 52, 53,
    60ff., 64-5, 73-4, 107, 111ff., 124,
    132-3, 183-4, 186, 192, 199, 215,
    225-6
Charity schools   10, 12
Child-centred education see under
    Education
Children   115
    development of   156-7
    imitativeness of   178, 186
Christianity   148, 193 (see also
    Jesus)

Church of England   10, 12, 14,
    15, 20-1
Civilisation   126-7
Civil Service, examinations for   22
Clarendon Commission
    1861-4   20
Classics   4-5, 10, 11, 19, 94, 103,
    147-8, 152, 160, 189-90, 200,
    203-4, 211, 212, 215, 218-19,
    220, 228
Coleridge, Samuel Taylor   104,
    204, 223
Commerce   130
Commercialism   126, 130, 133
Communism   90, 129
Competition   92, 130, 131
Comprehensive education   131,
    137, 140, 202, 217
Comte, Auguste   73, 75, 76, 115,
    192
Cooperation   127, 197
Cousin Report   150, 161, 187,
    193
Cowper-Temple, W.F.   19
Cram   92-3, 104, 148-51
Creativity   92-201
Curriculum   Part III chs. 4,5

Darwin, Charles   56
Day, Thomas   104, 198
Dearden, R.F.   xii
Deduction   see under Logic
Democracy   71, 91, 132-3, 139,
    177, 189, 197, 199, 215, 217,
    225, 226
Demosthenes   5
Denominational schools   14,
    17-19, 161
Despotism   132
Determinism see under Freedom
Deterrence   171-3
Dewey, John   102, 105, 106, 176
Dialectic   71, 72, 91, 149, 176
    (see also Discussion)
Dialogue   see Dialectic,
    Discussion
Dickens, Charles   104, 155
Difficulty, stimulus of   126, 129
Discipline   92, 95, 100, 119, 122,
    140, 144, 159, 162-5, 177, 191-2,
    196, 210-11
Discovery   7, 105, 145ff., 154,
    199

Discussion   5, 92, 102, 145,
    175-7, 221
Diversity   see Variety
Durham, University of   21

Edgeworth, Maria   104, 198
Educability   37, 42, 51, 53, 109,
    138
Education   17, 23-4, 38, 53, 62,
    66, 67-8, 71-2, 75, 76, 77, 80,
    85-8, 92-3, 94-7, 99, 100-1, 105-6,
    107ff., 120-3, 125, 127, 137-8,
    166, 167, 178-9, 228
    aesthetic   194-5, 221, 222ff.
    art of   62, Part II ch. 5, 101
    child-centred   73, 100-1, 144ff.,
        151, 155, 181, 199
    concept of   105-6
    elementary   10, 12ff., 183-4
    general   204, 207ff.
    of girls   9, 10, 20, 21-2
    importance (power) of   23,
        87-8, 96, 109-11, 112-13, 115
    of infants   14 and note 23
    liberal   177, 183, 194, 198.
        Part III ch. 5
    methods of   Part III ch. 3
    moral   87, 103, 144, 150, 173,
        193, 195-7, 214ff., 220, 225-6
    Parliamentary grants for   15,
        16, 17, 18, 23
    physical   197-8
    principles of   143ff.
    process of   85, Part III passim
    progressive   100, 102, 105,
        106, 142, 154, 155
    purposes of   67, 88ff., 105,
        106, 138, 153, 162-3, 199-200,
        201-2, 205-6, 209-12, 227,
        228-9
    religious   19, 22, 150, 161,
        193-4, 221
    in science   91, 190-3
    secondary   19-20
    state and   10ff., Part I
        passim, 92-3, 150, 159
    technical   22, 228
    universal   10ff., Part I passim,
        91
    university   10-11, 20-21, 145,
        183, Part III ch. 5 passim
    vocational   183, 205, 206-7,
        218, 227, 228, 229

Education Act 1870   14, 18, 19, 22
    1902   19
Educational philosophy   xi-xiii
    73, 79, 100, 105
'Educative society'   140
Eichthal, Gustave d'   127
Elenchus   153, 163, 176
Elite, elitism   98, 166
Emotion   6, 97, 200-1, 222-4, 225-6
Empiricism   29ff., 49, 93
Endowed schools   10, 19-20, 22, 161
Endowed Schools Act 1869-20
English (nation)   112, 127
Environment   25, 39-40, 43, 51, 53, 60-1, 63, 64-5, 73-4, 75, 76, 79, 86-7, 92, 93, 95-7, 100, 103, Part II ch. 2, 142-3, 177-8, 180, 194-5, 197, 217
Epistemology   77, 93, 155
Equality   89, 90, 97
Ethology   59ff., 67, 73, 74, 76, 85-6, 101
Eton   193-4
Evangelical movement   11-12
Examinations   18, 22, 156
Example   103, 110, 152, 158, 172, 177ff., 186, 197, 216
Experience   29ff., 45, 46-8, 49, 64, 93, 95-6, 100, 102, 109, 144ff., 210
Experientialism   29ff., 46-7, 48, 49, 77-8, 93, 94ff., 103, 106, 107, 123, 142-3, 144ff., 160
Experiment   43, 44, 56, 63-4, 66, 74, 75, 78, 93, 95, 102, 144, 210, 219
Eyre, E.J., Governor of Jamaica   9
Eysenck, H.J.   137

Fact   32-4, 38, 45, 68, 79, 177
Faculties, mental   94 (*see also* Mental power)
Family   *see* Home
Farrar, F.W.   203
Fear   164-5, 174
Feeling   *see* Emotion
Ford Abbey   87, 109, 136, 222
Forster, W.E.   18
Fox, W.J.   195

France   5, 7, 109
Freedom   38, 40, 44, 76, 80, 89-90, 92, 138-9, 142, 165-7, 181, 204, 217, 229
    and authority   165-7, 181 (*see also* Authority)
    and determinism   38ff., 74, 78, 93, 130, 168, 169-70
Freire, Paulo   102, 106
French   *see* Modern Languages
Friend, Charles   186, 198

Gall, Franz Joseph   116
Gardeners' Chronicle   136
Geography   162, 185, 188, 208
German   *see* Modern Languages
God   94, 110, 118-19, 221
Government, influence of   132-4
Grammar Schools   10, 19
Grant's *Arithmetic*   146, 147-8, 151, 152, 154, 156, 187
Greatness   4, 7, 42, 75, 89, 146, 148, 151, 166-7, 177-9, 185, 186, 189, 201, 215, 222, 225
Greece, Greeks   146, 148, 189, 204, 211
Greek   *see* Classics
Grote, George   15, 100

Habit   48, 103, 143-4, 152, 197, 214
Hamilton, Sir William   31, 56, 57, 115, 187-8
Happiness   6, 70, 72, 76, 80, 88, 89, 90, 91, 102, 118, 167, 169, 220
Hare, William   178
Hartley, David   49, 50, 51, 98
Hazelwood School   104
Hazlitt, William   104
Health and Morals of Apprentices Acts 1802, 1819   15
Hegel, G.W.F.   176
Helvetius   xi, 11, 14, 96 and note 30, 103, 109, 110, 111, 116, 153
Heredity   96, 109ff., 131-2
Heroic   *see* Greatness
Hirst, P.H.   xii, 227, 230
Historicism   220
History   179, 185, 188, 202, 209, 215, 219-20
Hobbes, Thomas   48

Home   103, 128, 137, 179, 194,
   195-6, 214, 216, 217, 221
Human nature   Part II ch. 2,
   101-2
Hume, David   30, 35, 46, 48, 49
Hume, Joseph   15
Huxley, Julian   97
Huxley, T.H.   18, 160, 228, 229

Illich, Ivan   102, 106
Imagination   92, 112, 135, 200-1,
   211, 220, 223, 225
Improvement   xi, xiii, 6, 24, 32,
   36-7, 50-1, 59, 73, 75-6, 78, 80,
   88, 89, 91, 95, 99, 101-2, 132-3,
   142, 206, 220
India Office   3, 8, 21, 22, 145,
   224
Individuality   25, 38ff., 52, 53,
   65, 71, 74, 79, 88-9, 91, 92, 96,
   97, 100-2, 124, 126-7, 133, 139,
   142, 166, 167, 195, 204, 213
Indoctrination   23, 80, 138-9,
   141, 159, 180, 217-18, 221, 226,
   227
Induction   see under Logic
Inquiry   92, 144, 145, 150, 159,
   199, 213, 220
Inspection of schools   16, 17
Instinct   53, 60, 96, 97, 113-14,
   119-20
Instruction, methods of   Part III
   ch. 3
Intellect   75, 90-1, 147, 199-200,
   201, 202, 206, 210-13, 229
Intelligence   111, 131-2, 147,
   153, 202
Interest   164, 165, 193, 199
Introspection   56
Intuition, -ism   29, 30, 31-2, 46-7,
   50, 54, 57, 65, 93, 94-5, 115
Irish   124-5, 132
Is/ought   32, 68, 79, 117, 118

Jesus   88, 148, 179, 221
Jowett, Benjamin   204
Junius Redivivus (Adams, W.B.)
   179, 195, 200
Justice   168-70
Juvenal   73, 77 note 25

Kant, Immanuel   46
King's College, London   21

Knowledge   29ff., 59, 77, 93, 95,
   107-8, 157-8, 184, 199, 207,
   209-11, 213, 214, 216, 223, 227

Lamb, Charles   104
Lancaster, Joseph   13, 101
Language   116, 118, 140-1
Languages, teaching of   103, 144,
   147-8, 160, 188-90, 212, 218
Latin   see Classics
Law, meaning of   117-18
   educative influence of   134
Learning   156ff., 167, 180, 199
Leisure   227, 229
Liberal education   see under
   Education
Libraries   12, 16-17, 186
Literary and Philosophical
   Societies   12
Literature   178-9, 184-6, 189-90,
   194-5, 204
Locke, John   10, 29, 30, 35, 44,
   46, 47, 48, 49, 96, 97, 103, 110,
   138, 142, 143, 153, 175, 197
Logic   5, 7, 34, 45, 48, 163,
   191-2 (of science), 200, 211, 223
   deductive, inductive   34-5, 63-4,
   66, 152, 191-2, 211, 212
London, University of   20, 21
Lowe, Robert   18

Manual skills   197
Martineau, Harriet   193, 198
Mathematics   19, 30, 48, 146,
   187-8, 200, 212, 215, 219 (see
   also Arithmetic)
Mayo, Charles   104
Mediocrity   23, 89, 93, 133, 215,
   226, 229
Memory   147, 149-50, 151, 154,
   155, 211
Mental power   147, 148, 151-3,
   163, 210-11
Mill, Clara (JSM's sister)   224
Mill, George (JSM's brother)   224
Mill, Harriet (JSM's mother)   3, 6,
   224
Mill, Harriet (née Taylor, JSM's wife)
   7-8, 87, 104, 224
Mill, James   xi, 3-7, 11, 20, 23,
   25, 49, 50, 52-3, 76, 96, 98, 99,
   100, 101, 103, 104, 105, 107-8,
   109-10, 143, 160, 163-4, 169,

178, 190, 198, 199, 212, 218, 221, 222, 226
Mill, John Stuart   xi, xiii, 3ff., 17, 18, 21ff., 30, 76, 97-8, 102, 142-3, 146, 153-4, 172, 199-200, 206, 221ff.
  beauty, sensitivity to   134-6, 194-5, 221ff.
  botanical interests   9, 136, 200
  conservationist   125, 134-6
  criticisms of contemporary education   86, 92-3, 147ff., 159ff., 164, 184-5, 187, 190, 192, 193-4, 211
  education of   4-7, 51, 93, 105, 107, 113, 127, 146, 148, 150, 153, 159, 160, 161, 164, 178, 192, 198, 199, 208, 211-12, 221, 222, 224
  education, views on   xi, xiii, 17, 21ff., 71-2, 85-7, 92ff., 100, 102, 105, 108, 115, 120ff., 142-3
  elitism   98, 215
  in France   5, 7, 109
  in Greece   5, 134, 224
  heroic, admiration for   *see* Greatness
  Member of Parliament   8-9, 22, 168
  mountains, influenced by   5, 87, 109, 194, 222
  music, pleasure in   222, 224, and note 68
  mysticism   6, 32
  nervous crisis   6, 36, 101, 108, 137, 194, 195, 222, 224, 225
  Parliamentary candidate   8-9
  religion, views on   115, 125, 216, 221-2
  science, views on   32ff., 36-7, 38ff., 59, 62-3, 66, 68ff., 190-2, 209 (*see also* Science)
  truth, devotion to   24, 36, 73, 90-1 (*see also* Truth)
Mind   65, 94, 95-6, 98, 99
  subconscious   57-8
Modern Languages   160, 188-9, 190, 204, 208, 218
Molesworth, Sir William   150
Monitorial system   13, 16, 101, 155, 160-1

Morality   40-1, 43, 166-7, 168, 169, 214-15, 220, 223, 225
Moral science   *see* Psychology
Motivation   95, 98-9, 100, 143, 167, 225
Music   222, 223, 224

National Education League   9, 18, 22
National Society   13, 14, 15
Nature   109ff., 116ff., 134-7
  educative influence of   136-7
  'follow nature'   116-19, 120-3
  laws of   33-4, 36-7, 44, 59-60, 62-4, 73-5, 116-18, 121
Negroes   9, 114
Neill, A.S.   102, 142
Newcastle Commission   1858-61   17-18
Newcastle College of Physical Science   21
Nightingale, Florence   91, 171
Nonconformists   14, 15, 17, 20
Norwood Report   131
Nunn, Sir Percy   102
Nurture   109ff., 131-2, 137-8

Observation   44, 56, 62-3, 64, 75, 78, 110, 121, 122, 144, 147, 152, 153, 191-2, 210, 211, 219
Ockham, William of   29
O'Connor, D.J.   xii
Opinion, public   127-8
Orbilius   154 and note 42
Owen, Robert   13-14, 39, 104, 168
Owens College, Manchester   21
Oxford, University of   10-11, 20

Packe, M. St.J.   42
Participation   87, 92, 93, 95, 132, 133, 137, 177
Payment by results   18, 22, 156
Pericles   178
Personal identity   53-6
Pestalozzi   14, 103, 104, 142
Peters, R.S.   xii, 76, 105, 106, 123
Philosophia prima   70, 71, 72
Philosophical Radicals   6
Philosophy   xi-xii, 201
Piaget, J.   121, 156

Plato 5, 32, 47, 71-2, 76, 78, 80,
  91, 97, 110, 140, 148, 151, 152,
  153, 163, 176, 178, 179, 189,
  202, 206, 212, 215
Pleasure 98-9, 107, 108, 143-4,
  173, 196
Poetry 186-7, 192, 195, 200-1,
  222-3, 225
Pope, Alexander 222
Popper, Karl 220
Population, growth of 11, 135
Praise 101, 108, 197
Press, influence of 130
Privy Council, Committee of 16,
  18
Prostitutes 9
Psychology 37-8, 44-5, Part II ch.
  3, 59-60, 63, 64, 74, 98, 156-7,
  208 *(see also* Association
  psychology)
Public Libraries Act 1850 16
Public Schools 10, 20, 22, 193
Public Schools Act 1868 20
Public Schools Bill 1868 9, 22
Punishment 101, 104, 108, 161,
  164-5, 168ff., 197
  capital 9, 168, 172
  corporal 173-4
Pupils *see* Teachers, Teacher-
  pupil relations

Quality
  of citizens 89, 213
  of education 25, 91-2, 150,
  158-9, 185
  of happiness 25, 88

Raikes, Robert 10
Railways 135-6
Rationalism 29-32, 78
Reading 150, 184-7
Reason, reasoning 113, 119,
  166, 191-2, 200, 201, 210, 211,
  219
Reform 171-2, 173 *(see also*
  Punishment)
Religion 115, 125, 193-4, 216,
  221
Religious teaching *see under*
  Education
Repetition 143-4
Representation of the People Bill
  1867 9, 21

Research 200, 205-6
Responsibility 92, 104, 122,
  127, 132, 169-70, 214
Retribution 171, 173 *(see also*
  Punishment)
Revised Code 18
Reward 101, 108, 197
Robson, J.M. 36
Roebuck, J.A. 15, 201
Romans 112
Rousseau, J.J. 11, 14, 103, 104,
  111, 117, 119, 120, 138, 142, 186

St. Andrews, University of 9,38,
  203, 220
Scepticism 152, 191, 215, 219
Scheffler, I. xii
School Boards 18-19
Science 19, 29, 30-1, 32-5, 43,
  59, 67-9, 72ff., 78, 80, 93, 152,
  160, 177, 190-3, 204, 209, 212,
  215, 218
  and human nature 34, Part II
  ch. 2
  methods of 32ff., 59, 191-2,
  209
  teaching of 190-3
Sedgwick, Professor A. 144, 204
Self 45, 47, 54-6, 79, 199 *(see
  also* Individuality)
Self-discipline 132, 162
Sexes, differences between
  111-12, 114, 124
'Sinister interest' 199
Skinner, B.F. 76, 80
Slogans 73
Social engineering 75-7, 80, 102
Socialism 90, 129
Society 73ff., 125-8, 132-3,
  139-40, 163, 169, 170, 172, 195,
  196-7, 213-14
Sociology 73ff., 80
Socrates 176, 178
Socratic method 5, 149, 153,
  163, 176 *(see also* Dialectic,
  Elenchus)
Solitude 87, 135
Southey, Robert 223
Sparta 115
Specialisation 199, 205-6, 218,
  227
Spencer, Herbert 49, 56
Stephen, Leslie 96

Style 223
Sunday Schools 10, 12
Sympathy 186, 196-7, 225

Taunton Commission (Schools
Inquiry) 1864-8 19, 20, 22
Taxation 134
Taylor, Algernon (JSM's
stepson) 224 note 68
Taylor, John (Harriet's
husband) 7, 8
Taylor, Helen (JSM's
stepdaughter) 8, 9
Teachers, teaching 16, 94-5,
98-101, Part III ch. 3, 145-6, 156-7,
167, 179-80, 180-1, 214-15, 216
training of teachers 16, 22,
162
Teacher-pupil relations 151, 154,
156-9, 179-80, 216, 221
Teleology 70-2, 73, 87
Tennyson, Alfred, Lord 112,
200, 225
Theory 78, 85
Thring, Edward 20
Tocqueville, Alexis de 86, 133
Truth 32, 33, 34, 36, 45, 63, 71,
72, 73, 75, 88, 90-1, 92, 93, 94,
102, 145-6, 149, 150, 152, 153,
158, 176, 177, 188, 191, 198, 201,
202, 207, 208, 210, 211, 212,
213, 215, 219, 221, 223

Uniformity of nature 34-5
Universities 10-11, 20-1, 92,
145, 166, 183, 203, 205, 217

Scottish 203
Royal Commission on 20
University College, London 20
Utilitarianism 3-4, 6, 11, 25,
70-1, 80, 88, 123, 169, 193
Utilitarians 11, 13, 15, 20, 23,
30, 101, 160
Utilitarian Society 6, 175

Value, values 32-3, 62, 66, 67-8,
71-3, 76, 79, 80, 87ff.,, 96, 120,
122-3, 127, 139, 140, 163, 180,
197, 199
Variety 88, 92, 93, 96, 97, 129
Violence 128-9
Virtue see Altruism
Volition 56-7, 98-9

Wales, University of 21
Ward, W.G. 169, 170
Whewell, William 31
Whitehead, A.N. xiii, 215 note
40, 228, 229
Wholeness 201-2
Wilderspin, Samuel 14 note 23
Women
character of 111-12, 124
education of 9, 10, 20, 21-2
status of 128
Woman's suffrage 9, 21
Women's Suffrage Society 9
Wordsworth, William 6, 104,
137, 195, 200, 223
Writing 150, 184

Zeno of Elea 176

DATE DUE

MAY 08 '91			
DEC 10 1998			
NOV 2 7 1998			